The Group Context

The International Library of Group Analysis
Edited by Malcolm Pines, Institute of Group Analysis, London

The aim of this series is to represent innovative work in group psychotherapy, particularly but not exclusively group analysis. Group analysis, taught and practised widely in Europe, has developed from the work of S.H. Foulkes.

Other titles in the series

Circular Reflections
Selected Papers on Group Analysis and Psychoanalysis
Malcolm Pines
International Library of Group Analysis 1
ISBN 1 85302 492 9 paperback
ISBN 1 85302 493 7 hardback

Attachment and Interaction
Mario Marrone with a contribution by Nicola Diamond
International Library of Group Analysis 3
ISBN 1 85302 586 0 paperback
ISBN 1 85302 587 9 hardback

Self Experiences in Group
Intersubjective and Self Psychological Pathways to Human Understanding
Edited by Irene Harwood and Malcolm Pines
International Library of Group Analysis 4
ISBN 1 85302 610 7 paperback
ISBN 1 85302 596 8 hardback

Taking the Group Seriously
Towards a Post-Foulkesian Group Analytic Theory
Farhad Dalal
International Library of Group Analysis 5
ISBN 1 85302 642 5 paperback

Active Analytic Group Therapy for Adolescents
John Evans
International Library of Group Analysis 6
ISBN 1 85302 616 6 paperback
ISBN 1 85302 617 4 hardback

Group
Claudio Neri
International Library of Group Analysis 8
ISBN 1 85302 418 X paperback

INTERNATIONAL LIBRARY OF GROUP ANALYSIS 7

The Group Context

Sheila Thompson

Jessica Kingsley Publishers
London and Philadelphia

First published in the United Kingdom in 1999 by
Jessica Kingsley Publishers Ltd
116 Pentonville Road
London N1 9JB, England
and
325 Chestnut Street
Philadelphia, PA 19106, USA

www.jkp.com

Library of Congress Cataloging in Publication Data
A CIP catalogue record for this book is available from the
Library of Congress

British Library Cataloguing in Publication Data
A CIP catalogue record for this book is available from the
British Library

ISBN 1 85302 657 3

Printed and Bound in Great Britain by
Athenaeum Press, Gateshead, Tyne and Wear

Contents

Dedicated to the memory of Dr Jack Kahn, with gratitude and affection. The precursors of this work were two books co-written by Jack Kahn and myself — *The Group Process as a Helping Technique* (1970) and *The Group Process and Family Therapy* (1982). These have now been completely rewritten as *The Group Context* to take into account all the changes within the professions and in my own thinking since then. A substantial amount of new material has been included. However the influence of Jack Kahn and my great debt to him remains. Some of his characteristic anecdotes have been retained to illustrate the text, and his friends and former colleagues will no doubt be able to identify them. Chapter 13 remains very much as it was when he and I wrote it together. It reflects his interest in multi-disciplinary work and draws not only upon his experience as a psychiatrist but also upon the many years he spent as a family doctor.

Acknowledgements

As well as Dr Jack Kahn there are two other people with whom I have had the good fortune to be associated in the past and who must be mentioned here. First and foremost there is the late Dr SH Foulkes whose teaching and example permeate so much of this book. In addition there is Dr Pat de Maré who drew me into his pioneering work with large and median groups.

Many other colleagues have contributed to my thinking, too many to mention individually – in adult and child psychiatry and community mental health, in the Refugee Services of Kenya, in the Hospice movement in England and in the USA, and within the Group-Analytic Society.

I also have to thank Anne Harrow, Joan Hutten and Kevin Power for reading and commenting on draft chapters; and my husband Miles for all his patient support and help.

CHAPTER I

Thinking in Context

If then, Socrates, we find ourselves in many points unable to make our discourses of the generations of gods and the universe in every way wholly consistent and exact, you must not be surprised. Nay, we must be well content if we can provide an account not less likely than another's: we must remember that I who speak, and you who are my audience, are but men, and should be satisfied to ask for no more than the likely story. (Plato, *The Timaeus*)

Consider this press report of a wedding. It was entitled 'Seven faint with bridegroom at wedding.'

Eight people, amongst them the bridegroom, fainted during a wedding ceremony at H— Parish Church yesterday. The bridegroom, Mr. A.G., 20, collapsed to the ground. After reviving he was supported by his bride, Miss G.T., 23. A few seconds later the best man, Mr. K. G., fainted and hit his head. He was revived with glasses of water. Another guest took over as a substitute and found the ring in the best man's pocket. Then a choir boy was carried into the churchyard, followed by a bridesmaid, Miss J.G., who collapsed in the aisle. Four members of the congregation also fainted. The Vicar, The Rev. P.R., who omitted the address to the bride and groom, said he had never known a wedding like it. One of the 180 guests said that the church looked like a battlefield. It seemed to be a case of mass hysteria. Mr. G. nearly fainted again when he left the church.

This report, taken from his personal file of newspaper cuttings, was once used by Dr. S.H. Foulkes to introduce a lecture on his concept of Networks in Group Analysis. What was going on here? he asked.

We can borrow this example and ask the same question in order to place the topic of the group context in a context in its turn.

A number of different people have fainted. To start with, each fainting episode could be taken separately and an enquiry made as to whether each individual was prone to have fainting attacks. Were they each reacting to the physical context, to a hot day and an ill ventilated church? Or were they each responding, still as separate even if suggestible individuals, to a structured social event which might also have a particular personal meaning?

We could also place each of them separately in the context of their past lives. Present events rest upon events in the past: past experiences remain a part of people's internal worlds and become transferred into situations in the present. What individual experiences in the past might have been impinging upon the behaviour of each of them at this wedding?

Before World War Two there would probably have been little inclination to look further. In Western society there has been a long, though not exclusive, tradition of thinking in terms of separateness and of treating the separate self, paired with the separate body, as data which does not have to be questioned, the point at which speculation can start. After all we can have little doubt that we exist within the boundaries of our own skin and that we each have a unique and distinctive place in the world with a personal viewpoint that can be shared by no one else. Hence came the familiar medical model, based upon the isolation and study of the single individual patient, the single illness and the single case file. Hence came the development of Freud's dynamic individual psychology in which the inner world of a single patient was isolated to be the focus of attention, and context was eliminated as far as possible and treated as either an irrelevance or an interference.

Today, more is required. Converging developments from different areas – the disruptions and social impact of wars; cross-cultural studies; changes within psychiatry, social work and other professions; theoretical advances; dissatisfactions with existing practice; the growth and influence of the child guidance movement and of therapeutic communities; and increasing multi-disciplinary practice – have all interacted to extend the focus beyond the individual and take in relationships between and among individuals, networks, family groups and the social community

Not one of us can escape from what Chesterton called the degrading servitude of being a child of our own time. If our forebears were the servants of assumptions that we now question, today we are no less the servants of a different system of ideas. The belief that man and woman came first and society came second, that the social contract came to rescue us from a solitary, nasty, brutish and short existence, that infants enter the world as separate individuals with innate drives which then come into conflict with the demands of society, that individual and context can be kept separate, has been largely replaced. We have an alternative concept today of men and women born into the world as part of a group and then slowly and with difficulty achieving a limited degree of separation.

This gradual process of differentiation within the group, never complete, has been traced in the broad evolutionary development of a human race always dependent on group living for survival, and in the growth and development of each human infant. This viewpoint is now well enough established so that it may seem to require little underscoring here, though the belief that the individual self exists prior to any experience is still implicit in many ways in our culture. It is enshrined in many religions and J. Klein (1987) has suggested an extreme example in those pro-life lobbyists who base their interventions upon the assumption that the beginning foetus comes complete with the differentiated soul or self that it is to have ever after.

Returning to that wedding, our task now is to look beyond each individual for a context that could give a different meaning to the events. The people who fainted were connected by their presence at the wedding, but what other connection could there have been? Were they each responding to the behaviour of the others and each having an influence upon the behaviour of the others in his or her turn – a follow-my-neighbour event, as it were, no matter who the neighbour was? Or did it matter? Were the people who fainted linked together in some way that distinguished them from the rest? Did they have some on-going relationship with each other, apart from the immediate occasion, as family members, friends or rivals which could have triggered the disturbance? Or could the on-going relationship have been one with a less visible meaning? Were they participating together in some undisclosed drama of which they were, perhaps, scarcely aware? Was it, as Foulkes was suggesting, a psycho-social network in action?

In this anecdote Foulkes was looking for an illustration, or perhaps a metaphor, for the way in which small knots of people can be held together through reciprocal psychological needs.

We are essentially responding creatures at birth and throughout life. As Erikson (1950) pointed out, our awareness of ourselves as separate individuals depends upon the recognition of others that we are who we are. The infant can only develop in association, and everything that we do from infancy onwards is in response to something that is being done by someone else, or is a response carried over from something done by someone else in the past. The behaviour patterns that we have developed over the years through interaction with other people still need the presence of other people who will play the complementary roles needed to keep our own particular drama going.

The word drama introduces another metaphor, and the theatre will continue to be a source of analogies and insights. An indication of changing perceptions about the nature of interpersonal relationships is shown in the adaptation that John Osborne made of Ibsen's *Hedda Gabler* (Osborne 1972) in order to reduce the excessive emphasis that he considered had been given to Hedda in production after production of the play at the expense of the interaction among all the other characters. 'Like most great plays,' he wrote in his introduction, (Osborne 1972, p.7) 'the apparent central character exists only by the favour of the other characters in the play, however small.'

In employing the term *network* for such a psychological web of relationships, Foulkes (1975) was drawing on the concept of the neurological network employed by the neurologist Kurt Goldstein. Goldstein pioneered the view that the nervous system can best be understood, in theory and in practice, as a system that reacts consistently as a whole rather than as a complex collection of individual neurons. In this neurological network the individual neuron cells form nodal points through which communications may pass smoothly until a disturbance at one point brings a disturbance in the whole and affects them all.

This neurological concept can be used as a model for the position of the individual within the group and for the way in which individuals are held together by connecting bonds within the system as a whole. Foulkes described individual members of a psycho-social network as being like the nodal points in a neurological network. Communications may pass smoothly enough, with a sufficient balance of give and take and reciprocal satisfaction of needs, until change and disturbance is brought into the network and destabilises the whole and the parts. But the term network is now widely used in many situations, and Foulkes later substituted the term plexus to apply specifically to the small intimate knots of people linked to each other through the interdependence of their psychological processes. The members of a plexus may be related in other ways, as spouses, relatives, colleagues or friends, but their on-going significance in each others, lives is something over and above this. Members of the same family, or of the same household, are likely to be drawn together into the same plexus, but not exclusively and not necessarily in the same way or to the same extent.

The principle to be drawn from this is that no part can be properly understood if abstracted from the whole. The stability of members of a network or plexus depends upon the (flexible) maintenance of the existing balance. Any intervention directed at one part is likely to meet resistance and bring unexpected consequences elsewhere – as when the treatment and recovery of one disturbed family member is closely followed by the illness of another one.

We might imagine, for the sake of argument, that something about the wedding destabilised such a psycho-social network, or plexus, bringing an upset that rippled through the whole system and caused it to react and reveal itself in such a public way. Individual members fainted but the precipitating factor was a disturbance in the network on which the relative stability of the individual members depended.

Whatever part of a field is abstracted for examination, it is always possible to look further. It could be that focusing on those who fainted, and thinking in terms of a single psycho-social network or plexus, gives too restricted a view. Perhaps we need to place the events in a yet wider context that includes the whole congregation, the church and the occasion. Not all those present signalled their distress, but we might go on to consider whether nonetheless they could all have been involved in some way. Were those who fainted giving expression to some group experience or conflict on behalf of them all? Where was the distress located? As Mrs Gradgrind said , in Dickens' *Hard Times*, on being asked if she was in pain, 'I think there's a pain somewhere in this room, but I couldn't positively say that I have got it.'

Suppose now that exploration of the sad situation in the church were not merely an academic exercise. Suppose that some intervention was required in order to prevent such a situation occurring again, in that church, among that congregation or in a sub-group of that congregation? Or perhaps help was requested for one or more of the casualties? If the unit of disturbance is not confined to the individual but is to be found in the relationships among a network or group of people, linked not just by visible family ties but by (possibly undisclosed) psychological needs, what then?

We can all recognise an individual, and an individual problem has a location and can be bounded and contained. But if problems are to be located not within people but in the spaces in between, then new forms of intervention and treatment have to be found. How is the significant network to be identified? How can the processes taking place in a group be understood and addressed?

There are a few recorded instances (Foulkes 1964) in dynamic psychiatry of attempts to uncover and then to bring together a psycho-social network through following up every clue leading from the central figure of the identified patient to another involved person, through analytic examination and observation of his or her inner world and its links to the outer world of relationships, and through the reconstruction of past history and interviews with all the persons involved. But the difficulties involved in this procedure meant that the disturbed or disturbing network itself has had to remain in most cases within the mental activity of the therapist. Some other means of working within relationships needed to be found.

Different networks are linked together in space and in time through the movement of individuals. Throughout life we are passing from group to group as we move among family, friends, workmates and associates, and so carry patterns of behaviour with us from one group into another. Joining any new group, the individual will try to use it as another psychological resource, even if a temporary and limited one, and will attempt to behave in a way that will elicit the responses required to create the type of network on which he or she has come to depend.

So an alternative approach was found through proxy networks that could be created for the purpose and linked via each individual member to the elusive real life networks elsewhere. In a treatment group of strangers the problems that the group members were having in relationships outside the group could be introduced and re-enacted with a new caste in a new and protected situation, and here these problems could be explored and addressed.

This development brought more than a new operational tool for the treatment of mental disturbance. In these treatment groups it also became possible to study the behaviour of a group as a whole. There was now a unique forum for the study of group activity *per se* in which processes belonging to the group situation in itself could be identified and observed. The lessons learnt could be applied to groups and associations brought together in different situations and for very different purposes. A new era in the understanding and use of groups began.

The shift in thinking to take in the spaces in between, to place situations, problems and activities within a group context, in part due to the arrival of new concepts, in part due to a return to an earlier tradition obscured by the rise of individualism, has required adjustments, and has led to changes in methods and techniques in the helping professions and also to a growing extent in education and in industry. But it has sometimes seemed as if a long ingrained habit to think in terms of separate individuals, which introspection does nothing to discourage, means that we now have less appropriate equipment available for thinking in terms of interacting processes.

The long familiar model of the separate individual is based upon another familiar model, that of linear causality. According to this model, causes and effects are separated and then paired together sequentially, the one following the other within a temporal sequence. Thus Cause A will be followed by Effect B, and Effect B may in its turn become the Cause of Effect C in a one-way progression.

This well established pattern of thinking, which helps us to process the raw stuff of experience and find an orderly pattern in the confusion around us, is supported by the structure of our language.

The language that has been passed on to us, and which incorporates the mental activity of past generations, provides tools for describing the interaction of two entities in terms of one side or of the other in a sequence of events: it is much harder to find language in which to describe the interactional process as a whole. We can speak of cause and effect, or of organism and environment, the one producing the other or responding to the other, but always we are, for our own needs, artificially separating one single field of forces into distinct parts. The grammatical structure of our language requires a subject and an object before any ideas can be formulated. D.W. Harding, (1970) in pointing this out, described as one of the 'pervasive pseudo-problems of psychology' the difficulty of finding a vocabulary in which to describe the reciprocal process of mutual interaction without separating it into two parts of stimulus and responding organism. We have to be able to describe interacting forces as related to each other in such a way that each acts as both cause and effect.

So, in order to study a total field of simultaneously interacting forces without verbal misrepresentation we are in need of a new grammar as well as a circular model of causality to replace the old linear model.

It can be easier to choose between two polarised viewpoints than to attempt to integrate them, but today it is often less a question of 'either... or' than of 'both... and'. The individual may be embedded in a group context throughout life, but the individual also sees him or herself as separate. Each episode of fainting in the church has to be acknowledged both as an individual experience and as a group experience. We need to work with groups in the knowledge that groups are made up of individuals and we need to work with individuals in the knowledge that individuals are embedded in the group.

If a first step came with the recognition of the psycho-social network, and a second came when connections were made between this network and the proxy stranger group of group psychotherapy, then a third step can be found in the further connections that could then be made between group and group which brought the use of the group process out into other group situations. The concepts originating in group therapy can be used to clarify the dynamic properties of many other groups in many other settings – functional groups, educational groups, problem solving groups, work groups and life groups. But the change has not come without dangers. Each different group context has its own parameters and own requirements and these concepts cannot be transferred from discipline to discipline or from situation to situation without paying attention to the nature of each particular group.

This book deals with the extension of dynamic group concepts into different areas. These areas include counselling and problem solving, education and training, team building and professional development, the use of median and large groups and work with family units. Awareness of the group context has also brought the challenge of bringing this awareness into other situations where group work is not an option, where individuals wish to come alone for help, and where the network remains invisible except for its presence within the mental processes of patient or client and in the interaction with the professional helper.

The starting point has to be the origins of the concepts which are being reapplied to different settings. One has to understand what therapy is before one can move beyond it. Any dynamic group work undertaken in other areas needs to be distinguished from therapy and to have an established focus of its own, with a clear understanding of aim, purpose and boundaries, and of what has been sanctioned.

These topics will be explored during the course of an attempt to look at a range of different ways and different situations in which working in the group context has been developed throughout the helping professions and has then been carried out into other areas.

CHAPTER 2

A Group and its Processes

Without contraries is no true progression. Attraction and Repulsion, Reason and Energy, Love and Hate, are necessary to Human existence. (William Blake, *Marriage of Heaven and Hell.*)

The making of a group

What is a group?

We see a number of trees on the skyline, more than a pair but not enough to be called a wood. We recognise that they are all trees and that this is something that they have in common. We can pick the trees out of their surroundings and look on them as one entity. Someone else with greater discernment or better eyesight might recognise a clump of hazels among the trees, finding a different entity and drawing different boundaries. In both cases it is someone's perception that turns the different trees into a group. This is similar to the perception of the Gestalt psychologists, and is based upon our capacity to organise the elements of perceived objects into a single whole.

Another context, that of dynamic psychology, has different criteria. A number of people sitting in a railway carriage might be made into a group by a painter who looks on them as objects in space and is able to fit them all into a single composition. But if each sits reading a newspaper or sleeping, with no communication taking place among them, they would not be considered a group in any psychological sense.

Suppose however that there is a breakdown, the train is delayed and the travellers' immediate future becomes uncertain. In these altered circumstances they begin to talk to each other and exchange and share feelings of indignation, anxiety and distress (and despite the discomfort, these feelings may have overtones which are not unpleasant). Each of them communicates something, and each of them responds to the communications of the others. These communications and responses can be linked together to form a pattern of interaction which relates each part to each other part and so forms them into a whole. So to the two factors found necessary to turn the trees into a group – defined membership and common boundary – we now have to add a third one: interdependence.

Thus we have a number of people coming together, sharing some purpose, interest or concern, and staying together long enough for the development of a network of relationships which includes them all. Recognition of this network brings the concept of a group. Each member of the group, though she or he may continue to behave in ways which are characteristic, is now influenced by the behaviour of each of the others and also by the prevailing mood or climate present in the group at any moment of time. This mood, or climate, is something to which each contributes but which no single person can control.

The group may consist of a number of colleagues having a drink together after work, a committee meeting, a psychotherapeutic group, or any one of the small face-to-face gatherings in which most of us spend a large part of our working lives. After such a meeting one may look back and wonder why each person behaved as he did, why one member talked so much and another so little, why this one was listened to so eagerly and that one relatively ignored. Why was one topic pursued with interest while another topic was allowed to drop? Why was so and so never mentioned, and such and such only treated flippantly? Why was everyone so lively at one point and so much quieter a little later on? What forces, in fact, determine the proceedings of a group, and, supposing there are such forces, how can one begin to study and understand them?

A student of individual psychology might focus upon the behaviour of each individual member in turn, and attempt to give separate explanations for each one in the light of what he can learn about her or him. But this would not give him much help if he wanted to account for the complete pattern of events or to answer the questions posed in the last paragraph. It might be compared with an attempt to explain the shifting pattern of a kaleidoscope by taking the tube to pieces and listing the fragments found inside. Something more than this is needed. It seems clear that in studying groups we are not dealing with a collection of different pieces of behaviour that just happen to be in juxtaposition, but with a complex and dynamic interaction.

In order to understand this interaction, it is necessary to take all the individual pieces of behaviour, the contributions of each different member, and treat them as if they were all parts of one meaningful whole. And in order to do this we have to make certain assumptions about the nature of groups. We have to form a concept of the group as a separate entity, to ascribe forces to it, and even to endow it with capacities for decision and action. We have to do this in order to be able to describe and explain certain aspects of human behaviour, and we are entitled to do this as long as we do not forget that the group is an abstraction.

Such a concept can be compared with the many other concepts in both individual and group psychology which do not refer to anything with an actual, concrete existence, but which provide the language which is necessary for the description of psychological phenomena. The Superego, for example, is not an object; rather, it is an abstract concept which embodies inferences from observation and perceptions of experience. If we treat this concept of the group too concretely it may lead us on to another error, namely the naive transfer of properties which belong to the individual onto the group as a whole. Some of the mechanisms familiar in individual psychology may have their counterparts at a group level (and ambivalence will be discussed later in this connection), but their presence cannot be assumed, and each needs to be discovered afresh.

The concept of the group as a whole can be illustrated by another analogy. When two football teams meet they are creating something new and unique together – a game of football which is different to every other game of football. It is something in which they all play a part and which no single player or group of players could create alone. If you were to isolate a small sequence, an incident perhaps where footballer A had the ball in a particular part of the field and was successfully intercepted by footballer B, and if you were to ask what it meant, why the ball was there, and what A and B were doing, you would have to look for an explanation in the context of the game as a whole.

The different levels are not necessarily alternatives. The football coach, whilst looking at the game as a whole, may also need to consider the part played by the defence or by a particular player. But no one level stands alone. For present purposes, while it is necessary to hold in mind a concept of the group as a psychological entity, it is always with the recognition that the group is formed through the coming together of a number of individuals and that it has no existence apart from the activity of its members. Any property or activity that we ascribe to the group arises solely through the normal psychodynamics and psychopathologies of people meeting together, through the ways in which people interrelate, and through their reactions to the external realities of the situation in which they find themselves. The activity of the whole and the activity of the parts must both be studied.

The assumption of group processes

The assumption that some connection exists between all the events taking place in a group rests upon another assumption that, at some level, there are group processes operating and exerting an influence over every single thing that happens. These processes must belong to the group situation itself; they are created through the group interaction and they occur inevitably whenever several people meet and form a relationship with each other.

So if one is trying to understand the meaning of the behaviour of any particular person in a group context at a moment in time, an exhaustive knowledge of that person is not enough; one must also look for the processes operating in the group which will have played a part in eliciting that behaviour. These processes are not usually within the conscious awareness of the group members who are participating in them, but they may be more readily apparent to a detached observer.

Hypothetical example

To illustrate this point, consider a summary of events in one particular group meeting.

A number of students meet together for a drink on the evening before an important exam. Several of them immediately start to talk about their work in a flippant and frivolous manner. Two of them begin to discuss an academic point, but the discussion soon peters out and they fall silent. A reference to exhaustion due to hours spent in study is ignored. A shipwreck, reported in the day's news, is mentioned, along with the fact that some of the ship's crew were drowned because they could not all fit into the lifeboat. An absent student with a reputation for hard work and academic success is mentioned, and criticised as unhelpful and unfriendly. Several students discuss his way of life with pity and with some contempt, deploring its narrowness and lack of social and sexual content. There is an argument about payment for the drinks, a refusal to let any one person undertake this, and finally an agreement that each member should contribute an identical amount. No one seems to want to leave and they stay until closing time.

If we look for some underlying process linking together every single separate incident that took place at this meeting, we find an attempt to reconcile two distinct and incompatible sets of feelings. On the one hand, there is the wish that the group should continue to exist and provide the companionship and support of peers; on the other hand, there are competitive and disruptive feelings, the fears of arousing envy and hostility in others by examination successes, or alternatively, of experiencing feelings of envy and hostility oneself because of the greater success of others. These are the feelings that are activated or emphasised by the actual group situation, and, whatever other needs and preoccupations the individual members have, they all share these feelings to some extent. Thus we find an area of common ground where the different problems of individuals meet in a group problem. The behaviour of each individual at this particular group meeting can be regarded as part of an overall pattern of behaviour which has as its aim the reconciliation of the two opposing sets of feelings and which represents the group's struggle to survive under the pressure of disruptive forces.

In the light of our assumptions, the events taking place at the students' meeting can be interpreted in the following way. The group at first decides to act as if exams are not to be taken seriously, and therefore the threat to the group can be treated as if it does not exist. This solution is not at first unanimous and some pressure has to be exerted to make it so. The students' wish to remain 'all in the same boat', and their fears that the group may break up violently, are then expressed symbolically, since the anxieties are too strong to be dealt with effectively by denial and must be expressed outwardly in some other way. They then find that they can broach their competitive feelings more directly, and without endangering the group, by denigrating an absent rival, and at the same time they are able to maintain the fiction that none of them is actually seeking academic success. No one is allowed to take on the superior position of host. At the end of the meeting anxieties and fears are still present since nothing has happened to relieve them, and a sense that a threat still exists makes it difficult for the group to disband.

This interpretation is based upon the assumptions that have already been discussed. To sum up, it is assumed that all the different events taking place in a group, though contributed by different people, can be treated as if they were the product of a single entity; indeed they cannot be fully understood unless approached in this way. It is assumed that these events are all connected through the operation of forces known as 'group processes' which are a property of the group as a whole and not within the control of any one individual member. It is assumed that, through the operation of group processes, attempts are being made to reconcile the opposing tendencies which are present in every group, and which by their opposition arouse anxiety in the members and can even threaten the group's continued existence.

In the group of students there was an over-riding preoccupation in which all members shared, though to differing extents, and the proceedings of the group were shaped by the need to address this preoccupation. This group had very little of the structure that can impose formal patterns and through its formality hinder the spontaneous development and expression of a common group theme In other more structured groups the group processes may be harder to discern and may be influenced by a greater number of variables.

The power of groups

Groups are made up of individuals who share (though to rather different degrees) the need to belong to some grouping, the wish to be well regarded by peers, and the fear of isolation and exclusion. Not only under the pressure of exams but at other times too the students would find comfort and safety and a sense of identity and self-worth in belonging to a group, and discomfort at being isolated. So underlying the differences among individual group members, and any competitive jockeying for position that there may be, there is movement in the direction of a basic consensus that will keep a group in existence. The movement is not irresistible, but is strong enough to give groups considerable power to influence the opinions and the behaviour of their members.

As a group becomes established it begins the process of defining its own reality and forming an opinion as to what sort of group it is and how it compares with the other groups around it. It may, for example, come to see itself as a progressive group, as an easy-going group, or as the group that gets all the bad luck. It can measure itself against other groups and decide that these other groups are more or less desirable, more or less effective. In fact a poor opinion of other groups around it is sometimes an important part of a group's own self-esteem on which the self-esteem of its members largely depends.

These shared opinions can refer not only to the nature of the group and its position in the world, but also to what is acceptable or unacceptable in the behaviour of group members; and once such group standards begin to be established they can be supported through the powerful sanctions of group approval and disapproval. Such perceptions then come to form part of the group's own reality and can become merged with other perceptions about reality outside the group that are not generally open to question.

Such powers, belonging to the group as a whole and not to any individual members, can be seen at work in schools, teams, organisations and departments of organisations, clubs and families, and also in the wider association of religions, ethnic and national groups and social classes. One often wonders at the strength of (misplaced) beliefs in groups other than one's own. Some people come out in opposition to their groups. Those who do this, making a stand as Saul of Tarsus did, or as Luther took at the church door at Wittenburg, are enabled do so because of the support they receive from an alternative group which they value even more. This could well be an 'invisible group' such as a strong family tradition or a spiritual belief system which provides an even more powerful sense of belonging and of personal identity.

Structure and purpose

Every gathering, if it is more than a random collection of individuals who have not begun to regard themselves as a group, will have a purpose, just as the purpose of our students was to hold on to the support and companionship of their fellows in a time of difficulty. This purpose supplies a reason for meeting, establishing a framework and a context and providing members with roles to play and expectations about the behaviour of other members, It may also impose a considerable degree of control over the proceedings.

A committee, convened to carry out a specific task, will need to have a structure designed to further this task and to exclude elements considered to be irrelevant and time wasting. There will be a leader, or chairperson, an agenda and rules of procedure. Members will come to the meeting knowing that a certain type of behaviour is expected of them, and equally they will have some expectations about the behaviour of the other members. If one looks at the record of the proceedings of a committee meeting, one would expect, and one might even find, a greater coherence in the discussion and a greater consistency in individual behaviour than is usual in less structured groups. In this situation, as in all group situations, the group processes play their part but their operation is likely to be more difficult to detect.

A social gathering will have a different framework. Though there will be no chairperson, there is likely to be a host or hostess. There will be no agenda or explicit rules of procedure, but there will be certain conventions influencing the way in which people behave and their expectations of the behaviour of others. The purpose is enjoyable social intercourse, and the members will be expected to behave pleasantly and refrain from introducing any disturbing elements which might interfere with the enjoyment or disrupt the harmony of the group.

It seems necessary for our comfort that the groups in which we take part should have a structure of some sort which can impose control over what may take place and set some limits to the behaviour of ourselves and others. It could be frightening to be in a situation where there seems to be no form of control, where we have no firm expectations about what may happen, or where we do not know how we ourselves are expected to behave. Such fears are within general experience and have been shown to exist in experimental leaderless groups and in groups that are kept unstructured for a psychotherapeutic purpose. Typically, in the beginning stages of these groups, there is a period in which the members experience considerable anxiety; and they may try to press someone into the role of leader, or attempt to devise some rules of procedure or agreed conventions of behaviour, even when this is quite inappropriate.

The individual within the group

Within the group structure which may be firm or weak, explicit or implicit, are the individual members, each with their own unique psychological make-up, their own problems and their own needs.

The behaviour of each of us is profoundly influenced by the emotional needs we carry about with us. Though we may not be conscious of the way in which these needs affect our conduct, we all try to arrange our lives and our relationships with other people so that these needs can find some satisfaction. We are each of us aware that we feel more at home in certain situations and less at home in others. We like to play certain roles, to make certain types of relationships, and to be treated in certain ways. We are attracted to the company of people who will allow us, or encourage us, to behave in the ways we wish to behave, and who will give us the responses we seek. Wherever we are, we try to influence or manipulate our associates so as to prevail upon them to behave in ways that suit us and will meet our needs. We try to avoid getting into situations that we find unsatisfactory, or disturbing, or frustrating. If we cannot avoid these situations, we look for some way to change them or to lessen their impact. These basic emotional needs, which determine so much of our behaviour, in groups as in other situations, have their origin in our constitutional endowment and in our earliest relationships, and are shaped and influenced, modified or confirmed, by all our subsequent experiences.

Different needs will be activated by different circumstances. When one is with a group of other people, the situation in itself and one's reactions to the other people present will determine which habitual needs will be experienced and which ways of satisfying them will be used. One's behaviour will also be influenced by feelings about the group itself, and the relationship prevailing between the group and the outside world..

To take one instance: in a group meeting one member is talkative and vivacious, responding to every topic and entertaining the gathering with his fund of stories. This could be part of a characteristic pattern of behaviour which he habitually employs in such situations; if a single interpretation for it is sought, it might be found in terms of early experiences which have made him equate lack of notice with lack of love and feel frustrated if he is not given attention. Alternatively, this behaviour might be the result of interrelationships in this particular group and be specific to this situation; there may be someone present whom he particularly wishes to impress, or someone else who arouses strong competitive feelings. At another level, it could represent his reaction to a particular topic under discussion; he might want to divert attention from this topic, or to ensure that it is only treated flippantly. Finally, his behaviour may be the result of feelings about the group as a whole; a wish to keep it in existence because it is serving some need juxtaposed with a fear that it is going to break up. At a social gathering similar behaviour can sometimes be observed on the part of anxious hosts.

How our man actually behaves will depend upon the other people present, each of whom will also be trying to arrange matters so that a predominant need is met. His behaviour will help, or hinder, the attempts of the others. and so will meet with support or discouragement in varying degrees. Similar processes can be observed in marriage. One can observe unions that appear to bring together pairs of complementary needs - to talk and to be talked to, to dominate and to submit, to protect and to be protected. These marriages may appear harmonious, but are hardly likely to encourage personal growth and development since they provide no stimulus for change; in fact the success of such a marriage may largely depend upon the maintenance of existing behaviour patterns. It does not seem probable that Jack Spratt and his wife ever changed their eating habits.

Such a consistent dovetailing of needs is not to be expected in a group situation. There we find constant adaptation and change as each member tries to influence the others to behave in a way that suits his own personal and particular requirements. The more structured the group, and the more stereotyped the roles that the members are expected to play, the less apparent will be the tensions and needs that each individual brings into the group. The needs will be there, and they will exert some influence, but they will be masked by the formal procedure and there will be less opportunity for them to obtrude into personal relationships.

One will not willingly remain for long in a situation in which personal needs are not being met in some way or other. If unable to influence a group to provide some minimal satisfactions, one will look for a way out. The committee members whose needs are only satisfied when in a predominant position will aspire to be elected to the chair. If unsuccessful in this, other means to satisfy this need may be sought. It may be possible by hard work to achieve a prominent position as an authority on some aspect of the subject at issue, or, alternatively, as leader or spokesperson of a minority group. If unable to obtain any of these satisfactions, the committee member may find fault with the committee's composition, terms of reference, or method of procedure, declaring it unworkable (which by now it very well may have become).

If attendance at a meeting is compulsory, the dissatisfied member may perhaps withdraw into sleep or daydreams, or express dissatisfactions through overt or covert destructive behaviour aimed at damaging or ending the group. Such behaviour would be satisfying the newest and most pressing need, a need that has been activated by the specific conditions and reactions encountered in the group. It is not necessarily a position of comfort that is sought: there may even be some who find a perverse satisfaction in demonstrating that none can satisfy them.

This example, illustrating the disruptive effect of a single dissatisfied participant, is likely to be familiar to those experienced in committees, and equally, those experienced in committees will realise that this is only part of the story. It leaves out of account the constructive and cohesive forces within the group forming the committee, expressed in the consensus of opinion and the decisions which lead to action. It is this aspect which is more generally recorded in the minutes. The destructive forces operating in the group are less likely to be observed as such, and certainly not in the terms used here. The individual expression of such forces may well be described, and may even find approval, under such labels as 'sticking to one's principles' or 'upholding the rights of minorities'. A group that accepts such labels is, in fact, offering its destructive forces a legitimate means of expression and may even be able to contain them in this way.

Despite its complex motivations, our behaviour usually remains more or less appropriate to the different situations in which we find ourselves. By and large, we observe regulations and conventions, we pay some respect to the personal needs of others and we still manage to achieve some satisfactions of our own. If a particular need is so compelling that it must be expressed, and if it cannot find expression through approved behaviour, then we have to behave in unapproved ways, and we run the risk of being designated unconventional, unreliable, eccentric, maladjusted, ill, or simply mad or bad. But most people are able to function at more than one level, satisfying at the same time, and through the same actions, something of their own needs and of the expectations both of society and of their own immediate company.

So if it is to continue in existence, and if it is to retain all its members, a group has to make some provision for the wants of each of the individuals who compose it, conflicting though these may be. Therefore the total proceedings of a group meeting can be seen, at one level, as a compromise which contains some part of the personal preoccupations of each member and which goes some way to meet the requirements of each. This is a dynamic position, that is to say, the compromise is continually being adjusted as the interaction taking place among the group members stimulates the perception of new needs and offers new solutions.

The success of the man who seeks to dominate the group will depend upon the way in which the other members react. His attempt might be welcomed by some for complex and personal reasons, and may be justified in terms of providing the group with a new direction, giving a firmer lead, introducing new ideas, or changing an existing unsatisfactory position. For converse reasons, it could be resisted by others.

If there is open competition for leadership, then the group will only survive if it is able to find a way of accommodating these rivalries. Such competition would pose a problem for individual members; it also poses a problem for the group as a whole, and one must look at the total pattern of behaviour in the group to see the way in which this problem is met.

One of the possible solutions would be for all members to take turns. This could be formalised in arrangements for different members to take the chair in rotation; informally, it could just happen that each member finds himself taking the lead successively while the other members acquiesce. Certain provocative topics which stimulate rivalry might be quietly dropped, as if by some silent agreement. Alternatively, some member who is not directly involved in the leadership conflict might come to occupy the position of arbiter and referee. These different patterns of group behaviour can be explained as alternative possible solutions to a problem belonging to the group as a whole; they only provide solutions to individual problems at the point where each individual problem and the group problem meet. They are not necessarily reached through any conscious decision. Rather, they are reached through the operation of the group processes which shape the proceedings of the group into a form that will establish some common ground, where the needs of each can meet and achieve some satisfaction.

Cohesive and disruptive forces

The drives that bring the group together to satisfy the needs of the members to belong and to be accepted are always opposed by the contrary fears and resistances that pull the group apart.

Example

An illustration can be provided from the record of a particular group consisting of mothers of young children with learning difficulties which met every week with a social worker. The aim of the group meetings was to help the mothers in relationship to their children, and the discussion, though focused upon the children, was otherwise free and unstructured.

In the first few meetings the mothers all related anecdotes about the behaviour of their children, and a marked uniformity in opinions and attitudes was shown. When one mother described the behaviour of her child at table or at bedtime, one or two of the other mothers would join in eagerly, claiming that their children behaved in just the same way. Inconsistencies and contradictions soon became apparent, and it appeared that the mothers were less concerned with giving accurate descriptions of their children's behaviour than with maintaining unanimity at all costs. Only one mother, at the second meeting of the group, described her child as being different, and she received exaggerated sympathy from the others. She did not come to the next meeting and the group immediately referred to her and discussed her situation at length, dwelling on the abnormality of her child's behaviour and criticising the ways in which she handled him.

These were women who found it difficult, because of their children's handicaps, to take part in the normal run of corporate activities, and they all, to some degree, felt painfully different from mothers in general. Their behaviour demonstrated the strength of their wish to be in a group where they could share freely and did not have to feel exceptional. But it also indicated the strength of the disruptive forces threatening the group. Side by side with the wish to belong to the group were strong competitive and hostile feelings which the group situation tended to intensify. Most of these mothers were prepared to fight to obtain special provision for their children and were reluctant to have them classified with other 'subnormals'. The other mothers were seen as allies but they were also seen as rivals. Not all the mothers, of course, experienced these negative feelings to an equal extent. But the conflict between disruptive and cohesive forces posed an immediate problem for the group and led to the adoption of a group solution, the solution of denying differences and being all alike, in which most participated actively and a few acquiesced. The one mother who refused to acquiesce left the group.

It was the strength of the conflict between these two opposing drives, to belong and to be separate, that was responsible for the establishment of the artificial uniformity. This behaviour on the part of the group members ensured that the group (minus one) could delay having to confront this issue and continue to exist over the early sessions. It was not until the group was more securely established, and the relationships among the mothers, and between the mothers and the social worker, were stronger, that the fear of the group's destructive potential was reduced.

It is this need to reconcile opposing drives which brings the group processes into existence. By means of a ceaseless, dynamic, interpersonal and transpersonal process, through perpetual compromise and adjustment, an overall pattern of behaviour evolves. Any coherency in the group is derived from the ways in which the needs of individual members are made to dovetail together. Figuratively speaking, it is like a jigsaw puzzle made up of a number of pieces drawn from other jigsaw puzzles and now brought together to make some sort of new pattern. But these jigsaw pieces have a life of their own and have some power to change their shape and adjust to fill the space allotted, pushing the other pieces around as they do so. And as a jigsaw, when completed, turns into a new picture that is more than the sum of its parts, so the group becomes a new entity with processes of its own.

These group processes are complicated in the extreme. No observer can stand so far outside them as to be able to understand them all. If it is necessary to force upon them the simplification of basic laws, then these laws can be found in the assumption we make that there are regularities in the group processes, no matter in what forms they show themselves.

Such an assumption is made in all dynamic group work, and, in fact, there are comparable assumptions which underlie every attempt to study the world in which we live. Science is based upon two acts of faith. First, there is the belief that the universe can be understood; and, second, there is the belief that the same causes produce the same effects. These beliefs are not subject to proof or disproof. An alternative set of beliefs would be, first, that the universe can never be completely understood, and, secondly, that every event is unique. But in order to study science we have to be content with the assumptions that serve us for the time being and hand over our doubts to the philosophers whose job it is to explore these other dimensions on our behalf.

To return to our concern with the limited subject of group processes, we believe that it is possible to provide a working basis for our study by assuming that two fundamental and conflicting drives exist in every group, originating in two fundamental and conflicting drives present in every individual: on the one hand, there is the wish to be separate, and, on the other hand, there is the wish to be one of a group. Both these components are always present, though not necessarily in equal amounts.

The quality and strength of these drives shown in any individual will owe something to constitutional make-up and to previous history as well as to the nature of the group situation in which the individual is placed.

All of us try to obtain, at one and the same time, the advantages of belonging and of not belonging. We conform to the customs and standards of our immediate social group, but within this conformity we try to establish the fact that we are different. We try to choose clothes that will be both fashionable (same) and individual (different). We fear loneliness and isolation in being separate, and we fear loss of personal identity and of freedom in being one of a crowd. Anyone who seeks to be the leader of a group is trying to achieve a position in which he can maintain an extreme degree of separateness while still retaining membership of the group.

The existence of these two opposite drives is shown in the two conflicting attitudes towards groups that one encounters. On the one hand, one finds the belief that the group diminishes the individual and that membership of a group entails a surrender of part of personal independence, a suppression of individuality and loss of uniqueness which is to be deplored. On the other hand, one finds an advocacy of group membership as an enriching process which can provide a cure for all manner of social ills from delinquency to widowhood. Clubs and associations proliferate to meet all tastes and needs and are regarded as being beneficial to both individuals and society as a whole. Both these opposite attitudes contain some truth; together they reflect a feeling about the powerful and mysterious nature of group forces and an acknowledgement that groups contain potentialities for both benefit and harm to their individual members.

The conduct of individuals can be explained in terms of ambivalence, i.e. in terms of opposing and simultaneously operating loves and hates. We find comparable forces operating at a group level, and these forces are represented by the tendencies of the group to continue, (i.e. its coherence) and the tendencies of the group to break up, (i.e. its disruptiveness). *The simultaneously operating coherence and disruptiveness constitute the ambivalence of the group.* It may well be that only one aspect of this 'group ambivalence' will find expression at any one moment, but in order to understand the behaviour of the group, the other component must be assumed to exist in an undisclosed form.

The first problem facing a group is to survive, just as the last problem is to disband. Groups survive when their opposing tendencies can be reconciled. They also survive when they are able to provide sufficient satisfaction for the needs of each of their members so that the wish to belong is strong enough to overcome the wish to be separate.

Thus, when we consider what happened at any particular group, and wonder why events followed the course that they did, we need to look at the following factors:

1 The overt purpose and structure of the group.

2. The problems and needs that each individual member brings into the group, and attempts to solve and satisfy through the group.

3. The conflict that each member experiences about belonging to the group. If needs are insufficiently satisfied, the wish to break away may become stronger than the wish to remain.

These three considerations come together in a fourth:

4. The totality, which adds up to a basic group problem, and which cannot be equated with the problem of any one individual member but which belongs to them all. This is the struggle for the group's survival through the promotion of its cohesiveness and the containment of its disruptiveness. It is within this basic problem that the group processes operate.

Latecoming as an example

Another example of the nature and interrelationships of the processes operating within a group can be given through a consideration of the question of latecoming.

Like all group events, latecoming can be considered to have meaning at three levels: the individual level of each group member, the interpersonal level of relationships between and among individual members, and the transpersonal level of interaction in the situation as a whole. These levels are interconnected and the separation is artificial though convenient.

At an individual level, a particular instance of latecoming might be seen as a response to a specific external happening, or it might be part of a temporary resistance, an expression of negative feelings, or of a wish on the part of one member of the group to be different from the rest of the group.

Chronic latecoming by one individual, in whom unpunctuality is a permanent trait affecting many areas of life, can indicate an established determination to resist the imposition of control by others over where one is and when. It may be linked to other experiences of resistance in the past, and in particular may have its origin at that much earlier stage of development when the child first comes into conflict with the wishes of dominant adults.

These individual causes for lateness may be present at the beginning and then go on to play a part in helping to shape the total proceedings of a group. If one member is habitually late, the group has to respond to this, perhaps by incorporating the behaviour into the overall pattern, perhaps by attempting to change it, perhaps by both.

For example, the latecoming member could be criticised and excluded, could become the group rebel and be used to challenge the leader, could become the focus of anger or could be used as a scapegoat, according to the other needs present in the group at the time. Latecoming, with all that it implies, could become a group preoccupation, expressed through the activity of only one member.

At the second level, latecoming might be related to particular interpersonal relationships in the group. One member might come late as part of his reaction to another member, to the leader, to a sub group, or to the group as a whole. And this too would not remain at this level but would be picked up and given additional meaning, to take its place in the proceedings of the group as a whole.

There is a different situation when the latecoming itself seems to start as a shared primary group activity. Suppose that all the members of the group have in common a reluctance to be the first to arrive. In these circumstances, there could be persistent lateness affecting a group of otherwise punctual people, not one of whom would wish to be late in other circumstances. The lateness would have to be considered as a property of this particular group, arising out of the situation as a whole, a situation to which all the members were contributing.

An example in which latecoming reflected processes taking place in the group as a whole can be found in the records of one particular group – one of the groups of strangers brought together for the purposes of psychotherapy that will be discussed in more detail later. When the purpose of a group is psychotherapy the boundaries become particularly significant, and it is often in relation to the boundaries, particularly the boundaries of time, that group tensions are acted out. Ideally all members of a group should arrive together so that all experience is shared and the group can begin as soon as all are present. Lateness interferes with the development of relationships, introduces a distorting element in the group's natural development, makes it difficult for the members to meet on equal terms, and encourages splitting and the formation of sub groups. Yet lateness is often a persistent problem.

The group to be considered, in which latecoming was general and habitual during the first year of its existence, was conducted by two co-therapists. The group consisted of three men and three women, all latecomers in different degrees during this period. The women were more often on time than the men, and their lateness averaged ten minutes. The men were rarely on time and quite often a man would be twenty minutes late or more. One man who was usually the last to arrive was an 'outsider' whose personal history showed a persistent need to set himself against all authority and to avoid close personal relationships. The other members of the group showed a concern about him and a tolerance of his often disruptive behaviour. He seemed to represent through his behaviour an anarchic and rebellious aspect of the group.

Reading through the records, several themes emerge which concerned the group as a whole, and which all seem relevant to the chronic latecoming.

First, there was a problem, both discussed and demonstrated in the group, with 'making the first move' in any relationship, particularly a sexual one. The fears that were expressed were of rejection or ridicule. Less clearly expressed but also present were fears of receiving a warm response. There was a wish to be given guidelines that would make relationships predictable and safe.

Second, and closely related, was a wish to become closely involved with other people, coexisting with a reluctance to do so. There was hostility to the therapists who were not breaking down the barriers and making it possible for the group members to become more closely involved with each other.

A third theme was rebellion against authority and a search for rules and regulations which they could rebel against. The therapists were criticised for not being more directive, and attempts were made to manipulate them into taking more of a lead.

Fourth, there was a fear of showing feelings openly; in particular feelings of anger as well as other instinctual urges.

These themes emerged slowly within the proceedings of the group over a period of months. They could be considered at more than one level, as they had some particular meaning for each of the members, separately and in relation to each other, and they were also connected to the total situation in the group. So for a time latecoming played its part in bringing together and expressing a complex network of preoccupations.

The latecoming also expressed the ambivalence that was present at individual and at group levels. It was noteworthy that at the same time that the members of the group were reducing the duration of each session and making the treatment less effective by their latecoming, they were energetically putting forward the suggestion the sessions should be extended by an hour as they found the time allotted insufficient.

CHAPTER 3

The Quest for Change

Change is not made without inconvenience, even from worse to better.
(Richard Hooker, quoted in Johnson's *Dictionary*)

The search for change

Picture a small number of people coming together regularly, perhaps at weekly intervals, and spending an hour, or perhaps an hour and a half, in each other's company. They meet as equals, and they sit round in a circle and talk together. There is a leader with some sort of special knowledge and skills who is there to help them. The leader may seem to exercise little direct control over the proceedings. It is not a business or committee meeting that has brought these people together, since there is no agenda, no chairperson, and no reference to any external task. It is not a social or recreational occasion, since there appears to be a serious purpose. No systematic instruction is given, so the purpose does not appear to be formal education. There does not seem to be any ambition to bring about changes in the wider community, so it is not a political meeting. There is no reference to supernatural forces, moral code, creed or body of doctrine, so it is not in any sense a religious assembly. The focus is upon what goes on in the group, on the interchanges taking place, the contributions of members and of leader, and on this alone. Whatever it is that the members are seeking, it seems to be contained here.

Such a meeting could be taking place in any one of a variety of different settings – consulting room, social work agency, clinic, hospital, prison, school, university or even workplace. The members could be patients, inmates, clients, members of a youth club, or students of such disciplines as medicine, psychology, counselling, teaching, nursing or psychotherapy, or else trainees in industry and this is by no means an inclusive list. The leader could belong to any one of a number of different professions, including the disciplines listed above, each with its own techniques and its own distinct body of professional knowledge. Thus the groups may vary considerably in setting, in composition, and in leadership. They may also differ widely in their purposes and in their proceedings, in what the individual members hope to gain and in what the leader attempts to contribute.

What do these groups have in common?

Each member of the different groups we are discussing has come because of dissatisfaction, at some level and in some degree, with current circumstances and current levels of achievement. It may be dissatisfaction with the whole of present life or with one small part of it. The dissatisfaction may be small or great. What is being sought may be relief from a severe mental disturbance, or help with some family difficulty, or something that will ease the transition from one stage of life to another. But whatever the problems and dissatisfactions of individual members, or whatever new satisfactions are being sought, they all have this in common: *all of them are concerned with relationships between and among people.* It is in this area that the dissatisfactions are being expressed, and it is through this area that the remedies are being sought.

The dissatisfactions, or the search for new satisfactions, may be related to the existing level of professional skills. There are professions in which the contribution made by skill and sensitivity in personal relationships is explicitly recognised, and any professional practice concerned with living beings in a face-to-face situation will require from the practitioners a deeper understanding of their own behaviour as well as of the behaviour of others. Such deeper understanding cannot be acquired by any intellectual process alone. It may sometimes be sought (as may the relief from mental illness and the resolution of personal problems) through participation in the activities of a group.

So the members of these groups, with different motivations and different degrees of commitment, are seeking to improve the quality of the relationships which they make with other people; to learn to recognise the contribution they themselves make to every personal relationship in which they are involved and to take responsibility for that contribution. They could be concerned with relationships in general, or with relationships in a particular setting. To this end they are prepared to expose themselves to new situations which contain the possibility of personal change.

This brings us to a further point that all these groups have in common. *The change that is being sought includes a degree of personal change in each of their individual members.* This change is not something that takes place through the influence of any external factor, nor is it change in some determined direction. The members of the groups are not converted, nor are they indoctrinated, nor, for this purpose, should they be instructed. The agent of change is participation in the group itself and in its processes, operating under exceptional and disciplined conditions. Though all groups have their dynamics, and there are potentialities for change, growth and development in every human encounter, we are considering very particular situations in which an attempt is made to be aware of these potentialities and to make use of them.

If this scenario is generally familiar today in the population at large, it is to some extent due to the growth of the encounter group movement which mushroomed in the United States and then spread beyond in the receptive culture of the 1960s. Though the encounter movement itself appears to have largely run its course, its influence remains. Encounter-type groups crop up under many guises. Yalom (1985) in a review of the encounter group movement, lists some of the many aliases of encounter groups, including human relations groups, training groups, sensitivity groups, personal growth groups, marathon groups, human potential groups, sensory awareness groups, truth labs, confrontation groups and experiential groups, in addition to the large number of self-help groups that were formed under encounter group influence, and other groups sponsored by new and not so new religions.

These groups have features in common with each other and also bear some similarities to the groups to be discussed and differentiated here. There is the face-to-face setting, the time limitation, the focus on the here and now; there is also the attempt at freedom from normal social conventions, the emphasis on feedback and on the 'unfreezing' of existing belief systems.

The encounter group movement led to an increased awareness of the potential contained in the group context that extends beyond the meeting of specific needs; it also led to some over-optimistic adoption of group methods without the safeguards and boundaries that professional group work requires. It must bear some responsibility for any blurring there has been between the boundaries of therapy and some of the other forms of group work carried on without the safeguards and constraints that therapy requires. It has sometimes been presented as 'group therapy for normals', the differentiation between encounter groups and other groups being founded upon the assumed normality of encounter group participants This is an assumption that cannot always be sustained.

Obstacles to change

Groups may be joined in the hope of change, but even when change is being sought it may also be feared and resisted. Change threatens the established structure and patterning that supports our internal and external functioning and so helps us to function with some consistency as individuals and as members of families and of society.

We tend to spend much of our energy trying to avoid change, or at least to slow it down, endeavouring to maintain an existing situation because of fears that any alteration might involve loss rather than gain. This perhaps explains the increased vulnerability that comes at transition points in personal and family development, and the way in which people often experience depression at moments of change even when the change appears to be for the better. Freud (1926) spoke of a force at work in his patients which seemed to be clinging tenaciously to illness and suffering and using all possible means to avoid recovery.

It can be hard openly to acknowledge a need, for we may fear that if the need is known it may be ignored and then our burden would be doubled. It can be hard to acknowledge ignorance and incompetence if we are afraid of contempt and loss of esteem: we may fear that others will take advantage of any weaknesses we reveal. Thus insecurity can make us assume positions that are hard to relinquish and that discourage change. Others, however, may cling to weaknesses as an entitlement to a special care and consideration that they are reluctant to surrender, fearing any change that might bring greater challenges and greater demands.

At another level, there are aspects of ourselves that we struggle to conceal not only from our associates but even from our conscious selves. We may fear that any slackening in our self-control could reveal and release primitive impulses of which we are only dimly aware, and which we fear might overwhelm us even to the point of disintegration and madness.

Within groups, unstructured situations are felt to be frightening. They contain a danger that too much will be revealed. The less structure there is in a group, the less are we able to hide ourselves in stereotyped roles and the less predictable will be our own behaviour and that of the other group members. The less, too, will be the restrictions on the free play of group forces, which are also feared.

But the group situations in which we customarily find ourselves in our day-to-day lives have most of their challenge removed through rules and regulations, social conventions and agreed standards of behaviour designed for this very purpose. There are hierarchies, chairpersons and procedures, and established forms of social behaviour. We have our selected circle of friends whose needs dovetail with our own. All these help to preserve our accustomed roles, and protect us from unexpected encounters and embarrassing revelations.

The groups we are considering differ from these situations. If the members of these groups are seeking the possibility of change, they must be ready to expose themselves to an unstructured encounter with unselected others. They will have to abandon some part of their habitual defences, to relinquish some part of their controls, to reveal more and to be more honest both with themselves and with others. Some of the conventions of social intercourse with which they would normally protect themselves must be abandoned.

Safety and the group leader

Changes may be desired but they do not come about merely by willing them. If members of a group are going to be able to behave in a different way, then they must feel they are in a different situation. If they are to modify the defences they are accustomed to use in order to feel secure, then, initially, alternative sources of security will have to be provided. The margin of safety has to be extended. This will not happen all at once, and the security of the group will have to be built up by degrees as the members are able to test out and thus extend the permitted limits. They are likely to be helped in this by the knowledge that they all have similar or comparable purposes, and by the gradual sharing of confidences and experiences.

But whatever may happen in the group to help or hinder the development of this process, the safety of the group and of individual members is ultimately the responsibility of the group leader. It is part of the group leader's function to ensure that free exchanges can take place without unacceptable danger, that no one is subjected to more stress than can be tolerated, and that the group does not break up until it has accomplished its purpose. No leader can expect always to be completely successful in this. It is also the leader's responsibility to see that the aims of the group are preserved.

These aims set bounds and limits to the proceedings, and any self-exposure should not overstep the limits set by the group's particular aims. The group members have to relinquish some part of their normal controls, and, in doing so, they vest these controls in the leader. Removing a layer of outer garments, they rely upon the leader to ensure that the room is kept warm enough for their body heat to be maintained. They also rely upon the leader to prevent them from taking off so many clothes that they will either catch cold or be improperly exposed.

In every one of these groups, an implicit bargain is made between each group member and the leader. Within the terms of reference determined by the aims of the group, the leader guarantees that the difficulties can be discussed and feelings ventilated in a situation that is safe enough though not without challenge. Outside these terms of reference, the leader guarantees that any wish for privacy will be respected.

The specific aims of these groups can differ considerable: in some the terms of reference will be drawn widely, and in some they will be drawn narrowly. In each situation, the group members will only be prepared to expose themselves to the extent that confidence exists in the power of the leader to guarantee safety when conditions in the group cannot do so. This confidence may be helped initially by the acknowledged position of the leader, but it depends in the longer run upon the leader's skill in this role.

The leaders have the responsibility for establishing and maintaining the boundaries, but may be able to limit their direct interventions. Sufficient conditions of safety at each stage may come to be provided by the group itself as it develops and matures. Through the operation of group processes, a broad, tacit consensus of opinion can be expected to develop about the behaviour of individuals in the group, the honouring of confidences, the tolerance of divergences, and the level of reciprocal disclosures. Most leaders of such groups would not wish to interfere with the free development of such a consensus, which, though constantly shifting, will be far more effective than any imposed ruling would be. However, the leader's presence is necessary as the ultimate guarantor, and will be a personal reassurance when the strength and cohesiveness of the group seem insufficient.

Some members of a group will always be more vulnerable than others, and sensitivity in different situations will vary. Sometimes one member will introduce a topic, make comments, or ask questions, for which others in the group are not ready and which they find disturbing. For various reasons, and in various ways, individual members may find themselves isolated and criticised, The result of all this may be one or more members who become unable to participate, or who may even leave the group. The disruptive forces in the group, of which all are afraid, will need to find some expression; but if they are expressed too openly and too early, before sufficient cohesion has developed to contain them, they may lead to the disintegration of the group.

So in any of the groups we are considering, the leader may be required to intervene to protect a particular member, or to protect the group as a whole, to increase the safety of one of them or of all of them, and to help the group to develop sufficient strength and cohesiveness for its purpose. The leader may also have to intervene to see that the necessary limits are observed and that the privacy of members outside these limits is respected.

The bargain with the leader

The concept of a bargain between group member and group leader, 'implicit' because it can seldom be explicitly formulated, plays an important part. It is included in the concept of the 'mandate' which is given by the party seeking personal help to the party offering it, and which must not be exceeded.

This concept has been questioned by Halmos (1965). It has been argued , in relation to social work and counselling, that the client of the social worker is rarely in any position to appreciate the nature and limitations of the help that is being offered, or to forecast what is going to be demanded, and that therefore it is an act of self-deception for social workers or counsellors to speak as if there were a contract freely entered into by both parties. Training groups, which may not be voluntary, are open to similar criticism. By the same argument, the individuals who elect to join any of the groups we are considering may well have no clear and accurate idea of what will be involved, but this does not mean that they are agreeing to participate in an unlimited process. One joins a group for some particular purpose, and one expects that the leader will do everything in her or his power to to see that this purpose is achieved. In this sense, the leader is empowered to act in certain ways. If the individual members do not understand what these ways are, they are able to support any initial uncertainty because of the belief that the leader understands them.

The fact that group members and group leaders are embarking upon a joint task of uncertain direction and outcome makes it all the more important that its ultimate aims and limits should be understood and respected by leaders who must take responsibility for them. The consent of the members may often be based initially upon an act of faith, but this consent becomes ratified by their increasing involvement in the groups which they have joined. The leaders are fully committed at the beginning, but the members may have to extend the area of their commitment gradually. For them, the bargain is not a static one but a living experience which makes possible the organic growth and development of the group as a whole.

So to summarise, all the groups that have been mentioned, with their wide range of parameters and purposes from therapy to experiential learning, from counselling to sensitivity training to team building, meet in their aim to promote a degree of personal change in their members through participation in the processes taking place in the group itself. Each member of these groups, moreover, is expected to be more ready to expose him or herself to the possibility of personal change than would be expected in other encounters, and depends upon a leader with special skills to be the ultimate guarantor that it is safe to do so.

The very similarities to be found in these different forms of group work make it important to be clear about the differences. They each take place within parameters that need to be carefully established and maintained, and continuous attention must be paid to them. The differences are to be found in the aims of the groups; in the nature, degree and purpose of the changes that are sought; in the commitment of the group members; in the consequent role played by the group leader; and in the psychological level of depth and particularity at which each group operates. And each form of group work also has its own additional roots in a different individual helping process.

But before distinguishing the different group work systems, we need to return to the group process. An additional point that these groups have in common is the part derivation of their theoretical base from dynamic theories of group psychology that have been developed since the 1940s through the work of group psychotherapists.

CHAPTER 4

Questions and Concepts

The questions

- Why do people behave differently in groups?
- What makes it difficult to work in groups ?
- What holds groups together – and what makes groups fall apart?
- Are there recurrent patterns in group behaviour?
- How does each individual member contribute to the overall culture and process of the group?
- By what means do the processes in the group impact upon the individual?

The presence and activity of group processes is something that can only be inferred after watching how individuals behave together in groups.

Though the actual data for studying these processes and for developing dynamic theories of group behaviour may be present whenever people come together and interact in a face to face situation, the business and 'busyness' of most everyday groups conceals and distorts it. In most working groups the emphasis is likely to be placed on content, and on getting on with the business in hand as quickly as possible, at the expense of spontaneous expression; and so all the information that is being conveyed in other ways is obscured and can go largely unrecognised. But psychotherapeutic groups, with their clear boundaries which separate them off from the rest of everyday life, with their lack of formal structure and imposed task, and with their reduction in the barriers to free uncensored communication, can limit this interference and provide near laboratory conditions for observation and study. It is in this situation that the group processes have been recognised and most systematically examined, where a vocabulary has been established, and where group concepts have been formulated, tested and retested. So it is to the ideas developed in treatment groups of strangers that one has to turn.

The practice of bringing small numbers of patients together to share their psychotherapeutic sessions may have been undertaken by a few pioneers even before World War I, but it is only since 1945 that it has been used on any large scale. The development of theory has followed upon practice, in the same way that psychoanalytic theory did not become formulated until Freud had used the psychoanalytic method for the treatment of patients. But there is no single theory of group psychotherapy as such, instead we have a bewildering variety of different theoretical systems labelled group psychotherapy, some differing quite radically from one another, and some separated more by degrees of emphasis. The present position of group psychotherapy could be compared to the early days of psychoanalysis, when Freud's followers were all laying their separate claims to new discoveries and formulations. Today there is a similar wealth in the contributions of group psychotherapists, and, as techniques have become more refined and have come to be used more precisely, so the terminology has become more complicated.

These theories not only establish different forms of group psychotherapy, they also offer models of group dynamics that can be applied to all other groups.

Classification of theoretical systems

One way in which the different theories formulated and applied by the leading group psychotherapists differ is in the context or perspective in which any single event occurring in a group is placed. Thus, a single incident taking place in a group can be looked at in three different ways. It can be seen as a result of the activity of one particular group member, as a result of the interaction between two or more group members, or as the product of the sum of all the interactions taking place.

The first viewpoint is found in theories which treat the level of activity taking place at an intrapersonal level, within the individual, as the most relevant and significant. Here the therapists make use of a model drawn from the two-person situation of individual psychoanalysis. They set out to treat the individual within a group setting and to carry out something resembling psychoanalysis in public with a participating audience. It has been claimed that this can provide a therapeutic advantage over individual psychoanalysis because the support that each member derives from being a member of a group increases tolerance of anxiety and enables deeper levels to be reached more quickly. There is also the vicarious learning that can take place through being present at the discussion of problems that are like and unlike one's own. Slavson (1950) with Locke and Schwartz are among the group psychotherapists who first began to work in this way, using the group as a treatment tool but focusing the treatment upon each individual in turn.

Others have placed their main emphasis upon events taking place at an interpersonal level, that is, as transactions occurring between more than one individual, and the products of sets of dynamic interpersonal relationships. An example can be found in the games or transactions that Berne (1967) has uncovered.

In distinction to these is the third point of departure in which each group event is regarded as being determined or influenced by all other happenings in the group, and by the complete network of relationships that includes all members. Thus each event has, in addition to its significance at an intrapersonal and interpersonal level, a significance at a group level, and the sum of all the transactions taking place has a meaning which can only be understood by considering the context of the group as a whole. The total group situation always has to be taken into account.

This last viewpoint, which was introduced earlier, is the one to be considered more fully now. It is the viewpoint associated with Foulkes and his followers, with Bion and the Tavistock School, with Ezriel and Stock Whitaker, and also with Agazarian. The theories they have developed are psychoanalytically orientated, and also focus upon the activity, in Agazarian's words, of the Invisible as well as the Visible group. They differ at some significant points, however, and at times make use of rather different terminology.

These different theoretical systems all share with psychoanalysis the belief that every piece of human behaviour has meaning at two levels, the manifest and the latent, the conscious and the unconscious. There is the level of conscious response to the situation in which the individual is placed, and there is the level at which behaviour can only be fully understood as a response to unconscious drives and basic emotional needs whose presence has to be deduced. Although it is usually considered to be a naive mistake to think that psychoanalytic concepts derived from the study of individuals can be applied directly to groups, the concept of conscious and unconscious levels is fundamental to both fields.

Concepts

Different theoretical systems derived from group psychotherapy will be considered in relation to the questions posed at the start of this chapter.

These questions have an importance that extends beyond group psychotherapy to other areas where groups are used for counselling or discussion or teaching. They are also relevant to people who work with individuals and need to understand the group and interpersonal contexts from which their students, clients and patients come.

Bion

- What interferes with a group's ability to work effectively?
- Why are there typical recurrent patterns in group behaviour?
- Why is leadership of a group often such a difficult task?

Though Bion's theories were developed in therapy, they have been applied to different group situations and many people have found them to be most useful in the understanding of organisations.

At the beginning of his book *Experiences in Groups*, Bion defines group therapy in two different ways: 'It can refer to the treatment of a number of individuals assembled for special therapeutic sessions, or it can refer to a planned endeavour to develop in a group the forces that lead to a smoothly running co-operative activity.' (Bion 1961, p.11). The starting point for his theory was his belief that, in the treatment of a group, neurosis always needs to be seen as a problem of the group and not of individuals..

Bion looked at behaviour in the group in the light of the tasks that the group has to perform and of the relationship between the leader of the group and its members.

He separated out the *work group*, which can be taken to correspond in many ways to the Freudian Ego, and which contains the rational, orderly aspect of the group's behaviour. This is the level which we all know and recognise. At this level the group can give some explanation of why it is meeting, and what it is doing, and can describe its procedure and purpose. A group operating exclusively in work group mode would hardly need a facilitator. The nature of the task would be the only determinant of number and content of meetings and choice of leader, members would cooperate without anxiety or competition, and neither emotional gratification nor emotional deprivation would interfere with effective task performance.

But the work group has a struggle to keep going. Work group activity is constantly being hampered and diverted by certain other mental activities associated with strong emotions. These mental activities were identified by Bion as following recurrent patterns, and he considered them to be responses to the collective anxiety that is always threatening to overwhelm the group but of which members of the group may be largely unaware.

So also present alongside the work group will be another level of activity, what Bion called *a basic assumption culture*, and this will be more or less dominant and apparent according to the strength of the work group and the coherence of the group organisation. The existence and continuance of a group, according to Bion, is always being threatened by a conflict between what he called *the group mentality*, to which all members contribute, and the individual drives of each group member.

The function of the basic assumption cultures is to meet this threat and to ensure the group's continuance.

He identified three basic assumption cultures, though he suggested that there are more. They derive from three different and distinct emotional states which may have control over the group at different times.

The first of these cultures is dominated by the basic assumption *dependency* (baD). In this culture the group appears to be seeking some leader (or it could be an external object, idea, creed or political cause) which will dominate it and give it protection and greater cohesiveness. When the group is behaving in an excessively or inappropriately dependent way, it is as if it is meeting in order to be sustained by a leader who will protect it and provide it with material and spiritual nourishment and protection. The group appears to want to hand over all power to act to a leader even at the cost of remaining weak and immature itself. The members of the group show no interest in forming a relationship with each other; only the leader is credited with any ability, and the talents and capacities of the other people present go unacknowledged.

The second basic assumption Bion called *pairing* (baP). The group will be operating in this mode when two members become involved in an interchange which is allowed to dominate the proceedings and appears to be being nurtured by the group. This pairing, which may sometimes take place symbolically or vicariously, can again be seen as an attempt to increase the cohesiveness of the group, this time by generating a mood of hopeful though unrealistic anticipation, and this feeling of hopeful expectation is always an indication that a pairing group is in existence. The group behaves as if it has met so that two people can form a pair that will lead to a new situation in the future. The unconscious expectation dominating the group, Bion thought, was of a fruitful and so essentially sexual union (however unrealistic this might appear) and of a new and as yet unborn leader. It is essential that this leader should remain unborn if the feelings of hope are to be sustained. The group is able to shelve its current problems because of the hope that something better is coming, but if this something better does occur it has to be rejected. 'Only by remaining a hope does hope persist.' (Bion 1961, p.151).

The third of his basic assumptions Bion called *fight/flight* (baF), and here the assumption that is being made is that the group is meeting in order to fight something or to run away from something. In this culture the dominant feeling is one of rage and fear as the group pinpoints a particular threat or a particular enemy who can be blamed for the group's predicament. This threat could be inside or outside the group. The choice lies between fighting or fleeing, and the group is therefore looking for a leader who will organise action in one of these two directions and thus ensure the group's survival.

Each basic assumption culture requires an appropriate leader – to satisfy dependency, to direct the group in the direction of fight or flight, or to support pairing. So the group is always seeking a leader of the type indicated by the particular basic assumption culture that is present in the group at that moment. The leader of the basic assumption culture will need to be suited to that particular purpose and so is unlikely to be identical with the leader of the work group. In a therapeutic group the therapist would not collude with the demands of basic assumption behaviour but would try to make the group aware of them..

For Bion, neurosis was not individual but a disability of the community or group. Improvement could only come when the group improved its capacity to work rationally and effectively, gained a greater contact with reality, and became able to tackle neurotic disability as a communal problem. The therapeutic task was seen as one of helping the group to recognise and address the problems caused by the shared unconscious fears, emotions and irrational feelings of its members.

In any group, one of the basic assumption cultures will always be present alongside the work group, even if not always very dominant or apparent. When a basic assumption is dominant, the group is having to use up much of its energy to deal with its own internal anxieties and the work group is consequently depleted and may be rendered ineffective. When a particular basic assumption culture ceases to give sufficient protection from anxieties, there will be a move into one of the other ones. Participation in basic assumption activity is instantaneous, inevitable and instinctive, and every group contains a spontaneous factor based upon mutual basic assumption needs.

Basic assumption behaviour is a defence against anxieties that threaten to overwhelm the group, but it can also be seen as reflecting the resistance of the group to carrying out whatever work is being required of it. It is a retreat from the work group into a more primitive mode of functioning.

Bion gave the term *valency* to 'the individual's readiness to enter into combination with the group in making and acting on the basic assumptions'. This readiness is always present, though it can at times become higher or lower. He believed that certain personality types are more predisposed to become involved with one basic assumption rather than another.

So every group is engaged in a struggle, which never ends, to make the work group overcome the basic assumption cultures; and, despite the influence of the basic assumptions, Bion concluded optimistically that it is the work group that triumphs in the long run. This is compatible with Freud's dictum 'Where Id was, Ego shall be.'

What is the basis of the anxiety that in Bion's view is always threatening to overwhelm the group?

The origin of Bion's theories in psychoanalysis has been mentioned. To be more precise, Bion regarded the group activity as a regression to the earliest stages of mental life, characterised by splitting and projection, persecutory anxiety and fears; he therefore found his explanations in terms used by Melanie Klein (1963). Participation in a group can bring the individual into a situation in which he is part, and yet also not part, of something much larger and more powerful than himself, a situation reminiscent of the helplessness and dependency of the infant at the start of life. 'The adult must establish contact with the emotional life of the group in which he lives; this task would appear to be as formidable to the adult as the relationship with the breast appears to be to the infant, and the failure to meet the demands of this task is revealed in his regression' (Bion 1961, p.141–2). Thus the coming together of the group can evoke for each member buried recollections of dependency on the mother's body and the regression that follows is a collective one.

Patterns of behaviour compatible with the operation of Bion's basic assumption cultures can be recognised in the wider society – for example, in the over-valuation and denigration of political leaders, in the bellicosity and fear sometimes stirred up by the actions of other countries, or in the popular hopes and excitement that have sometimes in the past been aroused by a royal wedding.

Basic assumption activity, Bion considered, can be taken on by subgroups on behalf of the whole. He located 'specialised work groups' operating as if delegated by society to carry one or other of the basic assumption cultures in order to leave the main group free to pursue designated work group activity. He suggested that the church is primarily concerned with basic assumption dependency, the army with basic assumption fight/flight, and the aristocracy, including (presumably) the monarchy, with basic assumption pairing, shown through the interest in preserving inheritance into the next generation.

Basic assumptions do not always hinder the work group, they can sometimes be used to improve the group's work and the leader may be able to promote this. If dependency is appropriate, the leader, through his own appropriate but monitored dependability, can keep this from becoming unrealistic and infantile. Fight can be an appropriate response if kept from being foolhardy and overly aggressive, and flight may be a realistic withdrawal from a difficult situation so long as it is kept from being a cowardly evasion. Hope in the future can be constructive optimism if kept short of unrealistic phantasy.

It is through a planned endeavour to promote smoothly running cooperative activity in a group, that is, by helping the group to understand and recognise patterns of basic assumption behaviour, that the blocked work potential of the group is released.

Foulkes

- How are all the events in the group linked together?
- What determines the meaning of any single event in a group?

The concepts of group-analytic psychotherapy formulated by Foulkes provide another framework which enables us to look at the way in which we are all linked as part of the one psychological field, and which brings together a picture of the activity of the group as a whole and of the place of the individual member in this total field. Group analysis has been particularly influential in the general development of group psychotherapy and much of its methodology has passed into standard practice and will be encountered again in the next chapter.

Fundamental to group analysis is the belief that the essence of human beings is social not individual. We are born as members of a group and remain deeply embedded, any separation we achieved later can only be partial. Any distinction that is drawn between the individual and the group is unnecessary and artificial; group processes and individual processes are two aspects of the same phenomenon and everything that happens in a group always involves the group as a whole as well as every individual member. The concept of the individual apart from the group is an artificial though plausible abstraction, as artificial as the concept of a fish out of water.

Foulkes used a neurological analogy comparing the position of the individual in the psychological network to the position of a nodal point in a neurological network. He pictured the individual embedded in the network, playing a part in holding the network together, and forming one of the channels through which communications can flow. Disturbance in the network and disturbance in the individual go together, bringing blocking and distortion of communication at more than one level.

The origin of neurotic illness (dis-ease) is to be found in the relationships between people, originally in an incompatibility between an individual and his original network which is then carried over into all subsequent networks. The neurotic individual then repeats the pattern of failing to fit smoothly into the network and instead of a nodal point carrying information becomes a point that distorts the information flow and goes on to bring distortion into the network as a whole. Then he or she, moving with the passage of time from group to group, becomes the conduit for carrying a set of disturbed processes from one network into another.

Foulkes developed and communicated his thinking about groups through his concept of the *matrix*. He used the matrix to convey the way in which social forces penetrate individuals and groups and bind them together so that every event is linked to every other event and to all that has gone before.

In a face-to-face group, the dynamic group matrix is the network of communications within the group which begins to be constructed from the first meeting and which continues to grow and develop. In Foulkes' words, it is 'the network of all individual mental processes, the psychological medium in which they meet, communicate and interact,' and again 'the hypothetical web of communication and relationship in a given group . . . the common shared ground which ultimately determines the meaning and significance of all events and upon which all communications, verbal and non-verbal, exist' (Foulkes 1964, p.282).

At any point in time, the matrix may be said to be composed of the entire past history of the group including everything that has taken place at group meetings and everything which has been brought in by the individual members. Nothing is lost. It is only against the background of the group matrix that any single event taking place in the group can be understood. A contribution made by a particular individual is determined not only by that individual's past history, constitutional endowment, present life situation, and relationships with others in the group; it is also determined by the position of that contribution in relation to the group matrix. It not only develops out of the matrix but it also adds to it, and thus has an influence over every subsequent event in the group.

Take one particular event in a group, let us say a comment made by one individual member. The comment may be linked to a particular personal preoccupation, it may be a specific response to another member of the group. But it was elicited, was made and was permitted to be made, in the overall context of this particular group at this particular time, and it adds one more contribution to the network of communication that is the group matrix. It will influence whatever happens next, and it will form part of the ground on which all subsequent happenings rest. Specific group events take place against this background and are a response to the growing matrix, and they cannot be understood in isolation. It is only when they are located in their context in the matrix that their fuller significance and meaning can be grasped. By analogy, a single figure extracted from a complex painting loses much of its meaning until it is restored to its position in the artist's composition.

In this situation, the group as a whole is concerned with themes and problems which arise out of the group matrix. These cannot be looked on as the property of any one group member. They are formed at the meeting point of individual preoccupations. Each member of the group will be related to the central theme in a different way, and so different aspects may be expressed by different members, but their communications are not for themselves alone; they are also being made on behalf of the group as a whole.

It is with the help of this concept of the group matrix that the group analyst is able to regard all spontaneous contributions as equivalent to the free association of psychoanalysis.

> Looked at this way, it becomes easier to understand our claim that the group associates, responds, and reacts as a whole. The group, as it were, avails itself now of one speaker, now of another, but it is always the transpersonal network which is sensitised and gives utterance or responds. In this sense we can postulate the existence of a group mind in the same way that we can postulate the existence of an individual mind. (Foulkes 1964, p.118)

So in this sense there is no such thing as an isolated mind or an isolated communication. Communications are always embedded in a context and are always part of a total pattern.

Thus in a group-analytic group, all processes being treated as parts of the one process, the focus can take in even-handedly the individual, the parts and the group as a whole.

A difference in the orientation of Bion and his followers (the Tavistock School) and Foulkes and his followers (group analysis) can be seen. Bion represented the group-as-a-whole approach par excellence and exclusively, and it seems that he always related to the group at this level, directing his interventions exclusively to the group and paying little or no attention to the individual members as such. Group-analysis, on the other hand, is concerned with individuals but always within the group context, and passes from considering the contributions of individuals in the light of their meaning for the group as a whole to considering the themes and patterns emerging at a group level in the light of their significance for the individuals. The analogy of figure and ground can be carried further, with figure and ground changing places according to the particular focus in which an event is viewed.

In addition to the dynamic group matrix that is built up in every face-to-face group Foulkes went on to develop the concept of the *foundation matrix*, based on our deepest shared biological, social and historical inheritance, which enables people to understand each other even when meeting for the first time. In addition we each of us have a *personal matrix*, the container for our individual history and all the internalised representations of past experiences and relationships which we bring with us into every network and group in which we come to take part. In these matrices, which of course need to be seen, too, as part of the one matrix, we have a pyramid from the less to the more and more individual, from species culture, class, occupation to family and individual. But it is the dynamic group matrix that is separated out as being of special interest in the context of treatment, since this is the matrix through which change can be introduced.

Stock Whitaker

- What is the group trying to achieve?
- How are all the disparate processes taking place in the group reconciled?
- What covert problem solving activity is underlying the observed behaviour in the group.
- How do group themes emerge?
- How do they offer solutions to the problems of coming together in groups?

Stock Whitaker (Stock Whitaker and Liebermann 1965) looks on the group as always being engaged in trying to establish a soluion to a current problem that is threatening its functioning.

Each individual brings into the group and expresses in the here-and-now situation of the group, some *nuclear conflict* carried over from early in that person's life and still active in the present. From the range of personal preoccupations and concerns that each individual brings into the group, some selection has to be made. What is selected and expressed will come as a response to the current group situation, and the other members will then respond to that contribution in the light of their own nuclear conflicts, selecting some aspects and ignoring others. The aspects which are picked up and built upon through their relevance to the preoccupations of others gradually become part of an emerging shared concern of the group, another level of conflict which now belongs to the group as a whole and which Stock Whitaker calls the *group focal conflict.*

The nuclear conflict of an individual and the focal conflict of a group have a similar structure and are both made up of three elements. There is a wish or impulse associated with strong negative or positive feelings (known in this context as a *disturbing motive*), a fear that is linked to the wish and to the perceived consequences of attempting to gratify that wish (*reactive motive*) and the search for a *solution* which it is hoped will reduce the anxiety aroused by the conflict between these two motives

In the here-and-now situation of a group, the problem that causes a focal conflict is likely to be concerned with the management of the destructive forces, the competing wishes, jealousies and rivalries that are threatening the group's survival. Such a conflict, representing covert shared concerns of all members, and including present concerns and those carried over from the past, emerges in every group; but the more structured, consistent and purposeful the group, the harder it will be to detect.

So at any time, the behaviour of members of a small group can be seen as determined by the need to find a solution not only to individual nuclear conflicts but also to an overriding current focal conflict belonging to the group. Attempts are made, at an unconscious level, to find a solution acceptable to them all that will reduce the fears while it permits the maximum possible satisfaction of the wish. Over a period of time, recurrent themes emerging in a group will reflect the focal conflict or conflicts arising from related disturbing motives.

Reference has been made earlier to a group made up of mothers of children with learning difficulties. In this group the mothers' angry feelings about authorities, and their wish to compete to obtain special provision for their children, could be considered the disturbing motive which was conflicting with the fear, or reactive motive, that their anger and competitive feelings would endanger the group which they valued. The problem of reconciling the wish and the fear created the group focal conflict, and the first solution this group of women established for this conflict was to act as if they felt their children were all alike. It reduced the fear but gave them little opportunity to express separate wishes for their children or to consider their situation realistically.

In Stock Whitaker's terminology, this would be called a restrictive solution rather than an enabling solution. Restrictive solutions reduce the fears by denying the wish, in contrast to enabling solutions which, while also doing something to reduce the fears, manage at the same time to permit some more direct expression or satisfaction of the wish.

It is likely in the beginning stages of a group that the solutions to the group's focal conflict will tend to be more restrictive ones, moving on to more enabling solutions as reality testing and feedback reduce the fears. Reactive motives and solutions can change more easily that the underlying disturbing motives, and a group will always tend to fall back on restrictive solutions when anxiety levels rise.

Ezriel

- How are individual (infantile) wishes and fears carried over into the group processes?

Ezriel, like Bion, worked at the Tavistock Clinic. His formulations (Ezriel 1950a;b) are to a large extent drawn from the unconscious object relations theories associated with Klein (1963) and Fairburn (1952) and now translated into group terms.

Object relations theory, while giving primacy to the separate individual, relates psychological disturbance to successive failures in relationships with others from infancy onwards. Each member brings into the group unconscious phantasies about relationships with objects and part objects, the residue of unresolved infantile conflicts, and then attempts to relieve the tension this creates through the relationships created in the group. To this end, each member seeks to manipulate the other members of the group so that they will respond and behave in certain ways which will satisfy that member's unconscious needs, 'like pawns in a private game of chess' (Ezriel 1950b, p.775). But though they are all moving on the same board, they are not all playing the same game. Some common denominator has to be found. It is by means of the interaction of each members' individual dominant (unconscious) tension that an underlying 'common group tension' is created. The members of group are not aware of this common group tension although their behaviour is determined by it.

Like Stock Whitaker and Lieberman, Ezriel describes the group situation in terms of a dynamic triad of forces though with a different terminology. The relationship which the group (and before the group the individual) is attempting to establish he calls the *required relationship*. It is required not so much for the gratification which it is expected to supply as for its power to prevent an alternative relationship. This alternative he calls the *avoided relationship*, for in unconscious phantasy this relationship must be avoided lest it lead to a third situation, the *calamity*. For example, a group may behave in a docile and compliant way towards their leader. This is the required relationship. Their concern is to avoid another type of relationship, the one they really want to establish, one perhaps in which hostility to the leader might find expression and which might then lead on to the 'calamity' of his withdrawal or retaliation. It is the required relationship that is apparent when one looks at the behaviour of a group, and from this one has to deduce what it is that is being avoided and what calamity is feared.

General Systems Theory

Before considering Agazarian's theory of the visible and invisible group, we need briefly to introduce systems theory (see De Board 1978). Systemic thinking is central to Agazarian's concepts, and indeed many others have found it a useful model to hold in mind when surveying a complex field and dealing with relationships between wholes and parts.

Systems theory provides a comprehensive model of near universal application. Applied to the organic world we find that wherever we choose to look, from (within existing knowledge) subatomic particles at the bottom to galaxies at the top, units are linked together within one vast hierarchical pyramid. Any single unit on which we may choose to focus our attention has a dual position, being on the one hand a whole made up of component parts and on the other hand a component part of some greater whole.

We can think of the human being as a system made up of a number of subsystems (endocrine, nervous, gastro-intestinal etc.) that can be further subdivided. We can also think of a human being, if we look in another direction, as being a subsystem in a higher system. Men and women, as social beings, can form part of different hierarchical structures at the same time, combining and recombining in different systems for different purposes and being at one and the same time, say, a member of a family, a household, a work team and a club. Any part of this hierarchy can be separated out for consideration on its own and for some purposes it may be appropriate to do so while for other purposes it needs to be considered as a constituent part of a higher system.

Over and above the individual and the family, we have bigger social organisations, all hierarchically structured and all needing to be so structured if they are to function at all. Government departments, armies, schools, scout troops, like ant or bee colonies, all have a structure in which smaller units are grouped together into bigger units, all the way up to the top of the pyramid.

So wherever we look we find something that is system, subsystem and super-system. Each system, at whatever level it may be found, exists within its own boundaries which separate it off from the rest of the field which contains it, but it is also linked to every other system at one or more removes, even though it is only in direct contact with the other component parts in the system to which it belongs.

All systems involving living substances are considered as open systems, with semi-permeable boundaries, in constant interrelationship with their environment, exchanging information and other material with other systems. Any change taking place in that environment will not only affect that system as a whole, but will also infiltrate through it into every subsystem and super system. But not every system is equally open - some boundaries are more permeable than others. Therefore we have to bear in mind the possibility of a closed system separated from an environment that can neither influence it nor be influenced by it. But for present purposes these are only theoretical possibilities, serving to remind us that human systems vary in the nature and degree of their openness and that these differences are very significant. The systems we are concerned with maintain themselves by a variable flow of material inwards and outwards, as a human being maintains herself by taking in oxygen and giving out carbon dioxide, and always remembering that some people breathe more easily and more deeply than others.

The emphasis in systemic thinking is placed squarely upon the shifting relationships and the arrangement and rearrangement of the constituent parts. Each system is at work trying to maintain itself in equilibrium, balance its component parts, maintain its boundaries, control and monitor the information exchange that is taking place across these boundaries, and adjust to the changes taking place in other systems within and without, above and below.

This recognition that life is organised in a structure of linked hierarchies brings us back to the dichotomy between 'togetherness' and 'separateness' in human life in all its aspects, and makes it possible to treat them as two aspects of one process which permeates the hierarchy from top to bottom. Every unit or system with its own unique arrangement of parts is trying to assert its own unique pattern of activity, constrained by the needs of the equally shifting overall order into which it has to fit. The degree of freedom possible depends upon the cohesion among the constituent parts. Any system is strengthened in its relationship with its environment when its own subsystems fit smoothly and harmoniously together.

Thus man is at one and the same time a whole and a part. Individual psychology and group psychology provide two ways of looking at the same phenomenon. By focusing upon the relationships among the parts and upon the relative openness of all systems, we are able to deal at the same time with parts and wholes, and to move up and down and in and out of the hierarchy. At every level of intervention, we are dealing with something which is both a system, made up of constituent parts in dynamic interaction, and a subsystem of some greater entity. There is no need to choose betwen individual and group orientations.

This model can be applied to living systems at all levels, to individuals, families and organisations. And to groups. A group, as Foulkes understood, is part of a hierarchy of systems. When he first encountered systems thinking, Foulkes exclaimed 'But that's group analysis!'

The treatment group is one system that is composed of subsystems and is in a relationship with a super-system. Each member brings into the group his or her own subsystem of internalised problems and relationships. Change can be introduced through involvement at any level, moving across the semi-open boundaries between the systems and using the links between them. It is through the relationship network that each component part influences each other component part as well as the system as a whole. And through the relationship, each component part is affected in its turn by each of the others and by the subsystem as a whole.

Agazarian

- How does the individual system of the group member link up with the system of the group as a whole?

Applying systems theory to group dynamics, Agazarian (Agazarian and Peters 1981) has developed a theory of the *invisible group* or group-as-a-whole, a construct reached by deduction and distinct from the *visible group* which is made up of the individual and visible members. The two groups, representing individual dynamics and group dynamics, form two distinct but interrelated systems, each system having to work to maintain itself and look after its internal and external boundaries.

Agazarian sees *role behaviour* as the link between the individual and the group-as-a-whole.

Each individual, (as Ezriel and others noted) has a repertoire of roles, or preferred ways of behaviour, at his or her disposal, and these roles are needed to maintain individual equilibrium and to give consistency and structure to the individual personality. Success in adopting and maintaining a role is dependent upon associates being prepared to play reciprocal roles. Coming into the group, the individual will have to find a role from the repertoire available which is not only personally sustainable but which is also fits in well enough with the preferred roles of others so that it can receive sufficient acceptance and support.

Then, at the higher systems level, comes the group-as-a-whole which requires there to be a certain spread or pattern of group role behaviour at any one time so that the group can keep itself in equilibrium. It seems that there are often certain roles on offer in any group, representing functions that have to be performed or emotions and feelings that have to be expressed if group tensions are to be contained. It is as if the group-as-a-whole allocates these different roles to different members, and at the same time other roles that are needed to facilitate the work in hand are being offered round to other members or subgroups.

A role cannot exist in a group as a function of an individual member alone as it has to be acceptable both as a role for the individual and as a role for the group. The process of selecting, matching, modifying and discarding, goes on continually. It sometimes happens that someone is pressured within a group to take on a role that does not suit; at other times someone may wish to abandon an outgrown role and find the group, ever conservative, resistant to this change.

Agazarian defined four hierarchically linked systems, two belonging to the visible group and two belonging to the invisible group, the linkage being demonstrated through roles.

It goes like this:

1. The individual person comes into the group

2. This individual person then tries to find some personally comfortable individual role from his or her available repertoire that seems appropriate to the group situation

3. This member-role has to be modified in order to fit in with needs of the other members of the group and be accepted as a group role

4. This group-acceptable role will then become a role that belongs not only to the individual but has been shaped to meet the needs of the group and so is also part of the process of the group-as-a-whole.

The dynamics of systems in the same hierarchy are similar in structure and function and have a similar goal. At the individual system level, member-role behaviour helps to keep the individual system in equilibrium, and in a parallel way group role behaviour helps to keep the group in equilibrium. Each system mirrors the structure and function of the other. It is only through the constant negotiation and renegotiation of roles at the four levels that the individual members are held together together in such a way that the needs of the invisible group-as-a-whole continue to be met. Thus the theory of the invisible group provides another observational framework which makes it possible to look on group behaviour from these two different but complementary perspectives.

A number of different theories have now been introduced, formulated by prominent group psychotherapists. They all have in common certain assumptions about group dynamics, but while they are all concerned with the activity of individuals in groups, there are differences in focus. Some pay more attention to individual experiences, including one-to-one relationships carried over into the group situation from relationships in the past, while others look beyond the individuals and concentrate the whole of their attention on the activity of the group as a whole. In different ways they are all concerned with the situation of the individual within the group and try to link the different levels of activity together. Each of these theories has its adherents. It is quite usual for group psychotherapists and other group workers to become familiar with, and make use of, a range of different theories.

There are many other people working with groups who draw on these concepts but do not draw on them exclusively.

CHAPTER 5

Psychotherapy in Groups

Since psychodynamic group concepts, and the disciplined uses of the group process, originated in group therapy, both concepts and uses need to be introduced and illustrated in this setting before they can be applied to other purposes elsewhere.

We need to look at what happens when the context of therapy is changed from the two person situation to the group situation. We need to identify the therapeutic (and also the anti-therapeutic) properties that can be found in groups. We need to establish the boundaries and parameters and conditions that belong to group psychotherapy alone and which distinguish group therapy from other forms of group work.

This last is important. All the groups to be discussed, whether their purpose is therapy, counselling, education or discussion, team building or direct experiential learning and development, share the same format in which group members and leader sit together in a circle for open discussion. They all aim to create a situation in which personal change and development can take place. But it is only in a psychotherapeutic group that each member is a patient who is exposing the self to the possibility of change that will effect not only a specific area of functioning but the whole of the personality, and is (theoretically at any rate) committing the whole of the personality to the therapeutic process. Analytical therapy, individual or group, demands commitment, a greater commitment than in any other structured encounter. It is likely that no-one ever commits the whole of him or herself to this process, not even in individual analysis. Yet in analysis, whether individual or group, it is not possible to anticipate or to define the areas of confrontation, or to contract out of any one of them in advance. *It is the potentiality of commitment that is without limits.*

All the other ways in which the group context can be used to facilitate change differ from group psychotherapy in that the group members legitimately make mental reservations which keep some parts of themselves untouched. Since these other applications have a more restricted and defined aim, there are differences in the role played by the group leader and in the depth and particularity at which each group operates. There are also differences in the way the groups are established, in the rigours of selection and in the establishment and maintenance of boundaries. These differences have to be recognised and understood.

The context of therapy

It is an axiom of all dynamic psychotherapy, individual and group, that problems of personality have their origins in early disturbances of interpersonal relationships, that they are manifesting themselves currently in disturbed interpersonal relationships, and that it is only in interpersonal situations that they can be treated satisfactorily.

But which interpersonal situations?

Individual therapy developed originally out of Freud's 'talking cure'. In the original psychoanalytic model the aim was to eliminate context - the patient lying on the couch, the analyst, outside the patient's range of vision, a neutral figure acting as a blank screen to be used for the patient's transferences as the patient responded to the recaptured memories of the past and not to any actual relationship in the present. This actual relationship, it was assumed, had been all but eliminated for immediate purposes.

Context came to the fore with the advent of group therapy. It became clear that no situation can be as neutral as the early psychoanalysts thought, that the material which is produced during a psychoanalytic session is in fact elicited selectively, within a particular and exceptional context which is likely to encourage the development of an early regressive transference. It does not give the whole story, the whole story seems to be unattainable. Psycho-analysis cannot be treated, after all, to use Bettelheim's analogy, as if it were an Archimedes' point divorced from the world of social phenomena that could be used as a fulcrum for a lever that would be able to take a person out of his social environment and show his or her 'true' picture. The patient is not presented with a formless 'tabula rasa' on which to inscribe the conflicts; what is offered more nearly resembles a blank sheet of paper of a certain size, shape and consistency which encourages the production of one sort of picture and discourages the production of another.

The context of treatment may change but the problems from which patients suffer, the dis-ease, the disturbances and the neuroses, do not. Seen in both psycho-analytic and group-analytic terms these are the conflicts with ultimate origins in remote childhood whose immediate expression is none the less in the patients' current day-to-day lives, in their on-going relationships of the present with spouses, parents, children, friends, lovers, rivals and employers

A disturbance has two aspects, there is the way in which it is being expressed in the present and there is its origin in relationships in the past, and in the psychotherapeutic group it is the present expression that comes to the fore. The transference that the group situation is likely to encourage is slanted towards the transference, or recreation within the group, of those aspects of a disturbance which are active in the real life, current situation, and which concern relationships with other people in the present as well perhaps as in the past. The participants in the group are sharing a current experience; their immediate shared problem is concerned with relationships within the group, and it is these shared aspects that are likely to be emphasised rather than the private and individual experiences of the past.

As in individual therapy, the patients in the therapeutic group do not have to take responsibility for what goes on, and can express what is in their minds freely, without fear of consequences. But the help and support is not coming from another and more powerful person, as happened in childhood. The members of the group do not come to receive therapy from a therapist but to take part in a therapeutic process on an equal footing with others. The therapy comes about through the interactive processes in the group.

Setting and boundaries

In our model, the psychotherapeutic group is composed of seven to eight members and a leader or therapist. This number is now accepted as one that is small enough to reflect intimate networks and family experiences, but large enough to include a variety of patterns of response and attitudes.

There will be some selection, although the criteria for selection vary from therapist to therapist and from group to group. In selecting the group, there is likely to be an an attempt to avoid great discrepancies in terms of age, intelligence, educational background and previous experience of therapy. There is also likely to be selection in order to obtain either a one-sex group, or, alternatively, a group in which the sexes are balanced in numbers, thus avoiding a situation in which either men or women would constitute a distinct minority. The same considerations apply to ethnic origins. Some forms of illness or personality difficulties may be considered unsuitable for groups altogether, or unsuitable for one particular group. Stock Whitaker and Lieberman (1965) attach importance to selecting a group made up of patients who are homogeneous in terms of 'vulnerability', meaning by vulnerability the extent of the patients' capacity, or lack of capacity, to deal with stressful situations and to tolerate anxiety.

Our model group meets at least once a week and remains together for a fixed period of up to an hour and a half, sitting round in a circle with the group therapist. They are expected to communicate freely whatever is in their minds, including their feelings about themselves, about the group, about the other members of the group, and about the leader. There are no limits to the communications. This form of communication has been described as the group equivalent of the 'free association' of individual psychoanalysis, in which the patient is expected to reveal all the ideas and associations which come to mind without regard for their apparent lack of coherence or relevance. Group members cannot be equally free and spontaneous as they each inevitably spend more time in listening than in talking. However they are encouraged, as far as is possible, to contribute uncensored thoughts and associations, the result being what Foulkes (1964) has labelled 'free group association'. This he treats as the group equivalent of the individual's free association, resting upon the dynamic matrix and coming from the group as a whole. It will be related to the current shared problem or preoccupation of the group as it emerges, and will contain something of the preoccupations of each individual member.

This form of communication requires a relaxation of the censorship that is normally applied to the expression of thoughts and feelings in social situations. It will develop gradually as members of the group come to feel more secure than they would in other settings, and free from the constraints, obligations, and fears that ordinarily prevail. This safety does not mean, of course, that personal criticism or direct verbal attack should be precluded. What it does mean is that freedom of expression belongs equally to them all, that it will be kept by the leader within 'safe' bounds, that it will develop at a pace that will not seriously disrupt members abilities to cope with everyday responsibilities, and that there will be no repercussions or leaks of information outside the group.

For this reason, it is important in our model that the members of the group should be strangers to each other, and that any contact between them outside the group meetings be kept to an absolute minimum. Relationships within the group must be kept strictly separated from the personal relationships of domestic and occupational life. These latter are relationships which should not be jeopardised, and the obligations and responsibilities to the continuing life outside the group should not be disregarded. It must be stressed that we are describing what may be considered by some practitioners an idealised model, and for present purposes we are disregarding certain group activities which in other contexts are included within the definition of group psychotherapy by other workers.

This psychotherapeutic group has no other structure. No focus is suggested, nor is any topic for discussion supplied. Any external control, however minimal, would deflect the course of the group's free development and interfere with the expression of fundamental conflicts. Members of the group may be told that they are expected to talk, since ultimately group psychotherapy must rely on verbal communication, but even this requirement involves some interference, and some distortion. Talking can itself be a defensive activity, used to prevent the development of revealing silences and to distract attention from imporant non-verbal activities.

Therapeutic properties

In this unstructured and protected situation, the newcomers to the group are likely to find themselves attempting to communicate with the other members about their personal lives and difficulties. The other group members may, or may not, have been selected on the basis of some shared problem, but in any case they are all people who have acknowledged the existence of difficulties and who are prepared to discuss them with others. This in itself provides certain opportunities and experiences. The newcomers will soon realise that they are not the only people with problems, and they will find that others too have feelings of fear, shame, resentment or inadequacy, perhaps not very different from their own. This is a simple group phenomenon which has been labelled *Universalisation*, and is one of the group specific factors identified by Foulkes as having no direct counterpart in individual therapy. It can help to reduce the sense of isolation and shame, and to encourage further communication and even greater frankness. Though not confined to psychotherapeutic groups, it is here that it becomes part of a disciplined therapeutic process.

The members respond to what is going on in the group each according to their own individual preoccupations, interpreting or misinterpreting it significantly, each according to his or her particular *resonance*.

> On the fact that meaning refers to different levels at the same time rests the specificity of meaning for each individual. Each individual picks out as it were, from a common pool that which is most meaningful to him personally... Meaning is thus always relevant in the context of the whole group in its different configurations, as well as for each participating individual himself. (Foulkes 1975, p.122)

Sometimes these responses take the form of a 'chain' in which each individual adds a different association to a common theme. Looking beyond the individuals to the activity of the group as a whole, as the different contributions merge and fuse and as associations are pooled, the loosening and stimulating effect this can have brings the expression and release of material previously outside conscious awareness – the *condenser phenomenon*.

The responses of others to what is being communicated in the group may help each individual member to see him or herself in a different light. They will all come to have access to information about the effect of their behaviour upon other people, and the different ways in which they are perceived by others, information which may never have been available to them before. The actions and reactions of the rest of the group may challenge the previous assumptions they have made about themselves and their relationships, presenting them with a different picture. This was called the *mirror reaction* by Foulkes, with resonances from the distorting mirrors of the fairground and seaside pier. The visitor entering one of these 'halls of mirrors' is surrounded by different and often surprising reflections, each of which may contain some truth but none of which gives the 'true' picture. This type of feedback is something that each gives and each receives, as increasing freedom of expression brings benefit to them all.

Something of this is contained in Primo Levi's (1990) story *The Mirror Maker* which describes the invention of a mirror showing a reflection of oneself as seen by the person who happens to be standing beside one. Perhaps it is not surprising that attempts to market this invention were not successful, too few customers being pleased with the images that the mirror revealed; and the mirror maker, finding that no two images that he saw reflected in the mirror were the same, finally came to the conclusion that he himself could have no real existence.

Spectator therapy is another group specific factor, describing the benefits that can be derived from listening to a discussion of some problem resembling ones own, and from witnessing attempts to find and apply different solutions, even though one may not feel able or willing to contribute to the discussion oneself. Any group will include both talkative and less talkative members. Although the importance of verbal communication is rightly stressed, the silent member will also be participating and communicating at a non-verbal level, even through silence. Even if one says little, one may be feeling much. None the less, the growth and development of the ability to communicate in words about personal difficulties, to make one's feelings explicit and understood and to help others to do the same, can indicate the progress of the individual and of the group.

A final group specific factor is the *exchange* of information, explanations and responses that takes place in a group and which can help to open up a range of fresh options and encourage the questioning of previous assumptions. Members of the group are more likely to be receptive to the responses of their peers, in the same way that children listen more readily (for better or worse) to their own age group than they do to the opinions of their elders.

Participation in the group provides the individual members with two different types of information: they hear about the problems of the other members and they perceive the reactions of the other members to their own communications. Each disclosure leads to another, and as some put more and more of their cards on the table others find it increasingly possible to do likewise. Thus the information available to them becomes more relevant and more important.

Problems that tend to remain invisible or unclear within family and personal networks outside the group will eventually become visible in a group of strangers. Outside the group we are likely to have surrounded ourselves with people prepared to support our own habitual ways of behaving because of their complementary needs, and so disturbed patterns can remain invisible. In the group this is unlikely to happen for long, and the presence and nature of interpersonal disturbances will gradually become clearer.

Members of the group, in this safe situation which is bracketed off from life outside, and in which their habitual ways of behaving are not receiving their habitual support, may be able or required to test out the possibility of behaving and responding in new ways. They may then find that there is no need to be so dominant or so self-effacing, so suspicious or so ingratiating, in their personal relationships. Such disadvantageous behaviour may have become established from fear of the consequences of behaving otherwise. In the special conditions of the group one may feel safe enough to modify one's usual way of behaving to others and only then discover for the first time that the feared consequences do not follow. This opportunity for reality testing that the group provides is stressed by some group psychotherapists, who see it as a necessary forerunner to any therapeutic change.

Cox and Theilgaard (1994, p.405) quote a patient in a therapeutic group as saying 'these are the days of gradual unmasking'. They point out that this phrase contains three linked components of group therapy, each equally important. Talk of 'these days' puts the emphasis on events taking place currently in the present; the process is 'gradual'; the task is one of 'unmasking'.

Some of the experiences described so far are likely to be familiar to everyone and are not the monopoly of psychotherapeutic groups. They may even be provided fortuitously in any small face-to-face gathering, sometimes in situations where one feels accepted and 'at home', sometimes at moments of heightened sensibility. A person may find that his life is changed through a conversation in a railway carriage with perfect strangers. But the method cannot be taught. Psychotherapy, whether individual or group, is different from these casual encounters in that these experiences are deliberately sought, and in that conscious and disciplined attempts are made to foster them, to maximise their impact, and to call attention to, and study scientifically, what is taking place.

'There are three things I want to happen in the course of a group,' wrote Zinkin (1984, p26). 'I want each individual to use the group to explore his own conflicts. I want each individual to participate in the experience of being *part* of something, to have a sense of not what belongs to him but to what he belongs, and I want each member to enter into dialogue. A "good" group is, for me, one in which all three develop.'

Transference

Though the theories and concepts described in the last chapter stress different phenomena and different experiences, when they turn to therapy all pay some attention to the concept of transference. This concept, central to individual psychoanalytic therapy, needs modification before it can be applied in a group setting.

In a two-person setting, the assumption is that the patient transfers to the psychotherapist feelings that were experienced in earlier relationships and that are still inappropriately active in current life. Thus these transferred feelings have two characteristics: their roots in infancy and their current distorting effect on the patient's interpersonal relationships. In most systems of group psychotherapy, it is not considered appropriate to trace transferred emotions back to their individual historical origins and emphasis is, rather, placed upon their second aspect, the role that they play in the 'here and now' situation in which all the members of the group are involved.

The transference that takes place in a group differs in several respects from transference in an individual psychotherapeutic setting. Essentially, it has more dimensions. The patient may at different times transfer to the therapist, to other members of the group, and to the group as a whole, or may transpose into the group some multi-person situation which can involve them all. The therapist, as a recipient of the transference of relationships, aims to remain neutral and to keep his or her own personality from intruding. This is not true of the other group members, who will react spontaneously and repudiate any transference roles that do not happen to be meeting their own needs at that particular moment.

The patient may attempt to re-create in the group the original 'network' of relationships in which the conflict was first experienced, using different individuals, including the therapist, to represent the different protagonists. Each member brings a personal or family script, in the hope that the other members will play the reciprocal roles. The nature of the script is revealed when this hope is disappointed. Small groups are sometimes described as familio-centric, as the size of the group encourages the development of structures based upon family experiences.

In a group any transference relationship may be shared around and divided among the different members in a cooperative patterning of behaviour that can include something from each of them. In the transference to the leader, which is a feature of all groups, each member may be expressing a different and complemenary component of a complex and many sided relationship that is involving them all. The roles that the members take up in the group may have the same complementarity as the roles assumed within a family, where the good son and the bad son enact their parts, each presenting one side of the child–parent relationship and fulfilling family expectations as they create and confirm them. Attempts are made to transfer whole networks from outside into the group where they compete for a re-run with a new *dramatis personae*.

The language used to describe the effect of these transferred relationships will vary according to whichever theory is being used. They influence the development of one or other of the basic assumptions; they contribute to the formation of the group matrix; or they help to determine what manner of group focal conflict, or common group tension, develops. The pattern of the communications in the group is likely to be influenced in some way by the theoretical position which the group leader holds.

Finally the group itself may come to represent or symbolise things of significance to the group members, and elicit behaviour based upon this transference. These significant things may be people, ideas, objects or situations. The 'matrix' of the group may, at times, appropriately stand for the mother. At other times the group may be used to represent home, a symbol of security or of confinement, or other past situations inside or outside the protection of the family.

The group culture

Every group will over time establish its own culture, containing a shared view of itself and of its expectations and standards. This developing culture needs to be given careful attention by the group therapist.

The task of the therapist is to influence the development of the group in such a way that each member is able to derive the maximum therapeutic benefit from attendance at the group sessions. It cannot be taken for granted that group activity (even psychotherapeutic group activity) brings automatic benefit. Groups contain potentialities for harm as well as for good. Fears and anxieties may be confirmed rather than reduced when they are found to be shared by other people; 'feedback' may contain distorted and misleading information; maladaptive patterns of behaviour may come to be shared and so receive support instead of being challenged. The group may fail to develop and mature; it may encourage regression to earlier levels of development; it may become dependent on its leader, and even seduce the leader into playing a directive role. Individual members may be victimised, isolated, attacked or turned into scapegoats, to a degree which they are unable to tolerate, Finally, the group may break up, leaving behind it a residue of disappointment, failure and mistrust.

In the same way that cohesive and disruptive forces co-exist in every group, so the effect of the group on the individual may be ego-strengthening or ego-weakening, therapeutic or anti-therapeutic, and any group will contain both elements. In a psychotherapeutic group, the very factors that support and sustain the individual member support and sustain in order to make tolerable the exposure to increasing strain and pain. As endurance increases, so one can be given more to endure. As the group gets stronger, so destructive aspects can be more clearly and openly expressed, and the group finds itself able to tolerate such expression and survive increasingly greater stresses. This cannot be achieved easily. But if the individual patient does not encounter difficult, unpleasant and frightening situations during group psychotherapy, he or she is likely to leave the group untouched, with the conflicts still unresolved.

When problems from life outside become replicated in the group, the special conditions in the group can provide opportunities to address them more openly and more safely than elsewhere. It is life outside the group that has an on-going importance and it is there that significant relationships exist which should not be jeopardised. But relationships within the group are proxy relationships and can be used for exploration and experiment and testing out. Any damage or hurt within the group is bracketed off from other situations and can be contained there.

The phenomenon known as 'scapegoating', for example, which can occur in all societies, in all families and in all groups, can be extremely painful both for the scapegoat and for the other participants. Impulses which a number of members find unacceptable in themselves may be projected and discovered in one of their number. This process allows the remaining members to acknowledge the existence of these impulses but place them elsewhere where they can be openly attacked and repudiated.

This way of dealing with what is personally unacceptable may not only secure the continuance of a group, but it may also provide an experience that is necessary for both 'scapegoat' (who will have some personal reason for accepting this role, however painful) and 'persecutors', involving and highlighting the basic conflicts of both parties. The two roles are complementary. Group and scapegoat alike may find that they can pass through a frightening experience and survive it. On the other hand, there is the possibility that either scapegoat or attacker may find the experience hard to tolerate and may wish to leave the group in consequence. There is also the possibility that the person selected to be the scapegoat is being made to stand in for someone else who is too important to the group, or too powerful, to be made the target of hostility.

The group therapist must be aware of all these possibilities, and must attempt to maintain the delicate balance. One side of the balance is to allow sufficient stressful interaction to represent the inevitable conflictual situations that have to be experienced, and which all recur in everyday life The other side is to prevent the stress on any individual from extending to a breakdown that would damage victim and victimisers alike.

In an earlier chapter the concept was put forward that group processes are determined by the struggle between cohesive and disruptive elements in the group, and, by the same token, in the individuals composing the group. The existence of the group is constantly threatened by the disruptive forces in the group and in the individual members, and measures have to be taken by the group as a whole to meet this threat and safeguard its continuance. Scapegoating can be one such measure. This concept seems to be present, if not aways explicitly stated, in most dynamic group theories.

A close analogy may be drawn beween the group and the nation state. The disruptive elements in the state can be dealt with in a variety of ways. A confident state may be able to tolerate rebellious and even subversive activity on the part of minority groups such as students and others, whereas a threatened or divided state is more likely to curtail freedom of speech and assembly, introduce censorship, and attempt to secure conformity to its rulings. In a similiar way, some groups may develop a 'culture' which discourages non-conformity, puts a virtual taboo on the discussion of certain topics, or makes it only possible to discuss them in certain approved ways. Even the theories believed to be held by the group leader may become an ideology which must not be (or must be) challenged.

The term 'culture' was used in this way by Stock Whitaker and Lieberman (1965) to include 'the practices, standards, and mutual understandings which regulate relationships within the group and define the character of the group world'. It is the culture which determines what is acceptable and what is not acceptable and where the limits of tolerance and acceptance lie. In their focal conflict theory, Stock Whitaker and Lieberman see the culture as being made up of the sum of all the successful solutions to the focal conflicts that have been preoccupying the group at an unconscious or near-conscious level. These solutions are described as either restrictive or enabling. A restrictive solution to a group focal conflict is like repressive state action, the group as a whole deciding to deal with subversive elements by a restriction of freedom.

The role of the group psychotherapist

In all discussions of group therapy, the activity of the therapist forms part of the process. The therapist has to bring the group together, selecting, starting, safeguarding survival, promoting the therapeutic function. Left to itself the group may manage, at least for a while, to establish standards and patterns of behaviour that will keep the group comfortable and untaxing and discourage change.

Group psychotherapists are also subject to the influence of the group culture, but must be able to maintain sufficient detachment from it to be aware of what is going on and to be able to intervene to influence it. They need to be able to recognise the group processes, and the way in which they themselves and all the other group members are contributing to them and are being influenced by them. They must be able to forecast how the group as a whole is likely to be influenced by any intervention, or lack of intervention, on their part.

We can distinguish a number of ways in which group psychotherapists influence their groups. Every intervention that group psychotherapists make, or do not make, will have its signifiance. First of all, there are their implicit attitudes. Their behaviour will to some extent serve as a model for the members of their groups. It is through attitudes rather than through anything that is said that a therapist can show a group the value of tolerance and promote a permissive and accepting attitude.

It is through their own ability to tolerate distressing experiences that group psychotherapists can help their groups to tolerate them in their turn. Initially, and in the last resort, the therapist has to guarantee the safety of the group, and all group members need to learn that their therapist is capable of doing this, and that, whatever they themselves do or say, the therapist will not be frightened or angry, wounded or destroyed. Such tranquillity provides some protection against the disruptive forces, the fears and conflicts and antagonisms, which might impede the progress of the group. If the therapist can withstand the contents, Pandora may open her box.

Group psychotherapists are used as transference figures by their group, and have to recognise this and accept it even if they do not deliberately encourage it. They wish to help all group members to become as fully involved as possible, to encourage them to relate not only to the therapist but to each other, and to look to each other for reactions to, and comments upon, their communications. They do not wish to be the main focus of the group, neither do they wish to 'lead' it. It is for this reason that Foulkes did not use the term 'leader' but preferred to speak of a group 'conductor'.

In explaining his choice of this term (and also saying that the musical connotation should not be exaggerated) Foulkes was searching for a way to convey that while he was refraining from producing the group's ideas and influencing it as little as possible, nevertheless he was doing something. 'I was not the composer who wrote the music, but the conductor who interpreted it, the conductor who brought it to light. I remember saying to my colleagues: I feel like a conductor, but I don't in the least know what is the music that will be played' (Foulkes 1990, p.130). In this sense the leader of a psychotherapeutic group is not a leader, nor a teacher nor yet a counsellor. The group may try to impose such a role, and this attempt must be considered along with all other group happenings, in relation to the state of the group as a whole and the processes operating in it at that time.

The progress of every psychotherapeutic group is hindered by obstacles. These obstacles are introduced by individual members and may be accepted by the group as a whole because they afford a temporary solution to, or respite from, a current group problem, or because they prevent change in an unknown and therefore frightening direction.

For example, a group psychotherapist might consider that, when an attempt is made to make her or him take greater control, the group as a whole is trying to avoid dealing with some particular problem, is showing a reluctance to take the next step forward, is wishing instead to substitute some magical solution and to return to a state of dependence upon a parental figure.

This is reminiscent of the basic assumption activity described by Bion (1952) as attempts to avoid the work of the group – and in this case the work that is being avoided is engagement in therapy. As well as the passive hope that therapy can take place through the exertion of others, there may be diversionary attacks directed at people outside the group or there may be an attempt to structure the group in mutually supportive pairs that resist change.

Everything that a group psychotherapist does, or does not do, in such a situation, will affect the outcome. He, or she, needs to be aware of the group processes, and of the relevance of the group processes to, and their effect upon, each individual. Through tacit refusal to accept any imposed role, by denying to the group a magical solution or a dependent relationship, the therapist may be able to re-confront the group with the problem which it is trying to evade. It may be judged necessary to put into words what is going on, and to draw the attention of the group to the meaning of its own behaviour.

This brings us to group analysis and the unique aspect of the group analyst's role; the analytic function of 'making the unconscious conscious' through interpretations.

In distinguishing group analysis from other forms of group psychotherapy, Foulkes (1990) wrote that the aim in group analysis goes beyond the direct treatment of symptoms and does not accept symptoms at their face value, but subjects them to further analysis in order to achieve insight and a more lasting change.

The interpretations of the conductor in our group therapy model differ from those of the individual psychotherapist in that these interpretations are not centred upon individuals in the same way and, therefore, they do not set out to trace the transference relationships back to their historical roots. For the past history of each individual is separate and unique and belongs to that individual alone; it is only in the 'here and now' situation in the group that individual concerns meet, and that a focus can be found which belongs to all members conjointly, and which conjointly affects them all.

Each member is a co-author of the theme. Even if the conductor does not presume to believe in something as mystical sounding as a 'group unconscious', it is still necessary to respond as if every communication can, in some sense, be taken to come from the group as a whole. This means that the assignment is to find the factor in the communication that has reference to a common proccupation of the group. References to individuals are not necessarily precluded. The conductor may need to make an interpretation about the behaviour of a particular group member, where the interests of the group and of the individual require it, but every decision will be made with reference to the processes operating in the group at that particular time and bearing in mind the longer-term context of the group. It will also need to be made in the awareness that the singling out of an individual by the leader can be destructive to both individual and group, and is not to be undertaken without good cause.

An interpretation has to be well timed. If given prematurely, it may seem like an attack, increasing the threat to the group and the need for a defensive solution; or it may bring a potentially valuable experience to an untimely end. It could also forestall the finding of the interpretation by the group as a whole, and the group would be so much the poorer. For each member of the group has a role as co-therapist, as well as patient, and needs to exercise that role. Rather than presenting the group members with interpretations (and thereby emphasising dependence), the conductor may help them to find their own, asking questions rather than suggesting answers, and encouraging the gradual shift from a 'leader centred' to a 'group centred' group. For there is no role, whether that of guarantor of safety, protector of the weak, interpreter, clarifier, or therapist, that group psychotherapists would not rather see exercised by their groups working together than arrogate to themselves.

This aspect of group psychotherapy has been articulated most clearly in group-analysis. Foulkes' phrase 'Trust the group' is widely quoted. It was Foulkes' contention that the group as a whole represents a normality from which each individual member deviates. Every deviation is individual and different and will be challenged by the other members of the group so that the total pattern of group responses cancels out the deviations.

Foulkes' optimism when considering the balance between cohesive and destructive forces has been questioned, particularly in Nitsun's concept of the anti-group (Nitsun 1991). It has been said that Foulkes paid insufficient attention to the widespread resistance to engaging in groups which is the result of an idealised longing to return to the two person relationship of the distant past. As the group fails to meet this longing it comes to be identified with past frustrating and persecuting bad objects. Thus there is a powerful process in groups which is always operating to undermine them and even to bring them to an end. But equally this process can bring an opportunity to recapture and work through early experiences of loss and frustration.

The development of the group's own capacity to deal with its destructive forces must not be weakened or impaired, since it is in participation in this development that we find a large part of the individual's therapeutic experience. However, the expression of destructive forces may at times outstrip the capacity of the group to tolerate them without damage, and the vulnerability of different group members will vary.

In the language of psychiatric practice the phrase 'acting out' is used to describe behaviour which is undesirable or even disastrous, whereas a description of phantasies of the same behaviour would be welcomed as a revelation of unconscious processes. Some of the activities and exchanges within the process of group psychotherapy might well be called acting out. For example, members of the group may make sexual challenges to each other. These might well represent the recognition of sexual feelings in their manifold form. There is a legitimate place for the expression of these feelings, which exist in human encounters in a variety of forms even if they often have to remain unrecognised and unexpressed. However, in group psychotherapy, someone must take reponsibility for preventing these expressions from becoming dangerous seductions or attacks. The absence of limits for discussion is not the absence of limits for action.

The group psychotherapist has a duty which in some aspects is similar to that of the individual psychotherapist. Necessary as it may be for the deep unconscious material to be revealed, the psychotherapist must at some point relate this back to conscious material. Insight is not the equivalent of the revelation of unconscious material alone, it is the perception of both conscious and unconscious meanings at the same time. So in group psychotherapy it is the function of the psychotherapist to remind the participants of the existence of the outside world.

The skills which the psychotherapist needs to have also include the ability to reintroduce limits in a situation where the limits have been removed. This is not merely the ability to restrict something which one fears or does not understand. One has to be able to perceive the trends and to be able to carry oneself along into the same depths as the participants. One has to have the ability and the experience to keep part of oneself as an observer of the conscious as well as the unconscious meanings, and to predict the way in which the discussion will affect the feelings and the behaviour of all the group members. One has to be able to intervene and, equally important, one has to be able to remain silent.

Finally, one can only agree with Foulkes that the responsiblity is great and that 'no one should embark on this who has not the measure and control of his power firmly in his blood and system, lest he will suffer the fate of the sorcerer's apprentice'(Foulkes 1964, p.287).

CHAPTER 6

Counselling in Groups

- What is group counselling?
- How does group counselling differ from individual counselling?
- And how does it differ from group psychotherapy?
- What are its parameters?
- Where is it practised?
- And by whom?

Outside the specific boundaries of therapy there is a wide range of group work that also draws upon dynamic group concepts and makes use of the group process as a helping technique.

Counselling groups differ in a number of important ways from the model of therapeutic groups described here. There is no commitment on the part of members of counselling groups to engage the whole of themselves in the treatment process; they are on the contrary committing themselves to a defined and limited process, concerned with solving particular problems and modifying specific situations. To this end it may be necessary to bring about changes in some attitudes and relationships, but, in contrast to therapy, fundamental changes in the structure of personality are not specifically sought. Such changes may however take place and and in that case they would not be discouraged.

It is important to hold these distinctions in mind. For one thing, group work that is not defined and limited passes over into psychotherapy, requiring the sanctions and disciplines of psychotherapy, and only someone possessing the training and skills of a group psychotherapist is authorised to practise it. Those who join a counselling group should come with an understanding of the limits of the process they are engaged in and they should not find themselves being drawn into a therapeutic process that they have not chosen or agreed to. Confusion can occur because it is not uncommon for the same practitioner to engage in both group psychotherapy and group counselling, though not necessarily under these labels; and in addition those practising group counselling may have received some of their training and later supervision from group psychotherapists.

But for all that, group counselling should not be considered a form of group psychotherapy that has been diluted in order to allow it to be carried out by less skilled practitioners. The limitation in aims means that group counselling is less intensive and less comprehensive, but, by the same token, it is more flexible and has a wider application, extending to situations where the rigorous demands of group psychotherapy would not be met. Members of a counselling group come for a limited purpose; they do not have to be 'patients', accepting a status that can for some have implications of weakness and dependency. Neither is it always a necessary pre-condition that they be strangers to each other, and nor are they always required to restrict their contacts outside the group meetings as members of a psychotherapy group would be. Group counselling need not be confined to the consulting room but can be practised in a variety of different settings, and it can be applied to groups that are already in existence as well as the artificial groups created for the purpose, though here care may have to be used to find and maintain an appropriate focus. While attention still has to be paid to the context and boundaries, more flexibility is possible.

The diverse aims of group counselling can include, among others, improving family relationships, promoting changes in attitudes and behaviour, socialisation, empowerment, giving support through transitional stages of life, promoting recovery from illness, easing the move from institutional to community life, facilitating the recovery from trauma. Some of these aims are likely to be recognised and claimed by group therapists too, and listing them highlights the overlap between the two disciplines. It also highlights this crucial distinction, worth re-emphasising, that *in group counselling a particular aim is detected and defined at the outset, providing a focus and setting the limits within which the proceedings of the group take place. Group therapy is not so bound.*

Counselling and social casework

Counselling, like psychotherapy, developed within a two-person relationship of client and counsellor. Social caseworkers were originally the main counsellors, and many of the concepts first developed in social casework are now incorporated in the theory and practice of counselling. But counselling has now broadened its scope and range and has developed into a separate discipline of its own with its own practitioners: it has also come to be taken up as an addition to the repertoire of a number of other professions and is now being used to augment and extend existing skills by such professions as nursing, medicine, psychology, teaching and the churches, as well as social work. However social workers have been among its principal and most steadfast practitioners and it is in social work settings that its concepts can be most clearly demonstrated. And as in the past the boundaries between social casework and psychotherapy have constantly needed clarifying, so now do the boundaries between group counselling and group psychotherapy. Social caseworkers are traditionally employed within specialist agencies and have definite terms of reference. A client will be referred to a particular agency because his particular problem falls within its terms of reference. Although the caseworker will need to make a complete assessment of the situation in which the client is placed, and may try to bring about a general improvement in the client's circumstances and system of personal relationships, the caseworker never loses sight of the original problem. The client is expected to talk frankly about the problem and its context, and expects that it will be safe to do so, but there is no expectation that 'everything' is to be revealed and nothing held back. Should the client choose to enter into other areas caseworkers need to respond and must handle the situation within the limits determined by their training and experience, making such use of the client's contribution as they can within the particular framework set by their agency. Caseworkers need to be aware that there are dangers in extending the treatment process to include a form of psychotherapy which has not been sanctioned.

However, workers have also to be aware that it is not possible to extract one aspect of a client's life and separate it from its context. While retaining a focus on the problem that is presented, they can take a holistic approach in making connections between the problem and other aspects of the client's life and situation in family and in society.

Caseworkers make use of the relationship which they have established with their clients, and this relationship furnishes the context in which other forms of help may be offered, material as well as psychological. They need to be aware of the transference (and of the counter-transference), but, even though they have to give it some recognition, they do not need to interpret it in the way that a psychotherapist would do. They may need to demonstrate how a client is carrying over attitudes and feelings from the past into the present, but the attitudes and feelings are more likely to be conscious or near-conscious ones, and they will be ones that affect the practical issues in the client's life. Compared with psychotherapists, caseworkers have more freedom to select and set limits to treatment aims and to the themes that are to be discussed. Although they may have to limit their focus to specific problems, they have the freedom to select from a range of different helping techniques; they do not have to take the care of a psychotherapist to avoid behaving in ways which might prejudice the untrammelled development of a transference relationship.

Casework in the group context

When casework is extended into a group context, it is clear that group work cannot be tailored to meet individual needs in the way that casework can, nor can it include such a wide range of individual helping methods. Members of such a group will share some common problem or situation which provides a point on which to focus, and to which everything that takes place in the group needs ultimately to be related. It is the task of the group counsellor to maintain this focus and to make the links that establish the relationships. Thus the proceedings of the group and the interactions between all the group members, the contributions and the responses of each individual, are all made to play their part in the problem-solving process. Group counsellors may themselves play an unobtrusive part in the proceedings, keeping their own personality in the background, and in this respect their behaviour may appear to resemble that of group psychotherapists. But they have other options too. There may be occasions when the counselling needs of individual members and of the total group require the leader to play a more active role and make a positive and direct use of the relationship between them. Here too we can find a counterpart in the different uses that caseworkers in an individual setting may make of their relationship with their clients.

The limitation in aims means that group counselling is less intensive and less comprehensive, but, by the same token, it is more flexible and has a wider application, extending to situations where the rigorous demands of group psychotherapy would not be met. To say that group counselling does not deal with the deeper levels of personality is not to say that it is less valuable. It may no longer be necessary to labour to make this point, though there have been times when the great influence and prestige of analytic practice have suggested that all other methods are second best, and in the past social workers have themselves sometimes helped to establish this hierarchy by valuing more highly those forms of casework that made most use of interpretations and the development of insight. However, there is now more recognition of the fact that treatment in 'depth' is not always to be preferred, that different levels of work are appropriate in different circumstances, and that the optimum level is often that which achieves sufficient result with the minimum of disturbance.. By analogy, you do not need deep mining to obtain open cast coal, and, for that matter, in some situations diamonds can be picked up on the surface. The only justification for going 'deep' is that in some circumstances it is necessary to do so.

Lessons from child guidance

In order to make the distinctions that have to be made and to trace these roots, child guidance practice is going to be taken as an example, and the role of the psychiatric social worker, with individual clients and also with groups, will be given some detailed consideration.

In child guidance practice the different areas of work and the roles of the different professions can be clearly seen. It was early recognised that when a child required treatment, his place in the network of family and school had to be considered. For this reason child guidance was the first service to attempt to deal simultaneously with several dimensions of a problem, and it has long had a multidisciplinary approach, including psychotherapy and social casework, group therapy and group counselling, within its repertoire. At first the specialist professional roles were differentiated and separated: some time later with changes in thinking they were largely reintegrated in attempts to treat the whole rather than the parts of a problem.

The social worker in a child guidance clinic[1] is traditionally expected to contribute to the treatment of the child through the family interaction. Let us suppose that the treatment plan includes a series of interviews with the child's mother. It is likely that social worker will keep the following points in mind.

The social worker's client is a woman who is meeting difficulties in her role as a mother, and who has enough awareness of these difficulties to accept treatment for herself, albeit a limited and focused involvement on behalf of her child. The social worker, in a stronger and more knowledgeable position, is there to help her. The mother–child relationship is therefore to some extent mirrored in the relationship between social worker and client. Attitudes that have been carried over from the client's earliest relationship with her own mother are likely to be brought into this relationship. These attitudes are likely to be relevant to the problems on which treatment is focused, since it was from this relationship that the client derived her own primary experience of mothering.

In addition, every theme of family life has its resonance in the mother's conception of herself as a mother. Her past recollection of being mothered by her parents, aunts, uncles, and older siblings, are accompanied by present feelings about her role as supplementary mother to other members of her extended family; and there is also the counterpart of this in her continuing need to be mothered herself by these relatives and even by the children. All this is ever present in the mother's relationship with the child who is the referred patient, and also in the mother's relationship with the social worker. The social worker needs to be aware of the range and extent of these feelings and the part that they play in these two significant sets of relationship, that is, firstly, the relationship between mother and child on which her work is focused and, secondly, her own relationship with her client which is her principal therapeutic tool.

In this professional relationship between social worker and client, the social worker will seek to create a situation of safety in which the client will feel free to discuss her difficulties and her feelings about them without fear of being criticised

---

1   In accordance with traditional (if now somewhat old-fashioned) practice, the social worker in a child guidance clinic is referred to as *she*. It has also been convenient to describe work with mothers, though the increasing role that fathers now take in child guidance treatment needs to be acknowledged.

or misunderstood. The social worker will try to use the relationship sensitively and flexibly to meet what she conceives to be the needs of her client as a person and as a mother. She may use the relationship to augment the client's experience, perhaps to make good some deficiency in the past or in the present that is adversely affecting her maternal role. She may use it to provide a counterbalance to recollections of faulty experiences in the past that the present situation has re-activated. Whatever she does, she exists as a model with which the client may identify, providing a pattern of behaviour which can be incorporated and applied in other contexts. Within the particular focus of child guidance, the way in which the social worker behaves towards her client may be taken to exemplify 'good' parental behaviour. Ferrard and Hunnybun (1962, p.65) discussed the help that can be given to such clients 'by slowly building up a relationship with them that offers warmth and understanding, thus enabling them gradually to take over from the worker, as they might from a wise and kindly parent, ideas and ways of behaving never learnt in childhood'.

Within this relationship, the social worker may employ other techniques. She may seek to promote the development of insight and understanding about the problem at a more conscious level. She may use some interpretations. She may encourage the ventilation of hostile feelings, which, once safely expressed and accepted in a casework situation, could lose some of their hurt so that they no longer need to be directed inappropriately elsewhere. She may also try to educate her client about the norms of child development and about different ways in which difficulties with children could be handled. In all this, the skilled use of the worker–client relationship remains an essential prerequisite and is the context within which all other techniques operate. It is only when these other techniques are employed in this context that they become a part of casework rather than of some other process.

Although present behaviour is affected by all that has happened in the past, the effect is not static or inevitable. Any fresh experience in the present can give a new significance to past events and modify their current influence. Thus help can be provided by means of such experiences, without the need to work at 'deeper' levels.

Extension into groupwork

How can this work with parents be converted into group work?

Parents attending a child guidance clinic may, as an alternative or in addition to individual interview, be invited to join with other parents and a social worker in a group. The focus is still upon the parent–child relationship and the aim is still a development of this relationship in the interest of the referred child within the context of the family. But the instrument to bring this about is no longer an individual relationship and an individual casework process. It has become a group relationship and a group process, making use of free discussion with others in a like situation and of the interaction that takes place among the members and the group counsellor. Although the members of the group are free to talk as they wish, the group counsellor will carry the focus in mind at all times, making the relevant connections, and taking care that undue stress, the type of stress that could be sanctioned in a therapy group, is avoided.

Attempts may be made to justify such group work as a time-saver, a device to reduce the waiting list since it enables one worker to see a number of mothers at one interview. Whether the process does or does not save time, some groups may well go more quickly and more intensively into the important areas of discussion simply because the situation itself provides a living experience of some of the issues which in individual casework can only be indirectly described.

In such a group of mothers, the individual member finds herself in a situation that is more complex and more diffuse than individual casework. Instead of a two-person relationship designed solely to help her, which can be tailored to meet her own particular requirements, she is placed in a group of her peers and is exposed to the demands of competing needs. It is a situation which is closer to real life, into which current problems and preoccupations may be quickly transferred, and in which feelings are more immediately aroused. The relationship with the group counsellor, although many of the characteristics of the individual relationship will remain, is a more diluted one, and some of its aspects are spread out over the other members; but its totality is not necessarily less intense.

As in a therapy group, each member is not the sole recipient, a position sustaining and gratifying to some, humiliating and threatening to others, depending on past experiences and the roles sought in the group. She is now a giver as well as a receiver; she contributes to its success and to its failure, and to the help that the others receive. She listens and reacts to the problems of others, and her own difficulties are not divulged to one helper under conditions of strict confidentiality, but are exposed to the reactions and comments of a wider circle. If, in an individual interview, she were to disclose emotionally charged information about herself, the response would be carefully handled by the audience of one. In a group, her contribution will be received by the other members, and responded to in the light of their different emotional involvements. Any response made by the group counsellor will have to be geared to the needs of the group as a whole, and not solely to the needs of one particular member.

Each mother brings to the discussion her own experiences as a mother in relation to her children, and these experiences, in which she may feel she has failed, are used to enrich the proceedings of the group and may be treated as a valuable contribution. Thus through her very failure she is given an opportunity to experience the satisfactions and reassurance of being able to help others. This is an example of the support which a group can supply to its members, which extends beyond anything which could be provided in an individual casework situation. Each mother does not depend upon the individual reassurance provided by a social worker, which, if given, and if received, would be likely to increase dependency and allay anxieties in an unproductive way. Instead, she creates her own reassurance from her growing ability to contribute to the group, from the use that is made of her contributions, and from the further contributions of others. While discussing the difficulties of the maternal role they all share, there are opportunities to build up confidence in the person behind the role. It may even be possible, in this context, to attack the activities within the role without damaging the person responsible for the activities.

Example

In one group of mothers, one member referred to the fact that her own elderly mother of eighty was ill. She described her anxieties about losing her mother, but accompanied the description with a brilliant smile which seemed intended both to reassure herself and to tell the other members that all her feelings were within her control. Another member questioned her as to whether she would be relieved of the burden when her mother died, and gradually in response to further questioning she was induced to acknowledge some of her long standing hostile feelings about her mother. At this point the group counsellor (in this instance a man and a psychiatrist) was about to draw the session to a close when another member said, 'Are we going to allow Mrs X to go away thinking that she is a bad daughter? Oughtn't we to recognise the fact that she is genuinely concerned about her mother?'

If this point had been brought in too early, or if it had been introduced by the person who challenged her, it would have been no more than the reassuring smile which the mother had used herself. It derived its value from all that had gone before. This reparative part of the work might well have been carried out by the group counsellor, but it was far better coming from a member of the group. Indeed, if it had occurred to the group counsellor to make such a contribution, he might on second thoughts have decided to withhold it. Opportunities need to be given to all members of the group to exercise the functions that would, in a one-to-one situation, belong to the professional worker: functions such as acceptance, tolerance, support, and acknowledgement of both aspects of ambivalence. Thus Parsloe (1969 p.5) wrote that the social group worker

> has to find ways of working which allow full scope for the ability of the members of the group to help each other. This can be difficult for caseworkers, for we have been used in the one-to-one interview to having all to ourselves the powerful and satisfying position of accepting, enabling, and helping . . . In a group one hopes such support will come from a member, and this may mean the

leader has to control not only words but smiles, nods, and hand movements as well, and thus allow space for members to move in to show their acceptance.

A member of such a counselling group will not only talk about her own individual difficulties, but will also listen to the difficulties of others, and hear descriptions of attempts to cope with the problems which are like and unlike her own. She may become interested in a problem raised by another member and take part in discussing it, without revealing, perhaps without acknowledging to herself, that it is in fact a resemblance to some part of her own situation that has aroused her interest. Thus she is working indirectly and vicariously on her own difficulties.

Example

The last example was of a woman who acknowledged, after active questioning by another member of the group, some of her negative feelings towards her own mother. This theme, expressed by one woman, was of importance to the whole group. The woman who had initiated the questioning went on herself to speak of her own mother in idealised terms and it took a number of sessions before she was able to acknowledge the hostility that she too felt but could only express indirectly and in other contexts by involving herself in the similar problems of others. This theme was taken up by the group, and they became able to see how unresolved difficulties in the relationship with their mothers sometimes made it harder for them to know how to mother their own children.

Members of the group find areas in common and areas that are different. Each member in the mothers' group hears of a wide range of attitudes and reactions to common difficulties in family relationships than her own experience could provide. She learns that there are many different ways in which children can be handled. Through identification, she is able to experiment in phantasy, to try on and adopt, or sometimes reject, different modes of behaviour. She thereby is able to extend the range of her own possible responses and repertoires. Participation in the group may help some mothers to relinquish defences which are preventing them from dealing realistically with their situation.

For example, a mother could be unable to give her handicapped child the help he needs because she is preoccupied with attributing blame to medical or educational authorities. It might take a social worker, who is offering individual interviews, a long time to work through this, as any direct approach to this issue would be seen as one authority defending another, and would be likely to reinforce existing attitudes. Comments from other parents with similar problems but different reactions would be very differently received. From an early age, we tend to be more easily influenced, favourably or unfavourably, by the opinion of our peer group than by any other.

The woman who, as a child at school, had to demand attention from the teacher which she did not always receive, and had difficulties in making friends, may start with similar problems as a member of a group of mothers. The very act of joining the group has some factors reminiscent of entry into school during infancy, when the child had to abandon her position of exclusive relationship to her own mother and begin one that is shared with other pupils. This new relationship depends for its character on expectations regarding the teacher as well as on the realities of her character and behaviour, these difficulties may form part of the mother's nuclear problem, but they are not the aspect that she would bring first into the individual relationship with a caseworker. The group counsellor needs to be aware of each mothers' nuclear problem in all these aspects, and also of the ways in which the aspects are interrelated. In this particular instance, her responsibility to the mother is to try and ensure that what the mother experiences is not merely another sterile repetition of the past relationship as pupil to teacher or among peers.

I have emphasised, though, the specific foci of counselling groups, and that the maintenance of the specific focus in each group is a paramount responsibility of the group counsellor. In the mothers' groups, the group counsellor must herself keep the mothers' problems with their children constantly in mind, and she must also find the connections between these problems and all the activities at different levels that are taking place in the group. This should not mean an unnecessary curtailment of freedom of expression, nor should it mean the introduction of artificial, or unhelpful, or untimely, comparisons.

The discussion will inevitably range over other topics. For example, the mothers may turn from discussing their children to discussing their husbands, and confidences about their marital situations may be exchanged. The group counsellor will have to respond to this apparent change of theme. There is a danger that the group may lose contact with its original purpose, becoming an unfocused group or even slipping into a form of group therapy that has not been sanctioned. There is the further danger of entering into the enjoyment of the 'pastime' which Berne (1967) described as 'lady talk' with such topics as 'Delinquent husbands', with a further development into 'Aren't husbands awful?' and then 'Aren't all men just children?' The group counsellor would not deal with these themes in terms of the individual personality of a woman and her relationship with her absent husband, as in individual psychotherapy; neither would the themes be interpreted as an illustration of the narrator's unconscious or undisclosed feelings in relation to other members of the group or to the group as a whole, as might happen in group psychotherapy. Rather, they would be dealt with as exemplifying the complex interaction between people. They would be placed in a context which includes relationships between parents and parents, parents and children, children and children, either separately or together. The group counsellor is again making links between one relationship and another, seeing both aspects as part of an interconnected network with which she is concerned and of which the relationships with the children always forms a part.

Example: a counselling group discussed

This extract is from the record of one session of an on-going counselling group. This group, which was led by a psychiatric social worker, met in the psychiatric department of a children's hospital. It was composed of mothers whose children had been referred because of asthma, and the children were receiving treatment from a child psychiatrist in a parallel group. The two groups were seen as complementary to each other.

In the counselling group, a common concern of the mothers was with their children's group treatment; and the focus of the group was upon the mothers' relationships with their children in the special circumstances caused by the children's illness and in the current treatment situation. The aim of the group counsellor had two aspects. In general, she set out to augment the help given to the children by affecting the relationship between them and their mothers. More specifically, she wished to give the mothers an opportunity to express and to share their reactions to the difficulties and frustrations of their situation, and their mixed feelings at being in a position in which they had to accept help from others.

This was the third meeting of the group and five mothers were present. Mrs C. started talking as soon as everyone had sat down. She described how she had taken her son to the local authority child welfare clinic to be immunised against polio, and a woman medical officer had refused to immunise him because he was wheezing slightly. The doctor's manner was felt by Mrs C. to be critical and unsympathetic, and, furthermore, the doctor had discussed asthma in the child's presence, something which Mrs C. had always tried to avoid doing herself. Mrs C. was agitated while recounting this, she flushed and stammered, and her eyes filled with tears.

The other members of the group all sympathised warmly with her, and spoke critically about the behaviour of the doctor. Mrs H. and Mrs Y. said that they would not allow such a woman to see their children again if they were Mrs C., and that they would have told her exactly how they felt.

Mrs C. said that she had felt very angry, and would have liked to express this, but 'I never can, I always have an inhibition about it.' She wished she could show her feelings more easily, in the way that other people seemed able to do.

The discussion remained lively and heated, as the members of the group talked of the difficulty of knowing what they should do in situations where the experts disagreed; for example, some doctors advocated immunisation against polio for asthmatic children, and some doctors advised against it. Mrs Y. then asked the group counsellor for direct advice about her boy's nail-biting. The books on child psychology that she had consulted told her to ignore it, and she had tried to do this but her son was now biting his nails worse than ever.

The group counsellor responded by saying she wondered if they were questioning the help that experts could give, as these experts did not always seem to agree among themselves, and that psychology didn't seem to offer much practical help either. Perhaps they were wondering about her, and how much help she would be able to give them.

This was greeted with a short silence, and then Mrs Y. denied that she had meant to be critical of psychology, citing at length the number of books on psychology that she had read. She went on to criticise the staff at her son's school. They made little attempt to understand his problems. She found it impossible to tell his teacher how she felt.

The other mothers all agreed that they could not talk to their children's teachers either; and they went on to speak of teachers, particularly it seemed women teachers, as dangerous and powerful figures who needed to be placated and who could make trouble for people they did not like. There was general agreement that it was important to appear pleasant and grateful in front of the teachers, and to hide any angry feelings they might have.

Mrs B., whose child attended a special, open-air school, made an exception for one teacher there. This teacher was a married woman, herself the mother of an asthmatic child, and she therefore understood about the difficulties. The other mothers said they wished their children could have such a teacher.

The group counsellor said that she understood that they might feel that another woman with a child with asthma was, in a sense, in the same group that they were in. She went on to say that they seemed to feel that teachers, and the staff of clinics and hospitals, who had not got the same direct experience of their difficulties and so were perhaps in a different group, were hard to talk to and might be likely to blame and criticise them.

Mrs Y. said that the doctors at the hospital, 'and I don't mean you', did not seem to understand how much the mothers wanted to be told about their children's illnesses, and to receive more direct advice. Several of the others agreed.

Mrs H. then said to the group counsellor that she wished that 'someone like you' would go to her son's school and explain about his illness and the difficulties it caused.

Mrs C. described her son's demanding behaviour, and how he insisted upon having his own way, and how he always seemed to have an attack of asthma if she did not give in to him. Mrs H. and Mrs C., described similar episodes involving their children, and said that the children's inability to tolerate any frustration meant that they had no friends, as other children did not want to play with them.

Mrs B., who had not spoken yet, and who was the only mother in the group whose child was a girl, said complacently that she did not have any problems of this sort with Jacqueline.

The other four mothers then vied with each other in giving examples of the ways in which their boys tried to dominate them and get their own way in every situation. They spoke of this behaviour as something abnormal, and they strongly approved of a firm attitude on the part of parents and school teachers.

Mrs Y. said she had been very relieved when Dr S. (the child psychiatrist) had told her that 'it was all right to smack Richard'.

Before leaving, the mothers asked in some detail about the arrangements for the next session. The group counsellor indicated that she would be looking forward to seeing them all again the following week.

Discussion

Reading the record, one finds a single major theme predominating. Throughout the session, the mothers seemed to be preoccupied with their feelings towards those people who were professionally concerned with the health, welfare or education of themselves or of their children. In the immediate context of the group, these people were assumed by the group counsellor to be representative of herself. This theme needs to be studied at two levels.

First of all, at the individual level, there is the meaning that this theme has for each of the women in terms of her own personal needs and her current life. Second, at the group level, there is the importance of the theme as an expression of the current situation in the group, and the contribution it was making to the solution of the problems posed by the juxtaposition of cohesive and disruptive forces.

It appears that the members of the group anticipated that 'the experts' would criticise and blame them. It could be assumed that this anticipation was connected with the feelings which they had about their children's illnesses and the degree to which they felt responsible for them – or wanted to pass the responsibility on to someone else. It could also be connected with the anger and resentment which they felt at the burdens which they had to carry, these feelings co-existing with their love and concern for their children. Not only did they appear to anticipate a punitive reaction, but their behaviour seemed actually designed to provoke this as if it were what they sought. If the group counsellor were to react in a way that could be interpreted as unsympathetic, or defensive, their already-existing feelings of hostility would be legitimised and a scapegoat found to take the blame for continuing difficulties.

The behaviour of the mothers in the group also needs to be considered as a product of their experiences of the parent–child relationship, containing something from their experiences as children in relation to their own parents, and also something of their self-image of themselves as parents in relation to their own children. The group counsellor made no reference to this at this session, although it might well have been a theme taken up at this stage of individual casework.

At the level of group interaction, the record shows an attempt to form an in-group consisting inclusively and exclusively of mothers of asthmatic children. Everyone not in this in-group was seen as unsympathetic. This served to ensure sufficient cohesiveness for the time being, and helped to contain the urge to compete for the individual attention of the group counsellor, which might have disrupted the group. It also diverted attention from individual problems and allowed responsibility to be attributed elsewhere. But, at the same time, the presence of the group counsellor aroused considerable anxiety, and her relative passivity provoked fears of retaliation and wishes for firmer control.

The first recorded contribution of the group counsellor was a comment on the mothers' criticism of the behaviour of the woman medical officer, an interpretation at a conscious or near-conscious level that attempted to link the description of an outside event, and their reactions to it, with their relationship to her in the group. The purpose of this comment was to explore ways of helping them to express their feeling more openly, to encourage a more direct consideration of significant relationships, and to help the group to find a less restricting solution to its current problem. This intervention on the part of the group counsellor seems to have been premature; at this stage it was too direct and too personal, focusing upon an area which they were not yet ready to consider. The covert attacks on her continued and became more specific, this time displaced on to teachers, and fears of retaliation were indicated. The next comment made by the group counsellor was more cautious, and was designed to show that she was aware of the hostile feelings without being afraid of them, and without losing sight of the difficulties which had brought the mothers together and which were real. After this the criticism shifted from the teachers to hospital personnel, and an inclination to test out the group counsellor's sincerity and capacity to help was shown. There was an apparent change of topic when they started to talk about their children's behaviour, but it seemed as if they were also talking about their own behaviour. While they discussed their children they were, at the same time, revealing their own fears of having overstepped the limit, their anxieties at the permissive behaviour of the group counsellor, and their fears that she might retaliate. Before they left they needed to be reassured that they would be welcome at the following session.

Two further points need to be mentioned.

This record illustrates the way in which all the different personal relationships that an individual makes can be considered as related to each other so that each forms part of an interlocking system or network. This system is in a perpetual state of adjustment and change, as an alteration in one relationship will have an effect upon all the others. Thus the mothers in the group could move from discussing their reactions to the doctor in the child welfare clinic, to the teachers, to the hospital doctors, illustrating throughout this their reactions to the group counsellor. They could describe their feeling about their children's behaviour in such a way, and in such a context, that it could be treated as illustrating their view of the group counsellor's relationship with themselves. Thus no single relationship which might be demonstrated in the mother's behaviour or described in their verbal interchanges could be evaluated or understood in isolation; each had to be considered as a fragment of an interrelated whole, and intervention at any one point could be used to influence the whole field.

The second point concerns the treatment of the material provided in this session as if it were the production of a single entity. It is important to emphasise again that attitudes and feelings attributed to the group as such are not identical with the attitudes and feelings of each individual member. The covert hostility shown towards the group counsellor has been considered as an attribute of the group as a whole, contributing to the temporary solution of a problem also belonging to the whole group. To the establishment of this group solution each of the individual members made some contribution. At an individual level, this pattern of behaviour in the group must have had some particular meaning for each of the mothers present: for Mrs C., whose frustration at being unable to express her angry feelings about people in authority began the session; for Mrs Y., who vigorously developed this theme; for Mrs B., who indicated through her complacency the satisfaction which she derived as a spectator rather than as an active participant in the conflict. Though each member would have a different individual attitude towards the group counsellor, the hostility could be treated as a common denominator, reinforced and expressed more clearly in the group situation. It had a meaning for each one within this particular context, and, therefore, a point was provided at which an intervention affecting the total group process could be made.

In such groups in child guidance and child psychiatric clinics it can be seen that the members of the group are not psychotherapy patients but have a different commitment and different expectations; that their personal problems are only relevant at the point where they can be recognised as impinging on the focal problem; that intervention takes place in the area of interpersonal relationships; and that the use of relationships is a primary part of the group counselling process.

The group process in counselling

Group counselling is likely to be a function of a particular agency or service, and to be rooted within its context, in contrast to group psychotherapy which tends to be more bracketed off from its surroundings. The aim and focus of the group work may be determined by the agency providing it, it may be determined by the group counsellor, or it may be negotiated by the members of the group. However it is reached, it is the responsibility of the group counsellor to carry it consistently in mind.

Whatever the nature of any group work, and whether it is limited and problem focused, or whether it is intensive and analytic and engaging the total personalities of the participants, the positive therapeutic factors that exist in the group situation will need to be recognised and utilised. Likewise these factors will have their negative, anti-therapeutic counterparts, which cannot be ignored either.

The factors existing in groups that were identified as group-specific by Foulkes (1964) include the sharing and socialisation which brings the experience of belongingness; the mirror phenomenon in which the group member can see his own problem reflected in the problem of another, and the exchange of feelings aroused by some shared theme. There is also the support that the group provides as the members identify with each other and help each other through painful periods, finding an outlet for action even if it is of a negative kind, and binding the group together in 'fight' (and possibly 'flight') responses in face of a common 'enemy'. This possibility should be borne in mind whenever it is possible to exercise some selection procedure for counselling groups. Such groups are likely to make more rapid progress if there is some diversity in the solutions that members habitually employ to meet their common problems.

The loss of uniqueness, the knowledge of shared difficulties, should do something to reduce the feelings of isolation and shame which cultural attitudes in our society help to induce, and by which problems are often exacerbated. We have already discussed how one confidence often leads to another, and how we find ourselves becoming franker about our own problems in response to a friend's disclosures. After this, problems often appear less intractable and solutions more attainable.

In a social setting, the sequel to frank disclosures may be embarrassment and withdrawal at the next encounter. This may also happen in a counselling group. The group counsellor will have to anticipate this possibility, and perhaps even discourage premature exchange of confidences in the beginning stages of a group. A group psychotherapist, on the other hand, may be able to permit greater tensions to develop from the very beginning, and the group then has more time to develop its own means for dealing with such problems.

The capacity of the members of the group to identify with one another, to discover the common aspects in each individual problem, and to give as well as to receive help, forms an important part of the group counselling process. It is something that the group counsellor may need to promote, intervening more directly to this end than a group psychotherapist would be likely to do. It is therefore important that the group counsellor should be able to identify correctly the cohesive factors that are present in the group, the areas which can be shared, and the conditions under which sharing is possible; otherwise she may find herself encouraging a spurious uniformity and delaying the discussion of real and important differences. She must also recognise and not be dismayed by the disruptive forces in the group, and these may have to be addressed if they are relevant to the problem on which the group is focused, or if they are seriously hampering the group's progress. However, she will not seek to bring these negative forces to the fore in the way that might be appropriate in some stages of group psychotherapy.

This skill, the capacity to recognise, and make use of, such therapeutic forces as are immediately available, can be studied and acquired; it can also sometimes be recognised in an unlearned, intuitive response.

Example

Some years ago there was a meeting of parents and staff at what was then called a junior training centre. About a hundred parents were present. After the formal presentations the centre head, who was in the chair, invited questions from the floor. 'Please, Miss,' came from the back of the hall, 'when will my Jenny be able to walk?' The centre head did not answer this herself but appealed to the audience. 'Some of you know a lot about this. Come along, you other parents with Downs children. Tell us when your children started to walk.' The meeting at once became lively, with a number of parents eagerly recounting their experiences and others listening intently. A large unwieldy meeting had become for the moment an effective group able to give and receive help. What the head had done, while declining to take the position of expert herself, was to make a relationship between the experiences of one member and the experiences of others – a relationship which could then grow and develop.

This was a large group, and large and median groups have rather different dynamics from small groups and will be discussed latter, but it illustrates something valid for all groups.

As well as the behaviour of individuals in the group, the group counsellor must be aware of what is taking place at a group level, and she will look on the selection of any particular theme for discussion by the group as the result of a group process which transcends but includes the activity of individuals. Discussion of this topic must be meeting some need in each of the people present: it is also meeting a need belonging to the group as a whole, and is helping to resolve some group tension. The temporary solution that it is providing to a group problem may be a restrictive one, hampering the further progress of the group. Thus it may be reducing tension by diverting attention from some more sensitive area, enabling members to conceal differences that might become apparent were another topic to be discussed. Another diversion could be the direction of criticism to persons not present in the group, and the group counsellor, like the group therapist, would need to bring attention back to the here-and-now situation in the group.

The group counsellor must be aware of these processes. She (or he) is concerned with what goes on in the group in so far as it relates to the terms of reference, as in the group in a child guidance clinic described above, she looked for its significance in terms of the mothers' interaction with their children. She may wonder, for example, whether the mothers who discuss their marital situation are feeling that they have been unjustly singled out to bear the burden of their respective family's difficulties. If she thinks this is so, she may make some comment designed to help the mothers to express their feelings more directly, on the lines of 'Perhaps some of us are feeling that the fathers ought to be here too'. She does not say, 'Perhaps Mrs Smith is feeling . . .', singling out the most vocal member; rather, she attributes the feeling to the group as a whole. In this example, by using the first person plural, she indicates that she associates herself with the mothers, and is not attributing more responsibility to them than to their absent husbands. By using the word 'father' she underlines the fact that it is their relationships with their children that are at issue, and so she helps to relate the discussion to the specific focus of the group.

The group counsellor makes use of the individual relationship she has with every member of the group, and she also makes use of the relationship which she has with the group as a whole. Her relationship with each member at an individual level cannot be ignored; she must be aware of it, and at times may have to direct her intervention to one particular person in the group. For example, if one mother remains silent, and appears to feel isolated from the others, the group counsellor might wish to respond to her silent presence in some particular way. The group counsellor might also think it sometimes appropriate to give some personal attention to an over-talkative 'monopolist' who is holding up the progress of the group. The behaviour of both these members, however, is also part of a total group process in which all are implicated, and the group counsellor might find ways of helping the individuals through intervention at a group level, and in this way avoid the risk of weakening the group, and of hindering the development of its capacity to solve its own problems. In the same way that the social worker, in an individual interview, identifies the needs of her client and responds to them, so the group counsellor needs to identify and respond to the needs of the group as a whole.

Suppose that in our group of mothers, one member were to complain forcefully that the treatment is a waste of time and that the group counsellor isn't giving her any help. Suppose that the other members of the group allow this member to speak but remain silent themselves. In any treatment situation, the expression of existing negative feelings can have value. Many patients or clients, however, while experiencing feelings of hostility, may fear to show them, and others may have to pretend, even to themselves, that these feelings do not exist. The angry mother in the group is verbalising feelings that all to some extent share, but which only she is able to acknowledge and furthermore express. In the allocation of group roles, she has been given that of spokesperson and ventilator of angry feelings. The group counsellor can respond directly to this mother, accepting her hostility, and demonstrating that angry feelings are present in every relationship and that their presence can be acknowledged without harm. This would be appropriate in an individual situation, but to do this in a group would isolate the angry mother from the rest and leave the hostility that is not being expressed to remain unrecognised, perhaps by implication making it into something that seems even more dangerous. What is needed from the group counsellor is a group response, an acceptance of the hostility as something offered by the whole group, and an underlining of the point that her relationship, which can absorb the anger without being damaged, is with the whole group. It is in this way that the group counsellor is able to make contact with a wider range of feelings in her clients than would be possible in individual work, since feelings which would not be expressed by many clients in an individual interview can achieve indirect and vicarious expression through the activities of a group.

The group counsellor coming fresh to the group process need not feel that her interpretations should match those of her mentors, tutors or supervisors or, for that matter, those described in books. Every interpretation is part of the interaction between the group counsellor and the group members, and the counsellor's experience and personality are part of that interaction; every interpretation is her own professional and personal response to the immediate situation. The question is not whether an interpretation is right or wrong, but whether it is appropriate, taking all these factors into account. In all groups some interpretations are noted by the group leader but stored away in the mind and not used at that time. Some interpretations will not occur until long after that group meeting is over, and then will form part of that group leader's own personal and professional development, if not the group's. In this sense one need never regret the afterthought 'Why didn't I say that . . .?' because the particular thought will not be lost but will become embodied in what the leader has to offer to subsequent groups.

Group counselling with young offenders

Child guidance clinics provide a medical setting, and however much they have moved away from the medical model they still have links with a culture containing ideas of pathology and treatment.

A different context is provided by services and institutions which work with young offenders. The strength of peer groups of adolescents, at the transition point between childhood and adulthood, is recognised. With their power to define their own standards, generate powerful emotions and control behaviour through giving and withholding approbation, such groups can also provide the context in which deviant behaviour, attitudes and values are learnt and perpetuated. Alternative peer groups, with a leader able to be both supportive and confrontational, may be able to make use of the same process in reverse.

Intermediate treatment centres were among the first institutions to use group methods of treatment, and probation departments have followed. In such a setting, groups may be conducted for young people who are referred by the courts. Such youngsters come from different backgrounds and have different motivations; they have in common the fact that they have broken some law and that that is the reason they are receiving treatment. The group counsellor will have to elaborate this common factor, or establish some additional and more specific basis for selection.

One explanation for delinquent behaviour is found in a failure to identify with an authority figure and therefore a concomitant failure to incorporate acceptable standards and modes of behaviour. Such delinquency is not something that has gone wrong — it is a deficiency in the provisions that are necessary for development to proceed normally. It is a question of what has not gone right. Such an assumption is one of many that could be used to provide a starting point and a focus for a counselling group, and enables us to discuss the role of group leader by means of a string of further assumptions.

We imagine the group leader accepting the focus that we have suggested for him, and selecting the members of his group carefully on this basis. He (or she) will consider the relationship between himself and the group in the light of the deficiency in normal provision that has been assumed, and which he hopes to do something to remedy. Whatever other feelings are transferred to him, he will also inevitably represent that authority, parental, educational or magisterial, with which his clients or probationers have had their difficulties in the past. They now have an opportunity to enter into a fresh relationship with an authority figure in the context of a peer group — or alternatively to reinforce an existing one. The leader will perhaps hope that through the use of group, rather than individual, methods, with the support that membership of a peer group provides, he can facilitate and expedite the open expression of feelings and attitudes, and enable the group members to test out the limits of the relationship that he is offering them. Phantasies will then be more quickly revealed for what they are, and strong feelings will become less frightening when known to be shared. He will be likely to take active steps to relate positively to the group, demonstrating his tolerance and his concern and his capacity to remain undamaged by overt and covert hostility.

Within this framework, one will need to keep anxiety within the limits of the group's capacity to tolerate it at any moment of time. One will expect to see an increase in this capacity and hope that the group will develop sufficient strength and cohesion to take over some of this responsibility for itself. It may seem appropriate to introduce certain experiences into the group sessions in order to augment their impact and to increase the focus upon the areas considered to be most relevant. One such experience might be an exposure to the demands of authority. In this way, the boys would be given an opportunity to develop new ways of dealing with the challenge they have been unable to deal with successfully in real-life situations.

One of the phenomena already noted as specific to groups is the capacity that the group has to define reality through consensus among its members. A shared view is likely to emerge about what sort of group it is and about its relationship with other groups and with authority. If the members can unite in attributing blame elsewhere, they are reducing their own feelings of guilt. Such beliefs can be very powerful. A group composed of people who all have in their repertoire similar ways of dealing with their problems may come to supply support and confirmation for maladaptive patterns of behaviour in which they all have a share. Challenge may be discouraged by powerful group forces. Though this can happen in all manner of groups, it is more likely to occur in groups that are focused upon a common problem. The danger lies in such behaviour becoming entrenched as part of the group 'culture', as may happen when the behaviour offers a solution not only to individual problems but also to the threat of disruptive forces in the group.

Group counselling with ex-psychiatric hospital patients

Another counselling group to be considered is one made up of patients discharged to the community after long periods in a mental hospital. Such a group can be used to extend into the community the support derived from living in a protective environment. This provides us with an example of a counselling group in a different setting, and focused upon different aims. If we look for a relationship, significant to all its members, on which this group could focus, we do not find it in that between parent and child, nor between youth and authority. In this situation, two sets of relevant relationships could be suggested: there is the relationship that exists between each patient and the psychiatric hospital on the one hand, and that between the patient and the outside community on the other. The group counsellor may be identified with either hospital or community – indeed, one of these organisations is likely to be the group counsellor's employing authority – but in the group the counsellor needs to represent both, and to make a link between the two.

Any leaders of such groups have to limit the amount of stress within the group, and to keep it within the tolerance of individual members who may be exceptionally vulnerable. They may have to play a more active role to meet individual and group needs, which could include a need to experience continued dependence and protection. Indeed, it may take time for such a cluster to develop into a counselling group. Given sufficient time, participation in this group may be expected to provide some sense of comfort and security, to reduce the feelings of alienation and stigma, and to provide experience in relating to other people within a safe environment; it may go on to extend the range of responses that are available to the members for meeting challenging situations. As the group coheres and manages to establish its own structure, then dependence on the leader may come gradually to be replaced at least in part by a sense of belongingness to the group which will enable them to develop their own independent helping mechanisms and support each other.

Group counselling for victims of trauma

In the past, studies of post-traumatic stress have mainly focused upon individual experiences, and counselling seems to be offered more often on a one-to-one than on a group basis.

Each method of work has its particular advantages, at different stages and for different forms of trauma, whether the trauma be the result of domestic violence or follows an external catastrophe involving a number of others. Individual counselling emphasises personal responses and the way in which traumas can reactivate former problems. A shared and group process, particularly where there has been a shared trauma, brings together people with an experience in common and places the trauma in a wider context, giving the event a meaning that extends beyond the individual. The rap groups set up by and for Vietnam veterans have been widely documented (Herman 1992). These groups were started because the survivors of the trauma had lost confidence in the ability of their community to support them and were turning to each other as the only trustworthy source of help available. Here the opportunity to give as well as to receive help proved important, bringing back a sense of value and empowerment.

A disadvantage of individual counselling is the risk that the feelings of weakness and dependence that often follow trauma will be emphasised. But there are also disadvantages to group work. Shared external stress brings groups of individuals closer together, and sometimes this closeness comes to be valued as an end in itself. A group may perceive itself as a collection of victims banded together against a hostile world. Care needs to be taken to ensure that this perception does not become fixed and permanent and so prevent further progress and the re-establishment of other relationships.

Herman has illustrated the importance of focusing post trauma work to meet different needs at different stages, and of distinguishing between different forms of group work. She identifies three main stages in the recovery of victims of such traumas as rape, domestic violence or political persecution, each stage having different needs.

First there is the immediate need for a place of safety in which information can be shared, needs acknowledged, and strategies for short-term survival found. The emphasis is on the present and on taking one day at a time. At this stage a focus needs to be placed upon cognitive and educational processes.

The second stage brings the need to talk about the traumatic event, to recall and to bear witness and to recover and share experiences. In a group it would be important to establish a culture in which sharing and supporting is emphasised with a minimum of conflict.

Both these groups, with their different aims, would be firmly led and focused groups with a closed membership of people who had been exposed to similar, sometimes to the same, trauma. Cohesive and positive group factors would be promoted, conflict kept at a minimum, and the group leader, or preferably leaders, would be supportive and interventionist.

The third stage brings the need for reconnection in the present, with attention given to re-establishing the capacity to repair relationships with individuals and with the community and to restoring lost trust and a sense of the integrity of the self. This level is seen as needing group therapy rather than more focused counselling, in an unstructured, slow/open group that can allow conflict to develop – indeed the expression of conflict is seen as essential to the therapeutic task at this stage. The commitment now would be a one of the whole personality, and the concern would not be with the sequelae of trauma alone but with the totality of the individual's experience and relationships expressed through the here-and-now interactions in the group. The group should have a diverse membership and would not be limited to people designated as victims.

Example

One instance of an attempt to respond quickly to a traumatic event was a rapid ad hoc convening of a single session counselling group in the day centre attached to a hospice. It also shows that assumptions about the impact of trauma need to be made cautiously.

The trauma occurred one afternoon when seven patients who had been spending the day in the centre boarded the hospice minibus to be taken home. They were all ill in varying degrees with advanced cancer and two were in wheelchairs which were bolted down in the mini bus. As the minibus was about to drive off one of the patients suffered a huge and fatal haemorrhage and quantities of blood spattered the other patients and the floor. It was several minutes before staff were able to unbolt the wheelchairs and remove all the patients.

A group counsellor who was one of the hospice social workers invited the patients and staff involved, including the driver and the nurse who had been at the scene, to take part in a group meeting a week later. All who were able to come attended.

The group counsellor was searching for an appropriate response. She wanted to acknowledge what had happened, to signal the recognition and support of the staff, to give those involved an opportunity to share their feelings about it, and also possibly to relate it to their present situation and to past events. Although on-going work was not possible, it was hoped that this meeting would open up opportunities for talking further among themselves, and would lessen any risk of a tacit concensus to behave as if the incident had never happened.

The group counsellor, the only person who had not been present at the time, was aware of her own anxiety about the event, and realised that her reactions would be different and must not be allowed to intrude and influence the group.

The group consisted of four patients and two staff members. The group counsellor started by putting the event in the context of the hospice as a whole, voicing the concern of everybody, and asking them to help her to understand how they were feeling. She also said that she thought that by sharing experiences they might be able to help each other and also others not there.

The members of the group responded at once and recounted and compared their immediate reactions of shock and panic, the patients showing their sympathy for the staff and the staff sharing their feelings of pain. Both staff and patients joined in remembering the person who had died. There was a lot of mutual support.

But they did not spend long on this. They quickly went on to exchange other experiences of sudden death, and seemed to wish to put recent events into a wider context, mentioning, for example, the loss of a family member in a road traffic accident and the sudden death of a husband from a heart attack. The emphasis was not so much upon sudden death as such as upon the comfort to be found in treating it as an experience in which all shared, along with the perception that life was a dangerous business and everyone was at risk. The members of the group asked questions and actively sought contributions from each other, including contributions from the staff members who they clearly wanted to share in their perceptions.

Although they were used to meeting every week at the day centre, they were telling each other things and expressing feelings in a way that they had not done before. There was, in fact, less immediate distress about the event than the group counsellor had expected, in this special group of people who had accepted the fact of their own grave illnesses. It seemed that a shared experience, however traumatic it might seem, was being valued for its cohesive effect and that it may have been a greater trauma for the staff than for the patients. When the counsellor asked them how they had found the experience of coming together and talking in this way, they spoke of the pleasure of being able to meet in a quiet side room, away from the large day centre room. The impression given was that the trauma had provided an opportunity to talk, and a safe and containing situation that they valued.

Who are the group counsellors?

Finally, we need to consider who it is who does all this counselling?

Counselling groups may be found in approved schools conducted by psychologist, teacher or doctor. Groups of mental hospital patients are often led by a nurse, a hospital chaplain, a doctor or a social worker, singly or in any combination. Staff often get their training on the job, first sitting in as an observer, and modelling their work on that of their mentor. There are special schools where teaching the children can merge into counselling, and where more formal counselling may be necessary for groups of children or of parents. Prisons have their need for group counselling at different levels, and here the leaders of groups may be staff especially appointed for this purpose, specialists coming in from outside, or members of the disciplinary staff who have volunteered for the job, in any combination.

The use of visiting specialists has its justification. If there are conflicts to be resolved within an institution, the presence of a facilitator from outside the conflict may be needed. Staff meetings are often helped by the presence of someone with no previous history in that group.

However, care needs to be taken to avoid fragmentation of the activities for which the different categories of staff have to take responsibility. The staff of an institution cannot expect to hand over to outsiders the responsibility for dealing with the emotional problems that life in that institution engenders. It could be argued that in each special situation the initiator of the group activity should come from the profession which is primarily concerned with the setting in which the group work takes place.

There are many other examples where fields of work, which properly belong to an established profession, bring emotional problems to light, and these have to be faced and cannot be denied or warded off. This is particularly true for those professions whose consumers experience anxiety about the nature of the services which they are receiving, and about their consequences. Here again, it is not possible or desirable always to call upon an outside expert to deal with the emotional difficulties which are revealed, and which present problems in other people's working lives. Many professional workers will, rather, see this as part of their own responsibility, and will elect to deal with it themselves. These workers need to have opportunity to extend and enrich their techniques with some of the concepts we have been describing as part of group counselling. Just as social work has borrowed concepts from psychotherapy, and group counselling from group psychotherapy, so other disciplines are borrowing from group counselling.

There are many situations outside structured group work where doctors, nurses, psychologists, health visitors or teachers meet groups of people in connection with some aspect of their own work and have to interpret to them their expectations of one another and the possible outcomes of their techniques. They can enrich these discussions with a knowledge of their own involvement in the group processes. They have to have some idea of the hidden questions behind the questions which they are being asked, and of the alternative meanings of the answers which they are giving. They need to be able to draw comparisons, to detect common themes, and to recognise and deal with some of the anxieties that will be only marginally expressed. They need to be able to answer question with question, so as to extend rather than contract the area of discussion. All this involves the application of techniques which have been developed in group counselling, and which may have been learnt and adapted in their turn from contact with group psychotherapists. This does not make these workers into counsellors, and counselling is not the object of the exercise. If they can benefit from learning something about group counselling methods, it is not in order to obtain an additional profession but to become more competent in dealing with some of the issues in their existing one. Any skill that they acquire must become built into their individual personal style, and incorporated into the practice within the boundaries of their own profession.

CHAPTER 7

Education in Groups

Tell me and I will forget. Show me and I may remember. Involve me and I will understand.(Chinese Proverb)

I pay the schoolmaster, but 'tis the schoolboys that educate my son. (Emerson)

How can the group process be used in education? What are the parameters of group discussion? How can group discussion be distinguished from group psychotherapy and group counselling?

The merits of free and open discussion and exploration were originally argued by Socrates (though we may question if they were always strictly adhered to by him), but in many areas of education they have not been well understood or applied. The emphasis that came to be placed upon the separate individual as universal education was developed in the last hundred years, with the stress upon individual achievement and competition, meant that less interest was taken in the benefits of cooperation and learning together and less attention was paid to the context in which education was taking place.

A change of emphasis has come in the last few decades with the development of focused group work and an increased use of the group approach in other settings. This change was also stimulated by the student movements in the 1960s, following the expansion in higher education that took place then and the demands that came from the students themselves for a less didactic and more interactional form of education. There should be more talking and listening, the students maintained, and less lecturing and reading. All these developments brought the educational process itself under more scrutiny, and since then there has been growing interest in the group processes that take place in the classroom, and in the nature and influence of the relationships between teachers and taught. The context of education is now being recognised and utilised, and group discussion has developed as a separate group work system alongside group psychotherapy and group counselling.

The educational process

> To learn something new entails changing one's whole attitude to a number of
> things, to oneself and to the world in which one lives. (Foulkes 1990)

This is true of education at all levels. As new information is absorbed, so old
attitudes may have to be reorganised and some past ideas abandoned. This can be
painful. Even when it is factual information that is being transmitted, students
have to select from the material that is being offered to them, and they then have
the task of linking their selections to existing knowledge and to past experience,
rearranging, incorporating and discarding. Assumptions and value judgements,
including some cherished ones, may need to be brought up into conscious
awareness and re-examined. Intellectual and emotional growth cannot be kept
altogether separate.

In addition, in any educational context students have to accept a teacher who,
it is at least assumed, is better qualified and better informed than they are, with the
potential for narcissistic hurt that this can bring. The subtext in all these
encounters, particularly important when both parties are adult, is the theme of
authority and dependence. The more didactic the setting and the teaching
methods, the more of a split there is likely to be between teaching and learning, on
the one side the knowledgeable one with power and on the other the ignorant
ones with none. Students will respond in different ways depending upon their
past experiences inside and outside the family, and their current state of
maturation. But whether dependent, grateful, passive or rebellious, their ability to
become creatively engaged with what is being taught is likely to be affected.

In the 1950s, Abercrombie (Abercrombie and Terry 1978) began studying
these aspects of the educational process and applying insights derived from group
analysis to her work with students of various disciplines.

She advocated three changes in perceptions and attitudes.

1. The main aim of education must no longer be thought of as the
    transmission of information, but rather as the encouragement of
    autonomous learning

2. The relationship between teacher and pupil must be regarded not as
    that of giver and receiver of information, but as that of co-operating
    explorers of knowledge

3. The relationship between pupils, instead of being ignored as of neutral
    and negligable value in the education process, must be recognised and
    fostered as a powerful medium for interaction or collaborative learning.

Abercrombie worked with small groups of students of such disciplines as
teaching, architecture and medicine, and she described her task as one of
encouraging and stimulating interest and independent learning, and of freeing

the students from a blinkering dependence upon authority figures and the received wisdom of the past.

More specifically, Abercrombie was 'helping students to become more effective in their chosen field by getting more understanding, and therefore better control, of those relevant parts of their behaviour that originate outside their conscious awareness and therefore are not subject to their own evaluation' (Abercrombie 1981, p.2). The unconscious processes that she recognised as relevant in this situation were not so much those resulting from repression to avoid psychic pain (the province of psychotherapy), but rather those she considered to be the results of habit and of familiarity with processes and things that can be handled without taking thought. These processes could act as impediments to learning, and hamper and distort the perception of new ideas. Her method was to establish situations in which the students could talk freely about their current behaviour in relation to their specific educational tasks, allowing their relevant assumptions, expectations and attitudes, of which they were scarcely or not at all aware, to become clearer to them in comparison with those of their peers.

The difference between this form of education and other more didactic methods is immediately marked in a physical sense when the serried rows of desks confronting a teacher are replaced by the circle of chairs in which students and teacher sit together. Though this change in physical setting is not enough of itself to produce group discussion, it is a necessary first step to promote equal and 'on the level' exchange and participation, and to discourage any hierarchy or subgrouping. Any departure from the circular seating arrangement gives the wrong message and hampers the group's activity; and the more there is a departure from this arrangement the more will the group tend to slide back towards the didactic model of teacher and taught.

Abercrombie worked within higher education in general, but the changes she advocated have a wider application. Harrow (1997) has described finding her way to 'group analysis in education by accident' when she was teaching a particularly disruptive class of eight-year-olds in a primary school. One day when there had been more complaints than usual about behaviour in the playground she threw away the timetable, rearranged the furniture, sat down with the children in a circle, and refused to go on taking responsibility for 'their' problems. The response came quickly. 'Bullies and scapegoats were identified. Feelings were expressed with sometimes devastating honesty. Solutions were offered with spontaneity, originality and care. Our group ... began to find the ability to release and direct energy to promote change and find a sense of well being' (Harrow 1997, pp.24–25).

There are other situations and other forms of education, such as training for the so-called helping professions, where the use of group discussion has a direct application to the subject being taught. Here students are required to learn about human behaviour and about relationships between individuals and in groups, and to make direct use of this knowledge and of their own selves in their work. In training for social work, counselling and psychotherapy the methods of group discussion have long been employed.

Outside the area of professional training are other activities that have made increased use of group discussion. For example there are the programmes in specific aspects of human relationships that are provided in many schools, churches and youth clubs; and there are the marriage preparation courses run by such organisations as Relate. And there is in-service training in organisations of many different kinds directed to team building, or to promoting and managing organisational change, with programmes in which the group facilitator now often replaces the formal trainer.

The task of group discussion

There are inevitably shared areas between group counselling and group discussion, and also between group therapy and group discussion, but there is one point of difference that always has to be borne in mind. *The participants in group discussion are not patients and they are not clients. They are students and they have come to learn. The leaders in group discussion are not there to provide therapy or counselling; they are there to teach by enabling the members of the group to learn together and from each other.*

So the processes that take place in the group are now used to facilitate teaching and learning together, to develop and elucidate a particular topic with all its ramifications, to involve the students more directly in the process, or, in the case of experiential groups, to provide the students with an experience that may have many aspects but which is intended to be educational and to promote professional development.

It would be misleading if we were to think of group discussion as a half-way house, placed somewhere between psychotherapy and education. It must always remain within the limits appropriate to a method of education. It is, however, a very special method that makes use of concepts of dynamic group behaviour and insights derived from group psychotherapy and group counselling, and which shares some part of their aims and methods. But careful distinctions have to be made and maintained. The focus is not upon the total personal situations of the participants, as it would be in group psychotherapy, nor upon specific personal problems, as it might be in group counselling. The focus is taken out of the individual and personal area and kept on topics that are presented for development and elucidation, or on the opportunities that participation in a group can itself provide for educational and professional development.

The particular problems which all groups and particularly such relatively unstructured ones, will have to solve are likely to be influenced, and even intensified in the case of group discussion, by the nature of the task before the group and the type of theme or topic on which each session is focused. Both these factors may increase the stress which is experienced by the individual members, and this increase is likely to be reflected in a strengthening of disruptive, as opposed to cohesive, forces in the group as a whole.

However, while the members of a discussion group have to be protected from unauthorised intrusion into their personal lives, their concern is with some aspect of human behaviour in general in which the behaviour of each individual member in particular is inevitably included. Such learning requires involvement at emotional as well as at intellectual levels. The success of the learning process can best be evaluated by the nature and extent of the modification that takes place in each member's subsequent behaviour in relation to their work or their studies.

How far this expectation can be made explicit at the beginning will depend upon the nature, purpose, composition and level of sophistication, of each particular discussion group. It cannot be determined by intellectual level alone, although some professional groups, whose members have had previous training in this field, could be expected to be more at ease than some other students with the concepts involved.

Learning to use the self

It could be said that one of the principal things students of the helping professions have to learn is to understand and express the feelings which they experience in any task in which the skills needed involve the use of their own personalities.

This task may be a specific one. Where group discussion takes place in a professional setting, the task will be concerned with the provision of an individual service to patients, clients, or customers, or it will involve working as a member of a team. All these activities involve the use of personal relationships, and the skills required cannot be learnt through academic means alone. Information provided through lectures can be absorbed at an intellectual level without being converted into increased insight into the behaviour of oneself and others, and may even defeat its own purpose by becoming encapsulated and divorced from everyday experience. Students need to participate actively in this learning process and relate it directly to their own experience if it is not to become a barrier rather than a stepping-stone to further progress.

There are some learning situations, some professional trainings, and some tasks and enterprises, where the relevance of an individual's capacity to make appropriate and effective use of his or her own personality is clearly seen.

Thus, at a conference of Relate counsellors, a psychiatrist leading a group discussion was asked 'What does a psychiatrist do?' The questioner added, 'I know that a surgeon uses the knife, a physician uses drugs, but what does a psychiatrist use?' The answer, reached by stages, ran like this. 'The surgeon uses his knife, but he also uses his personality. He uses his knife scientifically, but he uses his personality unscientifically even if he uses it effectively. The physician uses his drugs scientifically, but he also uses his self unscientifically. The psychiatrist (though perhaps it should be said not the psychiatrist of every school), who uses no knife and no drugs, is left with nothing to use but his own self; but there is this difference – he uses his own self scientifically.'

Other professions, including those of psychotherapists, counsellors and social workers, share with the psychiatrist in the use of concepts which have been developed in order to use the self as a professional tool. In these professions it has long been taken for granted that the relationship between the professional worker and the patient or client provides the context within which the helping process takes place, and that it is necessary to make it a subject for study from both ends. Any social worker, for example, even when dealing with some concrete practical difficulty and using well-recognised techniques, has to be aware not only of the client's complex emotional responses but also of the worker's own. Where there is a selection procedure for membership of branches of these professions, flexibility and a capacity for personal growth and development are stressed as desirable, even essential, qualities. During training, the student is encouraged to develop self-awareness and sensitivity. It is recognised that this is a part of the professional training that cannot be provided through academic lectures and the reading of textbooks alone. Well-established teaching methods that attempt to provide it include group discussion as well as individual supervision focused upon on-going professional work or on more general problems.

An interest in the professional relationship and an appreciation of its importance now extends to other professional groups. The same component, involving the use of the self, is present, though often less well recognised, in many other activities. It is acknowledged in the rules and customs, sometimes unwritten and unspoken, which exist in many professions and occupations to govern relationships between those providing and those receiving a service, between doctor and patient, solicitor and client, and even between sales representative and customer. Even where it is not considered a specific part of the professional process, there is an ever-increasing realisation that the interpersonal relationship through which the professional help is given occupies a central position and can help and hinder the worker's use of occupational skills and the client's readiness to profit by them. This applies particularly to all transactions where help is offered through a face-to-face meeting, and directly concerns professions such as medicine, nursing, teaching, the law and the church.

Groups in industry

Another field in which group methods are increasingly used is in the in-service training programmes in industry. Here there are expectations of gains in professional performance and relationships. The focus may be less upon the use of a particular professional relationship than upon a recognition of the importance of an individual's behaviour in the context of a team and in the role of colleague, supervisor, manager and subordinate. There is also concern with the capacity of individuals to absorb change in a field where organisational and technological developments often take place rapidly. The readiness and competence of individuals to alter habitual ways of behaviour, and to accept changes in the organisations around them, depends upon much more than individual comprehension of the situation; it can involve such additional factors as self-awareness, sense of security, ability to trust others, and the nature and depth of the satisfactions derived from their work.

Here intellectual methods of training and retraining, such as the didactic lecture, have proved inadequate; indeed, they may have hazards as well as limitations, sometimes serving to mobilise defences against change imposed by others. For example, a lecture describing and advocating new methods of working may be seen as a concealed attack on existing methods and on their operators, who may in consequence be stimulated to resist the proposed changes.

The resistance may be particularly strong, even if not openly expressed, if the whole experience comes as an addition to past experiences of being a child in relation to an adult, a pupil in relation to a teacher, a cog in relation to a machine. Alternatively, it may serve to change the workers' image of themselves and of the work they are doing, providing an illusion that something is different without producing any actual appreciable change in methods of operation. The illusion satisfies their ambitions and so makes further effort unnecessary.

In this dilemma, industry has turned to dynamic group psychology, and has adopted group methods, which have sometimes been known in this context as 'T-groups', following the original work of Lewin (1952) in the USA. The original T-groups have already been referred to as the precursors of the encounter group movement in the United States. By this means it is hoped that more fundamental changes in attitudes and behaviour patterns can be produced. It is anticipated that an increase in sensitivity and self-awareness resulting from an exposure to group interaction will reduce dependence upon stereotyped, habitual modes of behaviour, and that there will be an increase in flexibility and in readiness to experiment as a result.

A T-group may be composed of a number of people unknown to each other and drawn from different industrial settings. Alternatively, firms may set up their own T-groups as part of an internal in-service training programme, despite the complications that could be caused by the prior acquaintanceship and the hierarchical relationship of the people concerned. In each T-group there will be one, or perhaps two, group leaders who are known in this context as 'trainers'. The trainer may encourage the group to focus upon its own behaviour, perhaps during the performance of some task that it has been given. Sometimes the situation is left as unstructured and leaderless as possible so that the old landmarks and familiar roles that the members habitually use are no longer available or effective.

It would seem as if these groups are designed primarily to be of benefit to the organisations that sponsor them, and only indirectly to be of benefit to the group itself and its individual members. Traditionally, it has not been thought necessary to give consideration to those who have to leave a post in industry because of inadequacy revealed through the stresses of new demands and the strains of interacting personalities. The use of group methods, in which such stresses and strains may be deliberately introduced, creates new hazards. This gives added emphasis to the importance that we attach to seeing that the aims and limitations of a T-group, and the sanction that is given to the leader by the group, should be formulated and understood as clearly as possible. It should remain the responsibility of the leader of a T-group, as of all discussion groups, to see that the defences of individual members are in fact adequate (this cannot be safely assumed) and that the stress that is inevitable in such a situation is kept within the tolerance of the most vulnerable member. Responsibility should also be taken for any casualties of the group.

This last is a consideration that does not apply to industry alone. By the same token, educational establishments have some responsibility for the students whom they select or accept for a training course in which group methods are used in such a way that the vulnerable parts of the personality may become revealed. If, as a result, any of these students have to withdraw from the course, some responsibility remains with the educational establishment and attempts should be made to secure appropriate help if it is needed.

Other applications

Professional and occupational training of one sort or another is not the only field in which group discussion methods may be used: they are equally applicable wherever an understanding of human behaviour, which has to include one's own behaviour, is involved in the subject at issue.

Group discussion, for example, may be offered to young people in school or youth club as part of a programme of preparation for adult life and as a way of giving help with the difficulties of this particular transitional stage. Adaptations to the challenges and opportunities of each successive stage in life, whether of leaving school, of marriage, childbirth and the parental problems of child rearing, of divorce, redundancy, retirement and old age can also be looked upon as a task for which preparation is possible and in which different areas and levels of the personality are involved. These problems are conceived at this stage as being general rather than specific, anticipated rather than actual. Were they specific and actual, the group discussants might come instead as clients to counsellors, selecting a particular agency, accepting a different status, and anticipating a different process. Particular and specific problems are likely to be introduced in the group discussion, and cannot be disregarded, but all the same the leader has to keep the appropriate focus and not let the process slide over into either group counselling or group therapy

In schools and youth clubs, the adoption of group discussion methods has come with the realisation that instruction in the physical facts of sexual behaviour, coupled perhaps with moral precepts, is not an adequate way of meeting young people's needs. Sexual behaviour, it is now realised, needs to be included within the broad context of human relationships and is by no means the only preoccupation in this area; other relationships, such as those with parents, siblings, peer group, and people in authority, also need to be included.

Any such attempt at education in human relationships, if it is not to be sterile, must be linked with actual experiences that the young people recognise and the situations that most closely concern them, and must involve them as active participants and contributors in the process.

Though these groups may differ markedly in many significant respects, such as their homogeneity, the level of sophistication of the members, and the ability of the members to withstand stress, the same basic principles apply to them all. The same care is needed to make sure that the group remains within education and that appropriate boundaries are maintained.

Comparison with supervision

The processes in group discussion, and the role of the group discussion leader, can be clarified by making a comparison with the individual process of supervision of psychotherapists and social workers, as students and as qualified workers..

We have seen that one important application of group discussion is as a means of helping workers in the field of human relations to increase their insights and skills. This is not the only application but it is convenient to start here where an individual counterpart can be found in the supervision or consultation process in which a student (or it could be a qualified worker) will bring problems for discussion with a supervisor or consultant. While this provides some pointer for the students of group discussion methods, its application is so much narrower and more specific that it cannot in any way furnish an exact parallel. The use of group discussion methods now extends beyond the field of professional education and disciplined learning. Nevertheless, some lessons can be drawn from the ways in which supervisors may help students to understand and modify the part they themselves play in relationships with their clients and also in the relationship with the supervisors; while, at the same time, the supervisors refrain from intruding into the students' personal lives.

This is a form of learning which cannot take place through intellectual means alone. The general problems that the students encounter in their work, and their specific difficulties, are likely to be linked to factors in their own personalities, and resolution will largely depend upon the growth of self-awareness. However, the relationship with a supervisor is not a therapeutic one, nor does it form part of a casework or counselling relationship. This means that the supervisor as supervisor has no sanction to intervene in a student's personal problems, and should seek no direct knowledge of them. Both parties should understand this, and both should know that the other understands it. Details of the student's behaviour on the job and the relationships that the student makes with others in the course of the work may have to be discussed, but the supervisor as supervisor has no authority to make direct links between them and other aspects of the student's life revealed in other contexts. Attention may be drawn to aspects of the work discussed, and general observations may be made linking the material to other areas. Students capable of personal growth and development may be able to use this opportunity to make the personal links for themselves.

Example

A social worker brought a family case for discussion with his supervisor. He was having difficulty in communicating with the family and in particular was finding the two young teen-aged children resistant and hostile. The father of the family was absent but the student made scant reference to this. The supervisor happened to know that the student's own father had left his family, but she made no direct connection to this fact although convinced of its relevance. Instead she pointed out to the student that very little information seemed to have been obtained about the father in this case and about the circumstances of his absence. She said it was worth considering whether there was any particular reason for this omission. At the next supervision the student reported some progress. He said the children had spoken to him about their hopes that their father would soon return and had shown their suspicion of other adults, particularly men, who they thought might be trying to discourage their mother from taking their father back. Still no reference was made to the student's own circumstances. It would have been open to him, had he wished, to refer to it himself, in which event it would have been handled, in the first instance, in relation to his work and its relevance to this case. As it was, it was left to the student to make the connections for himself. His ability to do this was reflected in the progress of the work.

In practice, some information about students' personal histories is likely to be disclosed, and cannot be thrust aside altogether. Supervisors may find themselves in positions in which they have to make a response to such disclosures. Sometimes it may be necessary to distinguish this response from other supervisory activities, and to place it outside the narrow professional framework in which supervisors and their students have their disciplined and functional relationship. Even though a supervisor's responses are designed to be helpful, it is important that the occasion should not be converted into a therapeutic encounter. If more than this is needed, the student should be referred elsewhere for casework or therapy on a formal basis in which the therapist would not have a dual role and the student would have the right to disengage without fear of putting a professional training in jeopardy.

However, an open recognition of the boundaries sometimes makes it possible to step outside them for a specific purpose and then step back again without damage to the relationship or to the position of either party. But it can only be done in a disciplined way and after the boundaries that are being infringed have been acknowledged.

When it is not a one-to-one relationship but the group context that is being used for professional supervision, the method is more indirect and the focus more upon the general than the particular. The behaviour that occurs in the group has to be taken into account, and can be used to illustrate and test the validity of some of the concepts put forward. Members of the discussion group will also expect the leader to refrain from intruding into their personal lives, and to prevent others from doing so. They will expect to be able to expose their work problems without encountering personal criticism or ridicule, and in the knowledge that the other members of the group are expected to do likewise. In discussion, members will necessarily reveal the nature of their defences and the areas in which they feel less secure, and they will need confidence to reveal these areas. The leader may comment, as in individual supervision, on details of particular cases or individual professional difficulties described by members, or may concentrate comments on matters involving the group as whole. The leader will need the skill to make use of the contributions of the less confident and to construct a framework in which the contributions of all can be included. She (or he) will need to protect the vulnerable, and is more likely to repair defences than to interpret their meaning.

Experiential groups

Experiential groups need separate discussion. They present a particular challenge to a group discussion leader.

These groups are coming to play an increasing part in the training for many professions. Their purpose is education but their focus is more inward than outward, with the object of giving the students experience in participating in a dynamic and conscious group process. These are groups that appear to invite the involvement of the whole person, and it can be difficult to clarify the theme or task on which the group is being asked to focus. This makes it all the more important that these groups be distinguished from therapy, as they also have to be distinguished from academic education. Whenever possible the students' therapeutic and academic needs should be met separately elsewhere.

The conductor or leader of an experiential group does not have the responsibility that a therapist would have were it a therapeutic group. In a formal educational setting, the members are not free to disengage in the way that a patient or client in another sort of group is free to disengage: disengagement could involve withdrawing from the training course. Furthermore, since the experiential group is part of a course, the leader of the group is a staff member, and, even if employed only for that purpose, is likely to be required to report back and give opinions about the progress and suitability of individual students. The leader is identified with the management of the course with all its faults and merits. In addition, the members of the group are themselves colleagues and likely to be friends and competitors and to meet frequently outside the group.

However, for all the lack of overt theme, and the central part played by free, untramelled and undirected communication, a focus has to be teased out and maintained by the leader. Boundaries have to be established and preserved. Working on the boundaries between therapy and experiential groups, clarifying and maintaining the boundaries, provides a valuable means of learning to understand more about both forms of group work.

Hutten (1996) has listed seven training aims of experiential groups

- to heighten awareness of self in the here and now

- to heighten awareness of others in the here and now

- to explore the significance of the fact that individuals can and do perceive the same events differently

- to place responsibility for learning with the individual members

- to heighten capacity to think about feelings and observations as they happen

- to further the appreciation and use of difference

- to develop a capacity to monitor what is work (on task) and what is anti-work (diversion from task).

Despite some resemblance to the aims often ascribed to group therapy, (Yalom 1970) it is clear that there is a different slant here, and Hutten sees the experiential group as a group that is meeting in order to become mindful of what it is doing. The leader is not there to facilitate the free exchange of emotions and responses so much as to promote this mindfulness. The explorations and discoveries in the group will, it is to be hoped, lead to improved understanding and awareness. The impediments in the way of this increased mindfulness and understanding will need to be addressed within the group processes and the group as a whole. These impediments will include individual problems and situations carried over from the past and will come to play their part within the group matrix. Unless challenged, they can be regarded as the property of the group as a whole with a general application.

The leader cannot avoid making individual and personal responses altogether, as past incidents are described and current relationships in and out of the group come under scrutiny and may be acted out. Individual responses may have to be made in the interest both of the group and of a particular student. The leader will have to be alert to the presence of personal problems and psychopathology, and may have to consider whether they belong particularly to this group or are being expressed and known about elsewhere too. This means that the leader of the group needs to be in contact with other staff members from time to time.

The leader is likely to concentrate upon the processes taking place in the group as a whole, on the patterns of interaction, and also on the place of the individuals within the group and on the place of the group within the super system of the course and the college. Included within this will be the transference to the leader, and this will involve feelings about him or her as a representative of the institution.

The leaders of experiential groups are likely to be attacked on a number of fronts and to receive personal criticism that could well be intended for other targets. Their professional attitudes and their attempts to preserve boundaries may be challenged. Students of psychotherapy may well be enthusiastic about therapy and eager for therapeutic experiences. They may wish to recreate in this group any experience of therapy they are receiving elsewhere, and to use it to experiment with therapeutic methods and techniques.

Example

In one experiential group the leader began by trying to establish some contract with the students and explained how she saw her role, carefully distinguishing it from that of a therapist. The students (who were all in group therapy elsewhere) referred to this constantly and critically during the first year of the three-year group. Whenever they wanted to express some negative feelings about the group leader they would refer to the fact that she had said she was not a therapist in this group, and they chose to see this, at different times, as a rejection, as an evasion, or as a mistake on her part. This was an aspect of the transference relationship, but also reflected some anxiety about their own roles as therapists.

Openness about all these considerations is essential, including openness about any limitations there may be on the group leader's ability to preserve absolute confidentiality, so that the important work of distinguishing phantasy from reality can go on, and so that projections can be recognised for what they are.

The leader's task (1): Carrying the themes

In all discussion groups (even those that are designated experiential) some theme or topic has to be carried in the mind of the group leader.

The topics of group discussion may require some factual information, but they are also concerned with personal relationships. Therefore relationships in the group itself, and the behaviour of individual members, are likely to be relevant to what is being discussed. The members of the group are observers, but they also form part of the field that is being observed. It is in this respect that an essential difference between group discussion and other forms of education lies. It is because of this that the experience cannot be one that is exclusively intellectual. No member can escape involvement in the group and in the process as well as in the topic.

The theme on which the group is focused may continue throughout a series of meetings, or, alternatively, the leader or the members of the group may bring a different theme to each meeting, or a number of themes may have to be dealt with to meet the requirements of a particular syllabus.

In a group composed of caseworkers, for example, different situations containing casework problems of particular interest or difficulty may be illustrated and discussed. In a group of general practitioners, the relationship between doctor and patient may be considered. A group of school leavers may choose as their theme relationships between young people and their elders, or may be concerned with such particular problems as drug addiction or peer group pressures.

These are all themes which have many different aspects and which can be approached in different ways and at different levels. They can be related at one level to different systems of thought. To the individual student, a particular theme will have both its academic and its practical aspect. The student will bring to it theoretical and conventional viewpoints and, at another level, attitudes based upon personal prejudgements. All these different aspects can provide material for discussion and it is the leader's job to draw out this material and to make it available to the group. The leader must see that the theme is discussed as widely and on as many different levels as possible.

This particular task of a group discussion leader can be briefly described as that of making appropriate links and pointing our relevant connections and resemblances. In bringing together all these contributions, individual and corporate, verbal and non-verbal, and in showing the relevance that each one has to the topic, many leaders see their job as constructing a framework. Value is given to each contribution that comes from a member of the group, as the leader takes it, accepts it and adds to it or adjusts it, and places it within the framework. In this the leader is likely to be more actively involved than in group therapy or group counselling.

The different aspects of the theme that could relate to each other will depend upon the richness and variety of the material that the members of the group, including the leader, are able to provide, individually and corporatively. The leader's task is to point out to the group such connections as can be discerned between the topics under discussion, the contributions of each individual member, and the behaviour of the group as a whole. It is also to relate attitudes expressed directly or indirectly in the group, and attitudes attributed to others outside the group; to make links between theoretical knowledge and personal experience; and to use behaviour that takes place inside the group to throw light on the behaviour under discussion outside the group. Many of the topics that are dealt with in group discussion may depend upon factual information, but they are all also related to basic personal attitudes. These two aspects are complementary to each other and of equal importance. Both need to be brought out.

Example

The context on this occasion was a two day course for home helps organised by a local authority, and the topic was 'Loss and Bereavement'. The work of home helps brings them into contact with people facing the loss of independence, the changes of old age and infirmity, and often the loss or threatened loss of partners. In addition, it has to be assumed in such a group that some of those present will have experienced significant loss and bereavement themselves.

During a group discussion, following some more structured exercises, one member, B, told the group that her father had been murdered a few years previously, and that the murderer, although known to members of the family, was still at large in the community. The group was overwhelmed and frightened and struggled to find an adequate response. So did the group leader. It was important fully to acknowledge what had been said, but also to contain the distress and to continue to further the purposes of the group. The response of the discussion group leader was to ask B what had helped her, and what had not helped her, at the time. This enabled the group to focus on searching for, and evaluating, constructive responses. B described the way in which she and her family had felt isolated by the reactions of the community to their tragedy, and in particular how neighbours had crossed the road in order to avoid having to speak to them. The group had to struggle with its own wish to 'cross the road'. This was acknowledged, other instances were recalled, and there was a discussion about the embarrassment felt at not knowing how to respond or what words to use. Different responses and different words were suggested, B made her comments, and it was possible to link this back to their working situations as home helps The group leader asked B whether or not she was finding the discussion helpful, and B thanked the group for listening to her without turning away, and for being open about their feelings. She was told that though they had felt very frightened at first they had ended up learning a lot from her contribution.

Skynner (1989) has written extensively about the group consultation he has conducted with social workers and other professionals. He argues from his experience that homogenous training groups, if they are securely led in such a way that the interaction can be allowed to develop, will usually reveal that their members are joined in an attempt to solve vicariously problems of their own that are similar to those found in the clients with whom their agency works. He found, for example, that marital counsellors often revealed a shared need to solve some childhood problem in relation to their parents' marriages: that probation officers had issues about authority: and that child care workers tended to avoid conflict and disagreement as if sharing a personal and professional need to keep families together in the face of threatened disruption. In heterogeneous groups, on the other hand, in which a mixed membership was drawn from a number of different agencies and so the focus tended to be on difficulties in professional cooperation and sharing, the interaction in the group often reflected levels of family relationships containing envy and destructive competition. So all the themes presented in the case material of different groups of workers could also be discerned within the interaction taking place within the groups.

Skynner works by paying careful attention to the group theme as it unfolds and develops from session to session, by directing the attention of the group to this overall pattern at opportune moments, but always by trying to mobilise the group's own potential for self help. He does not avoid his own involvement in the problems that the group is trying to address, recognising that the position of group leader can also offer all the pleasures and dangers of vicarious experience in which personal problems can be confronted by proxy without self-exposure. The group leader, if he or she is not to model an uncommitted observer position, has to carry a double role in the group, to be at the same time both attached and detached. 'A correct detachment,' says Skynner, 'would lie not so much in maintaining a constant emotional distance or barrier, as in finding a degree of inner freedom that would enable one to move back and forth, as the situation demanded, between a position of human equality and the parental authority and distance which is a responsibility imposed by the therapist's or group leader's role' (Skynner 1989, p.11).

Skynner concluded that if those workers attracted to a particular field because of identification with their clients' problems could be given opportunities to develop insight into this they could well prove to be particularly suited to the work.

Non-verbal communication can be used to express feelings without having to acknowledge them openly and have them addressed. The topic or theme may be acted out in the behaviour of the group members. Their behaviour may also signal an alternative and preferred theme.

Eden (1994) has described working as an external consultant to a residential homeless project. She led a series of training sessions with the staff, the avowed objective being 'to work towards respectful and honest communication within the team to enhance a sense of trust with each other'.

'People came late, carrying hot drinks and layers of outside clothing. Each week the group was a different size, with different membership and shifting alliances.' She saw this behaviour as a powerful non-verbal communication to her about the difficulty of their working conditions and their identification with their deprived clients. It was 'a direct reflection of the shifting population of their client group... I had a strong sense of being punished for not having to suffer as they did' (Eden 1994, p.231).

When direct interpretations do not seem appropriate or opportune, the discussion group leader may have to find an indirect way in which to signal to the group that she has understood the communications.

The leader's task (2): Working through relationships

In the relationship between the group leader and the members of a discussion group there are present, inevitably, many of the same elements that are present in the relationship between parent and child or between therapist and patient. Whatever the leader's task in the group, it must be performed with an understanding that the disruptive and cohesive forces existing in the group are likely to be exhibited through opposition and alliance to the leader. This opposition and alliance may be shown towards the leader's person, towards the leader's topic, and towards the leader's profession where it differs from that of the other members. It may be necessary to recognise within the responses of leader and of members the repetition of conflicts already experienced with parents, tutors, children and therapists elsewhere. This is a situation that is shared to some extent with group psychotherapists and group counsellors: the difference lies in the use that is made of it.

The discussion group leader is aware that the students are responding to the particular topic at issue within a particular context, and that a major part of that context consists of their current relationships, in phantasy and in reality. But the leader's function is to enable the discussion to proceed in such a way that it will provide a positive and relevant learning opportunity for the members of the group, within the limits of what has been sanctioned. For this reason, and for this purpose, interpretations, if they are made, are not interpretations at an individual level nor are they necessarily interpretations of relationships in the group as a whole. Rather, they are directed to the topic that is being addressed and to its implications for them all.

Whatever use the group leader decides to make of the relationship with the members of the group, and this will depend upon its direct relevance to the group's topic, the maturity and strengths of the group, and its readiness to look at its own behaviour, another function with which the leader is invested must be borne in mind. There may be an expectation that the leader will provide a model with which members of the group may identify. Since group discussion is concerned with some aspect of human behaviour, including interpersonal relationships, the group leader may be looked upon as embodying and exemplifying that aspect of human relationships which is contained within the group theme. This is an aspect of the group leader's role which can provide an effective teaching tool.

This was expressed by Balint (1957) in his account of groups designed to help general practitioners to become more sensitive to their patients' problems. He wrote thus of the role of the leader in these groups.

> By allowing everybody to be themselves, to have their say in their own way and in their own time, by watching for proper cues – that is speaking only when something is really expected from him and making his point in a form which, instead of prescribing *the* right way, opens up possibilities for the doctors to discover by themselves *some* right way of dealing with the patient's problems – the leader can demonstrate in the 'here and now' the situation that he wants to teach. (Balint 1957, p.306)

The model that the leader wishes to supply may differ from that which the group assumes he is supplying. Either model may be tested for flaws. Groups of young people may attempt to shock or disconcert their group leaders, or inquire into the leaders' private lives, in order test their sincerity. The leader of a group of social workers may feel that he or she is being expected to demonstrate an invariably accepting and non-judgemental attitude, and may be presented with case histories of great length and complexity to test a capacity to listen with unwearied patience and attention. There are circumstances in which it is neither necessary nor desirable that the group's expectations should be met.

The leader's task (3): Turning obstacles into opportunities

Impediments to free discussion are always present, and the proceedings of a discussion group could remain sterile and unproductive, allowing little room for development and change to take place at any level, unless the group can be helped to address them. The leader, at the beginning of a course or at any subsequent stage, may have to take a more active part to liberate the discussion from the repetition of textbook knowledge or other conventional opinions, or from an embargo on any exposure of personal feelings. This may be necessary in order to establish certain basic conditions without which group discussion cannot take place in any profitable way.

But all dynamic group work requires that the major element through which psychotherapy, counselling, or teaching and learning, is provided should be the action of the group itself. In every case, the group must be given opportunities to solve its own problems, and to establish its own methods of working. The group discussion leader who exerts too great an influence over the group deflects the group's own purpose, and wittingly or unwittingly replaces group discussion with a form of that very didactic teaching that it is designed to avoid. So facilitation does not mean removing impediments in the way of development so much as helping a group to recognise and address the impediments for itself. When the group is able to do this, impediments can be reframed as opportunities.

Group discussion brings its own specific problems (and opportunities). The leader of a discussion group may have little or no chance to influence the selection of members, either in terms of personal suitability, or in order to secure a homogenous group, a diverse group, or a group selected according to any other particular principle. To a greater extent than in group psychotherapy or group counselling all comers may have to be accepted and some way found of accommodating them within the group. This could be seen as a disadvantage but it could also be seen as an opportunity that brings richness and variety and the stimulus of the unexpected into the group.

Many discussion groups are held under the auspices of organisations which embody some authoritarian function, or are known or believed to endorse some particular line - such as a university, training body, school or church, for example. Members of the group may feel it is expedient to adhere to what they imagine to be the 'party line', perhaps suggested to them by the nature of the training that is being offered or by the particular sponsorship of the sessions. Their educational experiences in the past may have led them to believe that this is the way to be considered a 'good' student and win the approval of their teachers. Equally, for converse reasons, others may feel it is incumbent upon them to oppose the 'party line'. But whether it is accepted or rejected, its real or imagined existence provides members with roles to play at individual and at group level, and so can be used as a diversion or a protection against the possibility of change. The group may need to be given some help in recognising this and relating it to its particular framework.

Like every other living organism, a group cannot by-pass necessary stages of development. Different stages have been identified in different types of group, and in discussion groups with their educational purpose four typical stages have been noted.

In the first stage, an apparently united and enthusiastic group is likely to show its readiness to accept new knowledge in the hope and expectation that this would change the whole pattern of previous work and answer all the problems hitherto found insoluble. The second stage is marked by growing disappointment with what is being provided, and the development of a critical attitude to the ideas being communicated. In the third stage there may be resistance or even open hostility shown to the leaders, lecturers and tutors, coupled with an apparent belief that a 'party line' is being put forward, opposition to which would be interpreted unfavourably. A realistic hope is that in the fourth stage there will be a shift to a position in which much of the initial ambitions and expectations are relinquished, in which small changes of viewpoint can be accepted and a few new ideas incorporated into a framework which also includes personal and professional experience.

Within the group discussion context, the members need to have opportunities to explore and experiment freely and to discuss and try out new concepts and new attitudes. But the assimilation of new ideas and the reorientation of attitudes is a process that cannot be imposed or hurried, the time available may be limited and the syllabus may impose restrictions. So the benefits of group discussion may not be immediately apparent, and the hoped for changes may have to be left to take place, or not take place, after the group meetings are over.

CHAPTER 8

Larger Groups

- What happens when groups increase in size?
- How can larger groups be used as a context for therapy, counselling or discussion?

Outside the model group of eight of group psychotherapy, the numbers in the groups so far discussed have remained rather less precise; it must, though, have become clear that to some extent in counselling groups, and to a greater extent in discussion and experiential groups, it is often the practice to work with rather larger numbers than in therapy groups. Often this happens without any clear perception of the changing dynamics or of the impact that the increase in numbers might have.

It is only since the 1970s that the question of size has begun to be systematically examined, notably at the Tavistock Institute for Human Relations, with their Leicester conferences, and at the Group-Analytic Society.

And just as the introduction of small-group therapy drew attention to the particular uses and limitations of two-person psychotherapy, so the development of larger groups has made it possible for us to look back on small groups from another vantage point and so get a clearer understanding of the nature of the processes taking place with their relevance and limitations.

The impact of number

When interest in larger groups began, the term *large group* was used at first for all groups that could not be described quite loosely as small. Largeness began at some point around fifteen members and extended almost indefinitely. But practical difficulties in bringing large groups together meant that, outside occasional and infrequent conference and training situations, the groups studied rarely exceeded thirty in number. This was clearly a different situation to the groups of one hundred plus, and provided a very different experience. And so the concept of number came increasingly to be broken down and refined. With this came an increased awareness of context.

In trying to understand the effect of the changes in context that take place as groups increase in size, we can distinguish between:

1. *The two person situation*, pair or duologue. Applied to therapy, this is the situation in which problems are likely to be expressed and interpreted in terms of a relationship between the patient or client and another. The nature of this two-person relationship became clarified when therapy was extended to groups. It requires a small-scale, containing setting with a minimum space for two chairs.

2. *The small group*. In therapy, problems are now expressed and interpreted in terms of interpersonal relationships and transferred personal networks, following on from earlier family experiences. The family-centric nature of small groups became clearer, in its turn, when the larger situation began to be studied. The model is a group of seven to eight. In terms of physical setting, it is the number that can sit around a coffee table in a smallish room, a situation which encourages an intimate atmosphere and a family pattern of behaviour.

3. *The median group*. Family and small group structures are now becoming hard to find and maintain as the group expands and becomes more complex and diverse. This is the size at which experience begins to be drawn into the group from the community outside the family and from the impact on the individual of forces that cannot be contained in the smaller setting. There are too many now to sit round a coffee table, but not too many for a large domestic room or classroom. This will be a number greater than 12, when any resemblance to a family situation begins to become blurred, and extending up to a maximum of perhaps 35.

4. *The large group*. This group has outgrown the living room and requires a large or double-sized room, classroom or church hall. The numbers will be more than 35 but still not so great that the members of the group are unable to sit in one circle, hear what is said without strain, and maintain visual contact with each other. This gives an upper number of about 100.

5. *The 'large large' or massive group*. This is the group that requires a marquee, a gymnasium, assembly hall or auditorium. While no precise upper limit can be set, there is now a body of experience of groups with numbers up to 450 meeting over a period for free discussion. When single circle seating has to be abandoned, it becomes impossible

to take in the group at a single glance or to see the faces of all the others who are present. The members of the group are no longer in a position of equality, since seats in the inner and outer circles provide different experiences. Though this brings a qualitative change in context, it has not been found to be a permanent obstacle to the development of discussion so long as the group continues to be conducted with the care accorded to psychotherapeutic groups, so long as careful attention is paid to time and continuity, and so long as the essential central structure is maintained using concentric circles or tiers that can be arranged compactly. Any other structure interferes with the development of free exchange – for example, the lecture hall format promotes control and dependency, and the House of Commons model encourages confrontation and the adoption of increasingly polarised positions. Both these structures impose their own constraints which hamper or prevent the development of free exchange and dialogue.

This is not the end. Foulkes (1990) pointed out that it is simplistic to talk of small and large groups when we are moving on a scale on which everything is relative. What we are calling the 'large large' group is small and intimate compared with a football crowd in which strong, shared emotional experiences nevertheless can take place.

However, the first task is to establish a simple and crucial distinction – the distinction between the small and the large, between the small group model which can represent the intimate network or root family, and the larger situation in which family structures become lost altogether. The first question to be asked is what happens when we leave the small group behind.

We need to return to the beginning. Our first experience in relationships is in a one-to-one, infant–mother context, (albeit within some containing network) establishing the binary or two-way model of the self and the other. The growing infant then moves on to awareness of the small group or family network and within this setting the intensity of that first relationship becomes modified and augmented. The outward movement to school and then on into other larger situations continues throughout childhood, and most of us go on to spend much of our lives in groups of different sorts. For the most part it seems we look back to earlier certainties and endeavour to make sure that the groups in which we spend our time remain small.

Throughout life small groups of a size to replicate the family can continue to serve a function that originally belonged to the family. The family buffered and protected the young child, and so the small group, like the family, buffers and protects the individual against the forces outside the family in large groups and in society. Small groups act as containers for the familiar and provide a barrier against the world outside.

When a group begins to increase in size, these familiar patterns of behaviour become blurred, harder to recognise and to establish. It becomes more difficult to keep a sense of belonging, to find a role to suit or an opportunity to contribute in the group. The experience changes and brings different recollections, shifting the focus away from personal relationships in intimate situations onto probably less familiar and less gratifying experiences outside the family, and involving relationships, status and survival in the larger social context.

We get back to size and number.

- At what size, we need to ask, do these changes begin to happen?

- At what size do family based patterns of behaviour begin to be lost?

- At what size, and why, and with what effect, does the group situation begin to be experienced by many as alienating rather than familiar, does the balance between group and individual tilt against the individual?

- At what size is one sometimes prone to feel no longer part of the group but alienated from it or in opposition to it, confronted by an undifferentiated mass rather than a collection of recognisable individuals?

- In what size of group do speeches start to replace personal contributions, do responses tend to be confined to agreement or disagreement, does polarisation become established, and positions that have been taken up become hard to relinquish?

- In what size of group do we begin to lose our bearings and the capacity to speak freely, do we find we are making prepared statements, thinking before we can speak, watching our words, and in so doing losing the capacity to be spontaneously ourselves?

The individual in the large group

What is likely to be the experience of an individual who comes into a large group of several hundred in the hope of being able to participate?

Many of us will enter such a large gathering, a conventional conference, a big political meeting, or a discussion following a public lecture, believing oneself to be a relatively effective, articulate and thinking person. But any expectations one might have based upon experiences in smaller groups are not met here. Personal relationships and recognition are all but impossible at first within the serried ranks of others. One can feel isolated and different. It is harder to get into the debate, harder to collect one's thoughts in time, harder to concentrate on what others are saying and at the same time compose a response that will be clever enough and succinct enough to be acceptable. And as one feels ever weaker, so the group can appear more and more powerful.

As it becomes harder for individuals to communicate sincerely and respond to each other, so large statements replace personal ones. The experience of being an individual in a crowd of others turns into the experience of being an individual confronted with a single entity, the group; 'me and *them*' becomes 'me and *it*', bringing the fear of being sucked in and incorporated into an it much more powerful than oneself. What in another situation could be a network of involved and related other people easily becomes seen as a threatening mass.

The frustration attached to the larger situation is not merely a product of the difficulty in speaking and the projection of negative feelings and power into the group. It is increased by the incoherence and the multiple participation which can lead to contributions not receiving a response in the pressure of competing voices, and topics being picked up and dropped before they can be dealt with adequately.

The feelings of panic that can be engendered and shared among many of the participants in such a large group situation can produce different responses at individual and at group level. But the responses can all be seen as an attempt to restore the familiar within this larger situation, and to get back to the firmer ground of a one-to-one or small group experience. After all, it was in small groups that the ego was formed and developed, and it is through small groups or networks that the ego's equilibrium is maintained; so this equilibrium can be seriously disturbed when the supportive and buffering structures of the small group are lost.

There may be an attempt at flight, a flight away from the situation altogether (by the individuals who leave or by those who stay but withdraw and try to detach themselves) or a retreat into small, family-sized sub-groups which attempt to reintroduce the familiar container. Conferences break up into smaller groups for discussion, and it is often found difficult to bring people together in groups larger than fifteen. People find some reason to leave before the final plenary session. In continuing groups such as political parties it is not unknown for sub-factions to appear with splitting and projection.

A strong leader may be sought. Most formal large groups with a specific task are structured with someone in the chair to enforce rules and procedures, and so spontaneous personal interchange is limited.

The installation of an authoritarian leader and a hierarchical system, restoring something of the sense of safety originally found in the hierarchical family, may be a response to practical needs, but will in addition relieve the fear of an unfamiliar large group situation bringing loss of personal identity. It brings back a familiar structure in restoring the one-to-one situation, now that of leader and led, a relationship to one simplified object replacing the chaos and allowing all other relationships to be ignored. And some escape from a painful situation may be found through submerging oneself in an anonymous mass, with a leader to be the guarantor that the situation can be controlled. The individual member then no longer feels so alienated and unprotected within the group, and is freed from responsibility or the need to take any action. The price, though, is a reduction in the opportunity to think independently and to make personal contributions, so much of this power having been given away to someone else.

There is also the danger that leaders put in this position may find it hard to retain contact with reality themselves, and may allow themselves to be seduced into believing that they possesses the qualities that the group wishes to attribute to them.

Sub-grouping, and splitting the group into two or more factions, is another way in which a familiar pattern of relationship, the binary relationship between two parties, can be reintroduced, providing the support of belonging to one party united in opposition to another or others onto whom everything negative can be projected. In such a sub group any position taken up can become a bulwark that has to be defended against all challenges and so meaningful discourse and exchange become less and less possible.

Klein and Object Relations

The mechanisms that can be released in response to the pressures of the large group can be said to parallel the infant's primitive responses to the pressures of external reality.

To the extent that the experience is one of losing one's individuality and of being overwhelmed by something larger than oneself, with persecutory fears stirred up by the fear of being swallowed up and obliterated, and with feelings of rage at being frustrated and deprived that can only be managed through splitting and projection, then one is in a situation that is comparable to the experience of the earliest stage of life described by Klein (1963). The feelings aroused can be said to parallel those the infant experiences when the breast is not available. These painful feelings are projected onto the breast by the infant, and then re-experienced as belonging to the breast itself, so that the breast (and later the large group) becomes the persecutor and the container of all the rage and hate.

Thus many attempts to explain the experience of being overwhelmed in a large group look back to the object relations theories of the Kleinian school which take as their starting point the personal inner world of the individual but always placed in a wider interpersonal context. The projective processes described by Klein involve not only the individual but the other party or parties on to whom the projections are made, and so are part of a multi-body, multi-personal framework, and ultimately of the group.

Large group behaviour has been interpreted in terms of 'psychotic' processes, similar to those processes that Klein found in the first stages of infancy. Bion has also already been mentioned in this connection. Bion considered that the task of establishing contact with the emotional life of a group 'would appear to be as formidable to the adult as the relationship with the breast appears to be to the infant, and the failure to meet the demands of this task are revealed in his regression' (Bion 1961, p.141).

So the individual, having struggled in infancy to emerge from a symbiotic relationship with an all powerful other, is, in the large group, having to face a return once more to face those infantile fears. In the large group, the experience is one of being beyond and outside the family: but at the same time the experience represents a return to the first, pre-family stage. The intervening, mediating influence of the small familio-centred group has been lost. The weaker the ego to start with, and the less complete the mastery of the anxiety carried over from infancy, the stronger will feel the threat of becoming submerged in a repetition of this early stage of development.

The coming together in the large group of these regressed infantile patterns of behaviour can result in the establishment of a group culture, a pattern of shared assumptions, beliefs and behaviour, that contains and reflects them. Psychotic processes, which are normally largely concealed from view except perhaps in our dreams, can be detected in a large group as it recreates the type of situation in which these processes first originated. That is why the large group, seen as a whole, is sometimes described as an equivalent to the unconscious mind as portrayed by Freud. If it can be treated as a representation of a psychotically fractured mind projected onto a grand canvas, it can provide an opportunity to explore this early psychotic core.

Individual survival in a large group

How can individuals remain in contact with reality and maintain their identity, and yet be part of a large group?

If misperceptions are to be corrected, and if projections are to be recognised as inappropriate and withdrawn, there have to be opportunities for reality testing through the obtaining and receiving of accurate feedback. In a small group, with a more familiar pattern of relationships available, and less of the frustration and hostility, the members of the group are able to stay in touch with more of their normal thinking processes. This means that there will be more realistic opportunities for testing out and withdrawing inappropriate projections in the light of feedback, and it is this that forms a significant component of small group therapy. But the larger the group the less likely is this option to be available.

But individuals prepared to engage in large groups and stay in them and to tolerate any initial experience of the frustration and panic, and who do not seek to escape from the predicament through endowing a leader with superhuman qualities, or through allowing the group to split into factions, will find their position and their relationship with the group gradually changing. They can begin to grapple with the problem of becoming integrated within the group and participating in it, and at the same time being able to remain themselves with their own separate and unique individuality.

Turquet (1964) studied the progress of the individuals who stayed in groups formed for investigative purposes and varying in size between 40 and 80. One problem he encountered at the outset was that of finding appropriate terms that could be used to describe the different stages that the members passed through as their status in the groups changed.

He introduced the term *'singleton'* for the individual joining a large group on his own. He (or of course she) is not yet part of the group and has yet to establish himself and relate to the other singletons. Some never achieve this transition but stay as singletons, unable or unwilling to engage in the group and go through the changes that are necessary. Those who manage to make a relationship to other individuals and to the whole, the 'converted' singletons, he terms *'individual members'*. Individual members have engaged successfully in the struggle to move from a non-role to a group role and now can contribute to other members and receive a response, no longer having to struggle to survive and imprint some presence of themselves upon an anonymous mass.

The task then confronting the individual members is to maintain this group role over time, to implement it in an individual way, and to resist the attempts of group forces to reduce them to singletons again or to move them on into a third stage, that of *'membership individuals'*. This third stage is the one at which group membership takes over at the expense of individual self-definition and needs. The competing pulls of fusion and separation thus appear again in an ever-present dynamic, with, according to Turquet, the former pulling the individual on to the group dominated status of membership individual, the other leading back to a singleton state.

These three positions present the person in the large group with the alternatives of being isolated in the group, of being related to the group, or of being swamped by the group. No position is likely to be static, and individuals will find themselves constantly moving, or being moved, from the one to the other. Those who manage the most complete expression of individuality within the group are those who are not confined in one role but are themselves able to exercise some choice in moving between them.

The established individual members can ease the way of the remaining singletons. They are able to treat the group in a matter-of-fact manner, make ordinary sincere contributions and respond to the contributions of others, no longer being under pressure to impress or harangue, or no longer prevented by unrealistic perceptions from making any contribution at all. They provide a yardstick against which others can measure the reality or unreality of their own perceptions. Thus such individual members can have a transforming impact upon the culture of the group.

The median group

Between the mass of the 'large large' or massive group and large group on the one hand, and the familio-centric structure of the buffering small group on the other, comes the group of something between fifteen and thirty that has been given the name of median group by de Maré (de Maré, Piper and Thompson 1991).

This is the group we have seen fitting into an ordinary class or large room, where names can be known, in which it is still possible for personal relationships to be established, but which has outgrown its ability to identify with a family situation. It is a familiar size of on-going operational group for many who teach or learn in classes or who are part of operational teams or work groups. And, as happened in the case of small groups, it became possible to begin to study median group dynamics when median groups began to be brought together in carefully established situations for free-floating discussion.

The significance of median groups lies in the fact that they stand between large and small and can form a bridge between the two and throw light on features of both. And, in addition, they are far more within our operational reach, being of a size that makes it a more practical proposition to establish them and then to keep them going.

To be classed as large in terms of process as well as size a group has to be able to produce a definable cultural context of its own which does not depend upon transferred patterns of behaviour from small group settings. It has to be able to separate itself from the type of family culture which can only treat issues from the world outside by redefining these issues in terms of personal relationships. The median group is beginning to be of a size to make this separation; but at the smaller end of the median range, or when any stress in the group encourages regression, it can readily slip back into reflecting a small sized or family culture in which familiar (family) forms of personal communication can still be used.

The median group, it has been found, has particular features of its own. It can be viewed as a group on the cusp, at a point between two different modes. The search to create family structures is not frustrated as it would be in a large group by the overwhelming pressure of number, but it is constantly being blocked by contrary movements taking the group in the other direction away from and outside the family.

Thus a median group contains a whole range of possible experiences and meanings, perhaps more meanings than either a small group or a large group – and can move among pre-family, family, and post-family, situations. It can at the same time invite and resist the imposition of structures originating in families and personal networks. Experiences in a median group can be confusing because of this tendency to swing from one mode to the other. In experiential median groups members often express some personal confusion and feelings of loss of identity. Who am I within the family? is a small group question. Who am I outside the family? is a question for a large group. The median group member, trying to engage with the group, can be confronted with both questions.

Whole previous contexts can be transferred or transposed into the group in a way that is comparable but distinguishable from the transference of individual relationships. As groups get larger, we find an increasing tendency to look outwards and to bring in experiences and problems from the world outside the family that aroused powerful feelings in the past. The larger the group, the larger are the experiences that can be evoked, until we find whole contexts derived from past situations, in which individuals found themselves confronted with mass impersonal forces, being recalled and introduced or transposed.

In median groups, as a range of situations of different magnitudes become available for recollection and transposition, we can find played out the tension between the wish to leave the family behind and the wish to stay with the family; the wish to experience, and the wish to avoid experiencing, the otherness of life outside. It is a transitional group and contains transitional experiences. It can recall the turmoils of adolescence. Situations and feelings transposed may be those attached to leaving behind familiar surroundings, to first leaving home, to the entry into school and into employment, and all subsequent situations in which new patterns of behaviour outside the family had to be found but in which the loss is not absolute and the more intimate structures may still be obtainable.

A group of this size differs from a larger group in that the option of helplessness and anonymity, of electing to stay as one of Turquet's singletons, is less available. It may require a struggle, needing more energy than at first appears available, to be a full participant, but it can also require a struggle to stay in the group without speaking. The option of being one of the silent majority/minority becomes harder to exercise as the silent sub-group shrinks and finally all but disappears so that non-participants are made conspicuous by their silence.

Facilitating change through larger groups

What might large and median groups have to offer in facilitating change at different levels in individual members, whether the purpose that has brought the larger group together be therapy, counselling, discussion or experiential learning?

There is now a growing body of experience of median and some large groups conducted along group-analytic lines. As with small group-analytic groups, this requires a circular pattern of seating and free-floating discussion with no defined topic or agenda. There may be one non-directive group conductor or there may be more than one. Interest in the larger end of the group continuum has even, as we have seen, brought a deviation from the single circular seating, hitherto a hall mark of all group-analytic groups, when greater numbers make this impracticable.

Very often, these groups are brought together with no other object than to experience the larger situation and to learn to participate and communicate within it. In these larger group-analytic situations, people come to learn how to talk to each other. If this sounds facile, it is only necessary to recall the problems of the individual in the notional large group already described, and recall how rarely talking 'on the level' occurs, and not only in large groups but in other group settings as well. Most of the time, it seems, we talk at one another, against one another, or past one another. We talk to persuade or impress or convince. We talk to establish our position or to confirm our identities. Listening and talking, openly, carefully, thoughtfully, mindfully, responsively, each one trying to find and establish an authentic personal voice, is something that can be learnt through participation in the development of open communication in the larger group. We may then be nearer to achieving in the group what Dr Samuel Johnson described as 'the happiest conversation where there is no competition, no vanity, but a calm quiet interchange of sentiments' (Boswell 1884,p.186).

When therapy is mentioned, the larger groups are frequently described as providing sociotherapy rather than psychotherapy. The group may also be concerned with the discovery, exploration and resolution of tensions, but these are less likely to be only intra-personal and inter-personal and are more likely to include the tensions that occur between and among groups. The larger the setting the more do problems of personal relationships recede and the more is the focus slanted towards relationships with the wider society. Where personal problems do come to the fore in these groups they are likely to be concerned with disturbances of social functioning, or with emotional disorders resulting from social disturbance.

So the emphasis has switched from the area of intimate personal relationships, which is where neurotic problems and illnesses originate, to the bigger arena where these same difficulties may have to be acted out, and where other problems may be added to them. Our lives may be caught up with personal relationships, families and small groups and networks, but families and small groups also are enmeshed in their wider social context. And so are we. But for all its importance in our lives, this context has been treated in the past as beyond the reach of therapy.

Foulkes (1990) saw the large group as a therapeutic instrument in the widest sense, and distinguished three possible types of group analytic large groups.

1. *Problem centred large groups*, in which the whole group would function as a problem solving unit. The focus in such a group would be maintained on the problem which would be concerned with difficulties of interrelationships in which all were involved and not with individual

disturbances: he described this as social-therapy rather than psychotherapy.

2. *Experience centred large groups*, sometimes described as a sensitivity groups or T-groups, and designed to open up as wide a range of experience of group membership as possible.

3. *Therapy centred large groups*, which differed from the problem centred large groups and the experience centred large groups in that the group would be free to investigate all aspects of group activity in the on-going situation, including unconscious, disguised and symbolic meanings. Total human beings would be involved without reservations. Therapy, he considered, in the group-analytic tradition, resided not in the group conductor but in the group, and it was the task of the conductor to establish a culture promoting free investigation based on unfettered and frank communication.

For the most part, Foulkes went on to suggest, when therapy does occur in large groups it is coincidental, and Turquet described any therapeutic gain as a chance though acceptable by-product. But it need be considered no less valuable for that.

However, since Foulkes' observations were made, a growing body of experience has encouraged the belief that median or large groups managed along group-analytic lines can indeed carry advantages for individuals able to make use of them that could be classed as therapeutic, and that, even though these groups may not set out to offer personal therapy per se, in themselves they can provide a context in which significant personal change and growth can take place.

The focus is upon staying with the experience, not running away or withdrawing from it, and eventually mastering the panic and frustration by becoming integrated into the group and able to take a full part in it. To return to Kleinian terminology, it means moving from a paranoid position to a depressive one. The anxiety provoked is not evaded or suppressed, and so attempts to deal with it through projection and splitting are likely to be experienced in situations where they can be brought into awareness and addressed. Thus the individual has an opportunity to begin to handle and contain the anxiety, and through this to learn to talk and to think spontaneously in the group. Any persecutory anxiety that may be left as a residue from infancy can be re-experienced and confronted, and in so far as the objective situation of feelings of powerlessness *vis-à-vis* the 'mass-out-there' is mastered, so the phantasy situation carried over and recreated from infancy can be mastered too.

Though there is less opportunity, and fewer invitations, to air intimate personal problems of relationships in large groups, there is not necessarily less interest. But the interest seems to take a different form. When personal problems do emerge, they are likely to appear in different ways and to be concerned with the impact on personal relationships of mass impersonal forces that cannot be ignored but have to be addressed in some way.

There is not a direct line from the helplessness of infancy to the helplessness in the large group. The effect of early events is always being modified by happenings coming later. Sometimes the early events may have been recalled and intensified by subsequent traumas which can link up with residues from the past and carry them forward into the future. These traumas can include wars, revolutions, persecutions, bereavements, losses of home, job or homeland, changes of nationality, racial tensions, redundancies, relocations, loss of job and status. They can also include natural and man made disasters, such as fires, train accidents, or even mass shootings. These are all topics that emerge less often in small groups, and when they do are likely to be treated as issues of personal relationships.

If we move from the group processes to the problems encountered, we have to consider what response, whether therapy, counselling or support, is appropriate in response to external traumas? Individual counselling, even small group therapy, brings a retreat back to a replication of one's primary support system, and there the trauma is most likely to be considered in the context of the inner world of intimate relationships and so be treated as a personal problem. This is one dimension of the problem, but not the only one and not necessarily the most significant one. As Herman (1992) has described, traumas that damage self-worth have a wide impact, and while they can affect personal relationships they can also damage and weaken the bonds between the individual and the wider group or community, impairing the sense of belonging and of being rooted in a sustaining environment. It is this level that emerges in the context of the large or median group.

Apart from the residue of trauma, there is now some experience to suggest that phobias of different kinds, including very specifically the panic occasioned by public speaking, are among situations at the interface between individual lives and the world outside the family that have responded to treatment in a median group. Successful attempts to confront panic in the group can carry over into other situations, and can bring an enhanced ability to confront panic experienced outside the group. Members of on-going group-analytic large groups have reported an increase in energy, a sense of greater personal freedom in other situations both great and small, and the power to make changes in their lives that they had hitherto found impossible (de Maré et al. 1991).

Median groups may be brought together to form a problem solving unit, as Foulkes suggested, with a focus maintained upon a problem of interrelationship in the wider context.

Problems of minorities can be hard to address in a small group where the minority may be represented by only one person, who in such a case may well be protected by the group and treated as a token victim in a way that leaves key issues unexplored. In a large group, on the other hand, the numbers involved will ensure that very few positions or problems are unique, and there is always likely to be a subgroup that forms around the problem and its exponent. Through this comes an opportunity to address situations that are habitually evaded or concealed in small groups, and which can now be considered in intergroup rather than solely in interpersonal terms. So differences of gender, age, race, sexual orientation and religion can be explored more openly and within a wider and less personal context. The very size of the large group can provide a ballast, permitting the discharge of extreme feelings, able to absorb violence and extreme attitudes, and allowing oppositional positions to be taken up and expressed with less hurt than would happen in a small group.

Racism can be taken as an example. Initiatives for addressing racism have too often tended to personalise it, turning it into a matter of separating out abused and abuser and so leading to a hunt for individual racist attitudes which then have to be dealt with individually. And so further opportunities for splitting and projection are opened up. This seems to be due in part to a reluctance to engage in larger contexts and address racism outside the familiar individual or small group perspectives. Small groups are not large enough to encounter cultural problems or to recognise the assumptions that are part of our cultural background without turning them into problems of personal attitudes and relationships. It seems that wider issues of sameness and difference, of inclusion and exclusion, and of the boundaries we draw between ourselves and the rest, need a larger setting in order to come to the fore.

Ferron comparing small and median mixed race groups, has found that in the small group dependency is a recurrent theme, while in the median group identity becomes a bigger issue. The culture that gradually develops in a median group 'can be explored in relation to the wider cultural context (the context which maintains racism) as well as the different cultural experiences of its members. The difficulty in accepting newcomers, the dividing into packs, the splitting and scapegoating, the building up of hostility between rival factions, the development of mythologies, are all problems that can be found in life outside the family group. In the (median) black and white group all these features were found and it was possible to bring them into awareness and open discussion and relate them to the cultural context' (Ferron 1991, p.201).

De Maré

De Maré has been the leading theoretician and exponent of larger groups, and he and his associates are carrying the use of large and median groups into different areas. He sees larger groups conducted along group analytic lines as an inevitable and essential extension of individual and small group therapy, and has emphasised the importance of addressing the problems of our cultural context which can only become accessible in the larger group. Large groups need to take over where small groups leave off and provide a setting in which we can explore our social myths (the social unconscious) and in which we can begin to bridge the gap that has opened up between ourselves and our socio-cultural environment. This is a gap which is too often accepted as unbridgeable and beyond our reach.

De Maré has repeatedly urged the importance of beginning to construct a bridge between the individual mind and the social context, maintaining that our task as citizens is not only to adjust to society but to also to enable society to adjust to us.

In particular he has sought to address the following questions – 'Why do intelligent individuals perpetuate destructive cultures?' and 'How can the gulf between the individual and family on the one hand, and the wider social context on the other, be bridged?'

The threat experienced in the large group is to consciousness and to the use of mind, to thought itself. The larger the group the greater the threat, the more the individual feels swamped and disempowered, and the more primitive the responses. So large groups operate as if mindless, and this mindlessness of large groups is reflected in the mindlessness of our social context outside the group and is what makes cultures so intransigent

We have to learn how to talk to each other in a social setting. The gap that exists between the individual and the sociocultural context beyond, that remote abstraction apparently divorced from human minds and human control, can only be bridged through sufficient numbers of people obtaining experience and involvement in groups of increasing size. Fear of the larger situation means that we stay in small group and family settings as much as we can, and in these settings issues of cultural context can only be treated in personal and interpersonal terms, and so tend to be infantilised or evaded. But the individual who becomes engaged in large groups is engaging in a process which can make it possible to approach and to examine the context that lies outside the buffer zone of family and small group, and ultimately to take part in restoring mindfulness to it. Through engaging with the mindlessness of large groups, and replacing this mindlessness with a human culture that we can relate to, we can make a beginning in bringing understanding to the mindlessness of society outside the large group.

The need now is to develop *outsight*. The small group, as it buffers us and looks inward, promotes the development of *insight* into the meaning of our personal behaviour and its origins, an inwardly orientated expansion of awareness that is no longer sufficient. In large groups it is *outsight* that develops, and with it the parallel understanding of social behaviour and its meaning and an outward expansion of social consciousness and mindfulness.

Large groups and the society beyond the large groups can be said to share a similar structure; like the large groups already described, this wider society can also be dominated by split-off projections that left to themselves will cohere into a culture that is inappropriate, out of date and unresponsive to current needs, but for all that hard to change. Such cultures, if presented in individual behaviour, would look like insanity. Although ultimately the product of human minds, cultures have escaped from the control of human minds and become mindless. There are many examples of the way in which this mindlessness can lead on to the psychotically cruel manifestation of unstable political structures and monstrous dictatorships.

Through his work and his writing about large groups, de Maré has introduced many of the large group concepts that are now being used – clarifying the difference between median and large groups, and introducing some key terms of his own.

Dialogue he uses specifically to mean the free lateral discourse that can develop in a large group, the large group equivalent to the free association of psychoanalysis and the group association of group analysis. *Koinonia*, a classical Greek word, is used for the impersonal fellowship that can develop in a large group when dialogue has been established. 'It refers to the atmosphere of impersonal fellowship rather than personal friendship, of spiritual-cum-human participation in which people can speak, hear, see, and think freely, a form of togetherness and amity that brings a pooling of resources' (de Maré *et al.* 1991, p.2). It is distinct from the love that belongs to the family and small group, and is what makes us able to engage in society and with our fellows. It powers citizenship.

Dialogue as a part of behaviour and discourse in a large group does not take place easily, it is something that has to be learned as members stay with the group and gradually become able to exchange talk with each other. Learning is frustrating, especially at the beginning when the network of communication is rudimentary. It is not an instinctual process in the way that discourse in a family sized group is instinctual. We cannot fall back upon earlier patterns of behaviour and relationship. Dialogue is a sideways horizontal form of communication as against the vertical form of communication only too familiar in most other large group situations in which opinions are handed down and attempts made to deposit them into other people. The development of dialogue replaces the superficial conventionality and conformity that often disguises the lack of lateral awareness of other minds and other opinions and so helps to counteract the mindless massification of the larger situation. In this context de Maré recalls Pericles' comment, in the fifth century BC, that rhetoric destroys democracy as opposed to dialogue which promotes a culture of fellowship

De Maré has emphasised the frustration and hate that is the initial response to being in a larger group. Hate and aggression are not the primary innate elements posited by Freud in his description of the death instinct, they are a secondary phenomena and the result of frustration due to lack of instinctual satisfactions. This hate may be left free floating, and either denied or evaded. But the large group provides a setting in which it can be experienced, confronted, addressed and so transformed. It is only through the development of dialogue that the malign consequences of splitting, projection and massification can be avoided, and that the large group can be cultivated. With cultivation the hate is replaced by the *koinonia* which is a feature of an established communicating large group. And with *koinonia* the powerful energy that is produced by the negative feelings and hate can be transformed and rerouted to become available for the further development of dialogue.

Through dialogue and exchange the large group negotiates its own cultural context of shared beliefs, assumptions and patterns of behaviour and interaction. The individual members are not helpless bystanders now but are able to participate in this process. This culture within the group will have things in common with the wider cultural context outside the group but will also be different. It can provide a perspective within which cultural issues affecting members and originating outside the group can be distinguished and viewed. Myths and assumptions embedded in the wider culture will emerge from unconsciousness and from the mindless acceptance that makes them so intransigent and self-perpetuating, despite their frequent inappropriateness. This can bring into examination areas hitherto considered beyond the control of individuals and provide a bridge between the inner world and the world of relationships on the one hand and the socio-cultural context on the other. It is a forum in which topics can be discussed in a way that is different from any discussion taking place in a small group. Issues are less likely to be personalised or related to individual psychology or psychopathology and so they can be placed in their appropriate social and cultural context.

De Maré defines culture as equivalent to the mind of the group. He distinguishes three different cultures: *subculture, microculture and macroculture*.

Subcultures, or biocultures, take us back to where we started. They are formed from individual contributions and projections containing individual infantile developmental stages that form an active part of family cultures. As we have already seen, in the unstructured and primitive large group these cultures are projected in an unmodified form. The group then shows all the typical features of the earliest stage of development – the splitting into absolute good and bad, the idealisation of leader and demonisation of an enemy, the location of all the goodness in one's own group and all the badness elsewhere, and the massification of hate and destruction and revenge.

The *macroculture*, or socioculture, is the wider context outside the group to which we all belong. This macroculture, originally created through the interaction of individual minds but now effectively cut off from them and so outside human control with little effective mediating influences, can take on all the malign large group characteristics. It remains for the most part dominated by old and outworn myths and assumptions which are largely outside consciousness and hence inaccessible to challenge.

The third culture is the *microculture*, or idioculture, (from idio – to make one's own) which becomes established in the large group as dialogue is developed, and which can come to be distinguished from the infantile subcultures and from the out-of-reach macroculture of the wider society. It is a culture that can be cultivated, influenced and made amenable to change through a process of extended dialogue and lateral affiliative developments, and which can bring control, order and meaning to any existing culture made up of infantile perceptions and projections. It is unique, original, and therefore creative. Such a microcultural context emerging in a group can provide a perspective from which the group is able to become aware and then examine the macrocultural assumptions of society around us on the one hand and the subcultural assumptions rooted in individual and family on the other.

> In the median group we consider the most significant feature to be the transformation of the chaos of mindlessness and hate in the initial rudimentary stages to the koinonic culture of dialogue in its later, more complex phases. It is as if the space of mind is initially peopled by subhuman subcultures based on infantile developmental phases and then becomes re-peopled through dialogue by later, more appropriate, and more human communions and inner dialogue. (de Maré *et al.* 1991, p.8)

Stay in the large group, he says, learn how to communicate with each other and take part in developing dialogue and get beyond the infantile subcultural stage, and we will have set out on the road of being able to examine, influence and humanise culture so that we no longer leave it to be dominated by infantile remnants from the past. We will have begun to be able to introduce mindfulness and thoughtfulness into the way we manage affairs outside the family in ever bigger groups and contexts.

So the larger group managed along group-analytic lines and meeting consistently over a period can provide a bridge, an operational forum in which individual minds can be brought into contact with the cultural context. Unlike the group-analytic small group, in which the individual is the object of treatment but the main therapeutic agent is the group, the group has now become the object of treatment and the individuals have become the treatment agent. If individuals can learn to operate within this context instead of separated from it and alienated from it, they will begin the process of humanising it and making it responsive to current human needs.

The large group convenor

The role of any group leader or conductor changes as the group grows in size. To mark the differences, the term *conductor* has been replaced in median and large group-analytic groups by *convenor*. In other larger groups with different purposes the term facilitator is often used.

Though some members of large groups have found them to be a powerful and exciting experience, bringing an opportunity to make significant personal gains, others have found them overwhelming or frustrating and in consequence reluctance to become involved in large groups is still widespread. Apart from this resistance, there are more practical obstacles in the way of setting up large or even median groups than there are to setting up small groups because of the greater numbers that have to be brought together in order to make a larger group viable.

Larger groups of different sorts have often been treated somewhat carelessly in the past, and the detailed attention that they require has not always been paid to them. Dynamic administration, with care given to the way in which large and median groups are set up, to their physical setting and to the maintenance of their boundaries, is as important and needs as much preparation as it does in small group psychotherapy. Not only does it need to be done but it needs to be seen to be done. This is all the harder because the convenor setting up a large group will be aware of having less control. The larger the group, the more difficult it becomes to exercise selection and to know who will come or how many will come, and the whole venture appears that much more unpredictable.

It is number that is of primary structural importance in determining the group dynamics, but number also has to be seen as part of a total situation in which other factors have their influence. Number can have a different impact in different physical settings. And apart from number and space a third important dimension which has to be considered is time or duration, and this dimension increases in importance as the group increases in size.

Experience has shown that the larger group needs a larger format in time as well as space, not just a larger room. The group has to have the time to find sufficient coherence to support further progress and to draw the contributions of the participants together into a whole. It takes more time for a larger group to reduce frustration, to bring about sufficient participation, and to ensure that topics mentioned and then dropped can be returned to again before the end of the group. Common themes do not emerge so quickly or so easily in such a complex and changing mass as they would in a smaller group: common themes do emerge, but they take longer to do so.

It takes time to reach the stage at which a significant proportion of the people present have been able to speak. Just as individuals who find it difficult to speak for the first time in a large group report feeling a crucial change in their position when they have managed to do so, a group as a whole will appear to enter a new phase in its development when a significant proportion (which will vary with the size of the group but in a large median group seems to be about half) has said something.

But as in all groups, speaking is not enough. Each individual contributor needs a response which recognises the relevance of the earlier contribution and relates it to the other contributions, and so affirms the presence of the speaker and brings him or her in touch with the others. Otherwise each speaker will continue to feel an isolate, still struggling for recognition and a place in the group.

This affiliative confirming discourse takes time to establish while the group is gradually developing a more coherent interpersonal structure. The larger the group the more unrelated each contribution is likely to appear to be to the one before, as each speaker remains more concerned with his or her predicament in becoming part of the group than in listening to the others. So responses at first seem to be adversarial or disconnected rather than as developments of a theme, and many individual speakers are likely to be left feeling ignored. And the larger the group is, the longer is this preliminary period likely to be.

Because of the advantages of a continuous span of time, some large group convenors consider it to be more effective to hold all day meetings, even if they take place at quite long intervals, than to hold meetings of an hour and a half once a week. Or alternatively there are the daily large groups now being held for the five-day period of a group-analytic conference or symposium. These seem to provide the time and continuity needed for the group to get past the initial stages, when pressure to find a way out of the frustration can bring a search for sub-groupings and a preoccupation with difference, and so begin to communicate in a more thoughtful and responsive way.

Initially, the large group convenor, like the leaders of all other groups, will have the task of establishing a sufficient degree of safety to keep the group from disintegrating before it can develop a strength and coherence of its own. The danger with larger groups is that the frustration at the start will lead to absenteeism and falling numbers, so that a large group becomes a median group and a median group a small group, bringing general disappointment and a sense of failure.

In trying to help the group through this stage, the convenor has to avoid collusively falling into the leadership role. The group will be both demanding and resisting this, and may well turn away in disappointment and frustration to seek an alternative leader who can be venerated or attacked.

The role of the large group convenor is paradoxical. Whatever the convenor says or does is likely to be treated as a model of group behaviour for members who are searching for a means of establishing some position for themselves. Many of the interpretations that a conductor would be likely to make in a small psychotherapy group, as Main (1964) pointed out, would not be appropriate here.

In particular, any generalisations about group behaviour coming from a lofty and detached position, and emphasising a separation of convenor and group, are liable in this larger setting to be viewed only as a model of disengaged observer-behaviour, tempting other members of the group to detach themselves in their turn. The end result could be a group composed entirely of observers, who have come not to participate but to learn by trying to study the group and the behaviour of others from a safer position outside the action.

In the place of lofty generalising statements, Main emphasised the value of 'non-interpretative interventions', including comments coming from a sincere and personal standpoint which may seem ordinary and banal to a group expecting 'deep' contributions. Such comments can provide an alternative model and help to bring the members of the group back to interacting and responding to each other in a more real and everyday way. Interventions of this type, though sometimes hard to find, can help individuals to recover and rediscover themselves and each other in the group, and so make it possible for them to own and openly acknowledge more about themselves and their situations. Such interventions should not come from the convenor alone, of course, and the group can benefit from the contributions of any of its members who have retained or regained contact with their every day faculties and so are able to relate to the group in a realistic way.

CHAPTER 9

The Family Context: Understandings

The family is the first small group and the prototype: the influence of the family group is discernible in all group settings.

- Can the family group be brought within the same framework as the other groups we have been discussing?

- To what extent, in considering the processes which operate in all small groups, shaping their proceedings and holding them together, have we also been considering the processes which operate in families?

- And how can processes in a family group be observed and studied?

The answer to this last question became clearer when the pioneer family therapists started to bring parents and children together in one room for treatment. In doing this, they were putting boundaries of time and place around the diffuse and multifaceted family network and so turning it into a face-to-face group. It was not until this had been done that it became possible to transfer to families the concepts of group dynamics that were then being developed within those other treatment groups composed of strangers, and to demonstrate the existence and nature of family processes that could be compared to the group processes that have already been described.

'The family is the problem'

The first approaches to the family as a whole came via the child guidance movement.

One of the pioneers of family therapy, John Elderkin Bell, (1970) described the point in his own professional development at which he passed from seeing the family as a group of separate if related individuals to seeing the family as a psychological entity with its own unique processes and problems and solutions.

I had to wipe clean the blackboard of my mind and find a fresh piece of chalk to write large: 'The *family* is the problem.' I learned to reject the notion that the child who brought the family to treatment presented the problem with which I was to work. The child might be *a* problem, his behaviour having provided the occasion for starting treatment, but I learned that I must not regard him as the problem for therapy. *The problem is the family.* Here was the crux of the matter. Here was the transition in thought that I must make. This is the new idea, seemingly so small, but actually so major. 'The family is the problem.' (Bell 1970, p.24)

But the family is not a group formed for the purpose of treatment, in which all its proceedings can be brought under controlled scrutiny. On the contrary, it is an on-going real life group with its own purposes and functions and its own history and existence elsewhere. It has a continuous life which spans generations. And it is the most hierarchical and role-structured of all groups.

Functions of the family group

In common with all other groups, the family has one prime and overriding task on which all other tasks depend; namely, that of staying in existence. And, as in all other groups, this depends upon its ability to promote cohesive forces and contain disruptive ones.

Alongside this, every group also has its specific and individual functions. The specific functions of family groups are likely to include the following: the creation of a home base, the provision of economic support for the family members, the nurturing of children, and the sufficient satisfaction of social, emotional and sexual needs to keep the family members in the family.

The life of a family, like the activity of any group, is a pattern of conscious and unconscious compromises. This can be illustrated by means of a physical analogy.

Imagine an established family with all its acquired possessions moving into a new house. These possessions are both an enhancement and a limitation. There is a fixed amount of living space, divided up in a particular way. Into this space the family members have to fit themselves, their furniture and their pets, and make provision for the carrying on of their family life. Space may have to be found where little children can play and older children can entertain their friends, where mother can do her sewing and father his carpentry (or vice versa). Space is needed indoors for the bedroom suite, the dining-room table and the piano; and outdoors for the tool shed and the rabbit hutch. There will have to be compromise and adjustment, some of the furniture may have to go and some of their original ideas may have to be relinquished. However, the final outcome is likely to be an arrangement in which some provision is made for the major family activities, and in which the individual members are left feeling sufficiently satisfied even if they have all had to surrender something. We see the operation of group processes translated into a concrete form.

If you visit the family, you will be shown what they have done – the wall knocked down here, the partition put up there, the space found on the landing for someone's desk that could not be fitted in elsewhere. What they are showing you is the solution that they have established to their problem of living together physically as a family. This problem is their own unique problem, and you cannot know its exact nature and extent. You may come away thinking you would have arranged the house differently. But then the problem that you and your family would be attempting to solve would be a different problem requiring a different solution.

The visitor will not only see how the living space and furniture is arranged. She will also see how the different family members interact and respond to each other, the types of behaviour which are permitted and the types of behaviour which are discouraged. She may well think that she can discern an overall pattern in which the behaviour of each member is linked to the behaviour of each and all of the others. She may go on to discover that she cannot understand this overall pattern by considering the behaviour of the individual participants alone. In the same way, one cannot understand the positioning of the desk upon the landing unless one knows about the competing claims for space of the piano and the television set, and the value that has been attached to the bookcase inherited from Uncle George.

The family process is a continuous one, but within this continuous process it is possible to distinguish successive family units, each of whom has a history of growth and development. It is convenient, in looking for a point at which to begin, to start with the young couple as they first set up house together.

The relationship is a new one, but both partners inevitably bring with them much from their previous life experiences and from their families of origin. Often, it has been observed, they bring with them similar problems, with fears of a similar calamity, and with a shared propensity to seek one sort of solution rather than another. They have to negotiate a customary way of behaving together so that, over time, every activity does not have to be set up afresh and every decision debated. The result is a relatively autonomous system based upon the maintenance of comparatively stable interaction patterns.

They soon establish, for example, that one makes the breakfast, that they both have toast and coffee, and that one locks up at night and puts out the cat. And so on, throughout the day. They both have to modify their original expectations, conscious and unconscious, about each other. These expectations come largely from their prior experiences in their parents' homes (or wherever else their formative early years were spent), including needs carried over from the earliest stages of life of which they are not consciously aware. But the modifications should not have to go too far, and at least some of their original expectations and needs should be satisfied if their solution is to be a viable one.

As time goes on, it becomes settled between them that there are some decisions which he or she makes separately and some which they make jointly. He may find that there are areas in which he must not query her decisions; she may find that she can rely on his support in some of her activities and not in others and that this support needs to be given a certain amount of acknowledgement and appreciation if it is to continue. And so on. They need to have an unspoken agreement about their behaviour to each other, and to be confident that this agreement will, by and large, be honoured. They begin to say 'we always do so-and-so' in an acknowledgement that their life together is patterned in a mutually reinforcing way. But for all that, negotiation and renegotiation is always taking place.

At one level, each family is working on its own unique set of problems. But at another level of generality it can be said that all family problems are the same problems. Sufficient satisfactions have to provided for each of them in order to keep that person within the family circle, contributing to the satisfaction of the needs of the others and to the continuation of the family as a whole.

And because of the hierarchical and diverse nature of families, the needs that have to be provided for are complex and diverse. They are the needs of people of both sexes and of different ages, with social, sexual, emotional intellectual and physical dimensions, and all the time they are changing both absolutely and relatively to each other. They may at times be antagonistic, at times complementary. No satisfactions are ever complete; but in a fortunate, relatively harmonious family, they will be complete enough; everyone will be giving something and will have the experience of receiving something back in return.

In the day-to-day life of a family, there will be shared activities and separate activities, there will be approved and disapproved ones, and these activities will all be brought into some sort of balance reflecting the position of cohesive and disruptive forces in the family as a whole. In the same way that individual defence mechanisms are needed to preserve the individual ego from destructive forces within, so family processes have their defence mechanisms which serve to contain individual strivings without impairing the unity of the whole. Both in the individual and in the family there are always some parts at risk which require defending.

Family solutions concealing problems

In some families the problem solving process is unobtrusive and proceeds without drawing attention to itself, leaving conflict and anxiety contained within manageable limits. The struggle is going on, nevertheless, and it is through these continuous attempts to find solutions that family life, in every family, becomes fashioned into certain characteristic patterns.

According to this formulation, a family is in distress when a solution is no longer containing the problem, or is containing the problem at too great a cost. The solution that a family has managed to establish may be restricting or distorting its functioning to an unacceptable extent, or it may be bearing too hardly upon one particular family member or sub group. Alternatively, or in addition, it may be causing trouble between the family and the world outside.

The family that signals its distress to the world outside and becomes known to the helping professions could be asking for one of a number of different things. It could be looking for support and confirmation for its chosen solution, or for extra support to be given to a solution that is not proving strong enough to contain the disruptive forces. It could be asking for help to make a solution unanimous within the family, or more acceptable to others outside the family. Even when a family comes with a complaint about the behaviour of family members, or about a defect in family circumstances, what we are seeing is still part of an attempted solution to problems the nature of which have to be inferred.

But families operate as systems in contact with other systems and forming with them part of a higher system. A solution that a family may appear to find satisfactory may be causing problems elsewhere.

Example: The Dartie family

Mr and Mrs Dartie with their eleven-year-old son Benny and their nine-year-old daughter Carol were showing no overt signs of distress and asking for no help. No one paid any particular attention to the problems and solutions of the Darties until a school medical officer decided that Carol Dartie was grossly overweight. The medical officer asked to see Mrs Dartie, a stout and cheerful woman, and gave her a diet sheet for Carol along with an embargo on sweets and snacks between meals.

At the next medical inspection, the doctor found that Carol weighed more than ever. Mrs Dartie was at first bland and smiling, apparently unaware of any problem, until pressed by the doctor when she became at first belligerent and then tearful. She agreed that Carol was rather big, but then so were all the rest of the family and it had never seemed to do them any harm.

The social worker attached to the school health team visited the home and found a cheerful affectionate family, all extremely overweight; a family tradition of good eating, and the frequent distribution of sweets and ice creams. It seemed that this was more than a long established habit; it was an integral and essential part of the life of this family and a pattern of behaviour that involved them all. It was inferred by the social worker that Mrs Dartie could only experience her goodness as a mother through generous over-provision, and from the satisfaction she derived from heaping plates high. Conversely, rationing, denying and disappointing signified badness. The giving of food had become the language through which she communicated with her children, and they had learned to read these communications. They had come to know that all was well and love was certain as they ate their way through lavish family meals. And Mr Dartie, the good provider, had come to find confirmation of his value in the well-stocked fridge and the generous margin they all consumed over and above their basic needs. He was also satisfied with the love and attention his wife showed him through the teas that greeted him on his return from work. Their happiest times were when they were all sitting around a table together. As other families might share other activities, they shared eating. But it was more than eating. Earning money to buy food, shopping for food, putting food upon the table, sitting in the kitchen while mother cooked, also provided a structure within which the family could hold together harmoniously. The consensus about food seemed to be complete. This was the reality the family group had constructed, and any interference in their eating habits became an attack upon the family.

But what the doctor had seen was an unhealthy child and a feckless mother who was ready to subject her child as well as herself to all the physical and social handicaps of obesity.

What was a problem when viewed at one level became a solution when viewed at another, holding the Dartie family together, containing disruption and promoting family cohesion. It was an entrenched and inflexible solution, and it seemed to work. There was none of the distress that is found when a solution is less than adequate, unequal or unfair or restrictive. There was no sign of the turmoil that comes when one solution is having to be abandoned in favour of another.

But the solution did, however, bring the Darties into conflict with the standards of the society around them. It is not enough for a family to be a harmonious self-contained unit. A family also needs to maintain smooth relationships, as a system, with the larger system of which it forms a part.

The nature of the problem underlying this solution was recognised by the school health team. Collectively, they were able to place the problem within a different context. They now saw the difficulty, even the danger, of any attempt to introduce change into these family patterns. They were able to look on the family as a developing and changing unit from which the children would eventually emerge. They hoped that the children would be able to develop interests outside the home which would lead them in other directions, towards other possible solutions, finding alternatives for themselves even if it seemed that their parents had none. They had to recognise the risk that the current family solution would be passed on as a family legacy, so that for Benny and Carol and their children the centre of family life would be forever a groaning table and love a plate heaped high.

At another, and perhaps 'deeper', level, one might have wondered about the nature of the underlying problem which required such a solution. Why, one might have asked, did they have to evolve this exclusive means of communication? Was there, somewhere, someone's massive deprivation for which they were having to make amends? Whose hurt, whose feelings of insecurity, were having to be assuaged? What hazard or calamity was it feared that another pattern of behaviour might bring, and what sort of emptiness and depression might then be exposed?

Though these questions might come to mind, no one, in this case, was authorised to seek the answers. This family was not asking for any form of treatment, let alone family therapy. But the concepts of group and family process were nonetheless relevant and become part of the thinking of the school health team.

The fear of a calamity

The mention of the fear of a potential calamity which another pattern of behaviour might bring recalls the concepts of Ezriel (1950) mentioned earlier.

To recapitulate, Ezriel considered that the groups which he observed were trying, through the operation of the group processes, to establish a particular pattern of behaviour or relationships, the main purpose of this pattern being the prevention of an alternative pattern which, in the unconscious collective phantasy of the group, risked bringing a calamity upon them. A shared fear is established in which all the individual fears of group members find a common ground. The group as a whole struggles to maintain a pattern of activity which will permit the threatened disruptive forces to be contained, denied, given symbolic expression, or projected elsewhere. In this, families have much in common with other groups.

However, a family, enduring over time and playing a more central and more fundamental role in the lives of its members, is a more complex entity than a therapeutic stranger group. Family solutions take a more permanent form, becoming woven into the fabric of a family's life, and receiving powerful support. They may be passed on from generation to generation. But not every solution is as monolithic as that of the Darties. For the most part the solutions develop gradually, and they are always in the process of being reinforced, modified, adjusted and augmented. At times a solution will be abandoned altogether in favour of some other pattern of behaviour. Most families have at any one time a variety of sub-problems, within the fundamental problem of staying together, each of them simultaneously seeking a solution. These problems can only be accommodated through constant compromise and rearrangement.

Rules which regulate family life

The pattern of family life continues to be built up from an accumulation of small details and individual transactions which unite into a repetitive pattern. It is from the details on which agreement has been reached that general principles or rules are evolved by which other details can be regulated. An outside observer sees the details, such as who sits in which chair, who gets up to make the coffee, which television programme is turned on (or off), and who speaks first and to whom. The observer notices, perhaps, that there is only one comfortable chair in the living room and that father is sitting in it. Or that the living room is covered with toys, and that the women are drinking coffee in the kitchen. Like one compass reading, one observation is not enough to plot a position or draw tentative conclusions about the implicit rules and practices in a family; at least two compass readings, converging on a point, are needed. Or, as Sherlock Holmes said, 'when you follow two separate chains of thought, Watson, you will find some point of intersection which should approximate to the truth' (Hardwick 1964).

There may be rules within the awareness of a family which come to be openly stated: 'We are a democratic family in which everyone has a right to be heard.' 'We all share the work and everyone knows what jobs they have to do.' 'We are easy going and everyone is free to do their own thing.' There are also rules which are not stated: 'Mother does all the nasty jobs.' 'No-one has to take any notice of Father.' 'We never show how angry we are with each other.' Sometimes these spoken and unspoken rules appear to be in conflict with each other. And then there are also the rules which operate outside the conscious awareness of the family altogether.

Each family will have its own way of coping with threats to its integrity. Many of the minor, or even moderately serious, disturbances which threaten families are made tolerable by the use of family clichés which diminish the importance of disruptive activities and help to hold the family together.

'It's just one of your father's little ways.' 'It happened on one of Mum's poorly days.' 'All the men in our family have hot tempers/weak chests/no sense of direction/an eye for a pretty face.' Some of these phrases may sound patronising when quoted here, but they are in regular use. They can perform the same sort of function for the family as a whole that the so-called ego defences perform for the individual.

Another way in which the impact of disruptive forces can be reduced and the balance maintained is through the use of stereotypes which give some members of the family permission to be divergent and still to be thought of as normal within the family pattern. It may be taken for granted, for instance, that someone studying for an exam, or with a very particular bent or interest, can be excused the evasion of shared responsibilities without the importance of these responsibilities being reduced. Even a few oddities of personality can be used as an explanation for some unsatisfactory behaviour which might otherwise be experienced as dangerously disruptive. 'He takes after Uncle George,' may be used to explain away such incidents as minor delinquencies, relating them to the family's continued existence, and, at the same time, making the behaviour more tolerable because the person who is alleged to have set the precedent had some likeable qualities which kept him within the family and for which he continued to be valued. 'But the girls in the Smith family have always settled down in the end,' removes some of the threat from awkward behaviour by placing it within a family tradition which is recognised and accepted so that the individual does not have to be considered deviant. This is the process of normalisation which is part of flexible family growth and development, enabling the range of the acceptable to be changed or increased to fit the changing reality of a particular family.

'Science advances by relentless examination of the commonplace,' wrote Jules Henry. 'If a man reads a newspaper or watches television; if there is dust or no dust on the furniture; if a parent kisses or does not kiss his child when he comes home; if a family has eggs or cereal for breakfast, orange juice or no orange juice, and so on through all the trivia of everyday life – this is significant to me' Henry (1972, p.xix) This recalls Jane Austen writing to her sister Cassandra and appealing for news, '…you know how important the purchase of a sponge cake is to me'. She too understood all the complex issues involved in the purchase of sponge cakes.

The metaphorical unity of the family

The big events may give the signals about the problems and solutions, but we enter into the family process through the small change of family life. The regulation of this small change, and thus of the rules, stated and unstated, conscious and unconscious, takes place through the interplay of the cohesive and disruptive family forces and so through the action of what we have called the family processes.

In order to reach this level, which transcends individual activity, we have to treat families, like the small groups discussed earlier, as if each family were a psychological entity. This has been made easier for us by recourse to a metaphor, and also through a return to systems theory (Skynner 1976).

The individual body is seen to have its physical boundaries, and most people are prepared to treat the individual as constituting a separate and distinct whole. But, in fact, the unity of the individual could, in certain contexts, be considered to be no less notional than the unity that we are now attributing to the family.

The unity of the individual is a concept which is needed in order to describe certain activities, but which can be abandoned in other instances when there is a need to consider the individual as a collection of different and separable parts, Sometimes it is important to be able to give separate descriptions of the endocrine system, the central nervous, the autonomic nervous system, and so on, and to trace connections between these systems and the activities of respiration, metabolism of foodstuffs, and the chemical and electrical activities within the tissues generally. All these systems interact, but all the same it may sometimes seem a desirable aim to intervene exclusively in one or more than one of them. Sometimes the emotional life is treated as a separate existence, but this, too, can also be related to activities in these other systems.

Thus the individual can be considered as a unity; but, for other purposes, the individual can be considered as a collection of different systems related to each other in different ways. Thus an individual, depending upon the viewpoint of the observer, could be considered as a system, as a collection of subsystems, or as a subsystem that forms part of a larger system such as a family or group.

The concept of homeostasis

One of the observed characteristics of the individual, which can be described only by assuming a unity made up of interrelated systems, has been given the name of 'homeostasis'. In an individual physiological sense, the term 'homeostasis' is used to describe the tendency for an organism to return to a state of physiological balance after a disturbance of metabolism.

There is nothing inevitable about this return to the previous state, but since such a tendency has actually been observed, a word is needed to refer to the observation. Through repeated use the term has become to some extent reified, and, in consequence, people sometimes talk as if there is some force called 'homeostasis' actually in existence. From here it is not difficult to make the further assumption that it is through the properties of this homeostatic force existing in the individual that the return to a state of physiological balance takes place. But we are still talking about a tendency which can only be observed if and when it is present, and, in fact, there is no guarantee that, after an upset, such a restoration will ever take place.

Family homeostasis

The family group can be considered as an entity which operates according to a system of 'rules', some inside and some outside conscious awareness. These rules limit and circumscribe individual behaviour as they work to establish and maintain a viable family solution to the family problem.

Within this limiting system of rules, the amount of flexibility permitted may be small or great; there may be much leeway or there may be very little. But, in every family, however securely it appears to be able to handle the disruptive forces, there must come a point where deviations from the code of behaviour which the family has established as its norm have to be corrected. The family which is based upon a democratic conception of family life in which no one is overly dominant may not be able to allow one member to take charge. A family based upon the principle that 'father knows best' cannot allow father's authority to be seriously challenged. A family in which there are shared fears of separation and loss will have difficulty in permitting risk taking. If a rule has any force at all, then it must mean that any family member stepping out of line is pulled back before he takes a step too far.

Suppose we have a family which has established a tacit rule that certain topics which could cause friction are not to be discussed openly at family gatherings. This rule, of course, will itself be one of the things that cannot be discussed. Suppose that one family member draws dangerously close to a forbidden topic. Family cohesion is threatened and there is fear of the release of disruptive forces. There may be a withdrawal from the person who seems to be about to flout the family rules, or perhaps an attempt at a diversion, or a display of the symptoms of physical illness. For example, mother may develop one of her headaches, serving as a reproach, a warning or a distraction. It then becomes hard for the deviant member to proceed further. The moment of danger passes and the rule is tacitly re-established.

There may be other times when a challenge to the rules leads to some appreciable change in the family system. The family may find that the rules have somehow come to be modified, that the boundaries of what is permitted have been extended, and that more deviations from the former norm can now be tolerated without any increased fear that the family will be put in danger. Conversely, there may also be times when the response to challenge is a tightening of the rules. At such times any threat, external or internal, to the family established solution is likely to lead to an attempt to do something to increase conformity and cohesion, and strengthen the solution.

It is here that we can make use of the term 'family homeostasis'. We apply it to describe the way in which deviations from the norm which a family has established for itself are corrected through some process in which all the family members are involved. But, as with the application of the term to the individual, there is a danger that 'family homeostasis' may be used as if it were describing something with a reality of its own, apart from the perception of the observer who is using the term because he needs some language with which to enclose his observations.

The use of the term homeostasis applied to the family group is as valid as the use of the term applied to the physiology of the individual, with the qualification in both instances that it is only valid if and when the individual or family group can be seen to restore a balance after a disturbance. It is improper to speak of homeostasis as a force before such an observation has been made. And family homeostasis also resembles physiological homeostasis in another particular; there are times when the balance is *not* restored.

Maintaining the balance, or homeostasis, in the family means the application of constant repairs, sometimes requiring an amount of family effort (and often including unequal amounts of individual effort) which may seem disproportionate to the advantage gained. There are reparative activities which drain off so much energy from other more positive family undertakings that they leave the family unit weaker rather than stronger, and so less equipped to deal with subsequent threats. Opportunities may have to be relinquished, and controversial undertakings abandoned, in order to keep a vulnerable family unit together. Individual members may have to remain within the limitations of their socially defined family roles in order not to fracture a rigid family structure.

For many families, some sort of working balance is usually maintained. Solutions are created which fit with sufficient comfort into the fibre of family and social life, evolving and developing to meet changing circumstances, so that for many families it is only occasionally, at some particular point of stress, that the nature of the underlying problems become apparent.

There are transition points in the lives of all families which strain the existing solutions and demand adjustments. These are among the 'crises' described by Caplan (1961). Transition points provide opportunities for growth and development, for the abandonment of solutions that are failing and for the establishment of better ones; but they can also bring a slide back to a former solution that had appeared to have been outgrown or the adoption of other more restrictive coping mechanisms. Such transition points could be, for example, the death of the grandparents, the departure of the adult children, or a change of job, all having an impact upon the family problems and family solutions.

The family and its environment

A family is not a closed system, and so it is in a constant interaction with the larger system of which it forms a part. The nuclear family is embedded within the extended family, within the neighbourhood, the community, and the wider society at large. Dynamic interchanges are always taking place, and information is being passed back and forth through the permeable boundaries of all these interconnected systems. No solution at any level is ever established in isolation from the wider environment, and no solution can be maintained without the co-operation, acquiescence or collusion, of other people and other groups.

There are families which appear so disorganised, so inconsistent and inefficient in carrying out the family task, and so incomplete as a psychological entity, that only repeated activity on the part of helping professionals can keep them together. These are among the families who become well known to social service departments, to probation officers and to health visitors. There are other families that obtain the help they need from elsewhere, and a relative or even a family friend may play a similar, though probably more concealed, role.

There are also families that are held together by solutions which appear to be satisfactory to themselves but which are considered too deviant or too anti-social to be acceptable to others. These are the families that are delinquent, or that offend in some other way against the standards counted as normal by the community in which they live. Sometimes they are clinging to standards which their contempories are busy abandoning.

The Darties can be considered in this context, since their family solution, satisfactory to themselves, came to be challenged by the school medical service. In this case, the Darties seemed to 'win'. Such a challenge leads to change somewhere in the system, but it is not always the identified 'deviants' who do the changing. The result in this instance may have been a change in the conceptions of the school medical team itself rather than a change in the system that the school medical team was trying to modify.

Working with fragments

An observer can only obtain a little glimpse into the life of a family. Any opinion or diagnosis has to be based on an accumulation of fragments and assumptions.

One assumption that the family therapist has to make in order to carry on the work is the assumption that family life is all of a piece, and that the visible portion contains a decoction of it all. Family life has to be thought of as a bowl of soup, in which one spoonful is sufficient to convey the flavour and quality of the whole, rather than as a plate of mixed salad made up of disparate and unrelated elements. Every little interaction, every gesture made and every word spoken, is considered to contain something of the problem within it. Like group therapists, family therapists work with the processes before them, and equally like group therapists, they inevitably contribute to these processes. Unlike group therapists working with stranger groups, however, they have to relate the processes to the on-going life of the group which continues when the therapists have left the room.

'The Power to guess the unseen from the seen'

A social worker once said that she did not need to go inside the house of one of her clients in order to know what it was like. It was enough for her to stand on the doorstep, to see the knocker on the front door and the curtains at the window and to glimpse the tiles in the hall. Making these observations, she would then know what to expect in the sitting room and in the kitchen, In saying this she was making two assumptions. She was assuming that the rest of the house did exist so that what she was able to see was not all. And she was also assuming that what she could not see, although different, was, at the same time, all of a piece with what she could see; that the relationship between the one and the other was such that clues as to the nature of the one could be found within the other. She was also, of course, claiming that she had the experience and the knowledge to make these assumptions. And she had to be ready to be proved wrong.

A very similar idea was expressed in 1884 by Henry James (1987).

I remember an English novelist, a woman of genius, telling me that she was much commended for the impression she had managed to give in one of her tales of the nature and way of life of the French Protestant youth. She had been asked where she learnt so much about this recondite being, she had been congratulated on her peculiar opportunities. These opportunities consisted in her having once, in Paris, as she ascended a staircase, passed an open door where, in the household of a pasteur, some of the young Protestants were seated at a table round a finished meal. The glimpse made a picture; it lasted only a moment, but that moment was experience. She had got her direct personal impression, and she turned out her type. She knew what youth was, and what was Protestantism; she also had the advantage of having seen what it was to be French, so she converted these ideas into a concrete reality. Above all, however, she was blessed with the faculty which when you give an inch takes an ell, and which for the artist is a much greater source of strength than any accident of residence or of place in the social scale. *The power to guess the unseen from the seen, to trace the implication of things, to judge the whole piece by the pattern, the condition of feeling life in general so completely that you are well on your way to knowing any particular corner of it, – this cluster of gifts may almost be said to constitute experience.* (James 1987, pp.194–95, italics added)

Whatever the range of observations available, we have no choice, when working with families, but to act upon the basis of the small part which we can perceive, and to assume that it is not random or arbitrary. Indeed all of psychotherapy, whatever school it represents, is based to some degree upon the inference of the whole from the part.

Freud in his *Interpretation of Dreams* (1963) made the point that having no direct knowledge of the dreams he was claiming to interpret he could only work on fragments mutilated by the untrustworthiness of memory and embellished by subsequent false elaborations. He based his work upon an assumption that a direct relationship existed between the unconscious processes which had given rise to the unknown dream and the distorted fragments presented for analysis – 'these arbitrary improvisations, hurriedly patched together in the embarrassment of the moment' – so that the very distortions and the selectivity of the recollections were not themselves arbitrary but were part of the same mental processes that had brought the dream into being. The part and the whole are all of one piece, linked together through the pervasive processes from which there is no escape, and the one contains the essence of the other.

Perhaps Freud, as he concentrated exclusively upon the inner world of his patient was able to make a virtue of necessity, using the part to lead him to a whole.

Therapists in general are faced with a similar necessity as they struggle to make sense out of the fragments they observe. To find this sense, they have to add some fragments of their own. This brings the very real danger that they might come to reconstruct a complete drama out of their imaginations and out of their own personal family experiences. Their interpretations are based upon the few lines from the script that are being played before them, and they take it for granted that this bit of the action is the equivalent of the original play which they can never completely know.

The analogy of a play is irresistible. For the therapists, it is as if the stage curtain rises for a moment and all the action is before them on the stage. Only a fragment is seen, but the assumption has to be made that all the essentials are contained within it, including the theme of the play as a whole. Nothing can be treated as random or arbitrary, everything is taken to be significant and full of meaning. The task is to bring these fragmentary observations into some sort of meaningful order, and to arrange them into a pattern. This can only be done through the use of the therapists' past experiences, the professional framework, and the concepts and theories that happen to be available.

Bertrand Russell (1960) used an analogy from the theatre in his *Sceptical Essays*. It serves as a warning against the dangers implicit in any such task.

> *Hamlet* is a well-known play, but few readers would have any recollection of the part of the First Sailor, which consists of the four words 'God bless you, Sir.' But suppose a society of men whose sole business in life was to act this part; suppose them isolated from contact with the Hamlets, Horatios, and even Guildensterns; would they not invent systems of literary criticism according to which the four words of the First Sailor were the kernel of the whole drama? Would they not punish with ignominy or exile any one of their number who would suggest that other parts were possibly of equal importance? (Russell 1960, p.26)

Those who work with family groups are given the task of intervening in the whole drama on the basis of an observed fragment. It has to be assumed that the fragment that is available is enough for the immediate task.

The need for a storehouse of knowledge

To use another analogy, archaeologists with a few pieces of pottery can infer the existence of a whole culture. But before they can do this there are a number of stringent requirements that have to be met. There is the disciplined approach, the familiarity with the skills of digging and handling artefacts, the knowledge of the shapes of pots previously discovered. In addition, they need a knowledge of cultures in general, and the ability to enter another culture free from the distorting influence of one's own.

Family therapy needs no less stringent requirements. The fragments of family life observed in clinical situations can only be understood in the light of an understanding of the broad sweep of family life, of individual families, and of families at large, both inside and outside the particular culture in which one is living.

For this sort of knowledge, we have to draw not only upon clinical observations but also upon the work of the historian, anthropologist, novelist and dramatist. We have to study family life as a continuing saga spanning generations. We have to escape the confines of our own experience, so that we do not risk finding that the only family which we can use as a template is one based upon (falsified) recollections of our own.

This wider knowledge has to come from many sources. It has to come through personal experience and through entering into the lives of others. It has to come through the work described by doctors, nurses, health visitors, social workers and other helping professionals. It can also come through reading newspapers and novels, seeing plays, and listening to passing conversations in bars, supermarkets and railway stations. All this and more is needed to give the would-be family therapists, and others in this field, a storehouse from which reference points can be derived, similarities and differences discovered, patterns recognised and validated or discarded, anomalies noted and remembered. The need for such a storehouse precedes the need for the disciplined structure which comes with formal training.

Wider applications

All this is a two-way traffic. Family therapy has done more than add another option to work with families in distress and open up a new therapeutic approach. It has added a new dimension to the study of human behaviour at large, and it has brought new insights into the field of literature and the arts. In this, the impact of the new whole-family psychology could be compared with the advent of psychoanalysis as a metatheory outside the consulting room, which led to a major reappraisal in, for example, the fields of history, biography and literary criticism. It has also fundamentally affected the work of other professions. For example, we have already noted how at one time a large proportion of social workers began to describe themselves as psycho analytically orientated. They were not psychoanalysts, they continued to consider themselves social workers and to practise their original discipline, but they mastered and applied many psychoanalytic concepts. When these concepts were truly incorporated and assimilated into existing practice, they enriched and extended it.

As in the case of the concepts of psychoanalysis and group psychotherapy, the concepts of the family process are not the exclusive property of the family therapists who first formulated them, to be passed on within a closed profession. The next stage is the outward movement of ideas and concepts into the work of other disciplines and into the understanding of human behaviour at large.

CHAPTER 10

The Family Context:
Interventions

If a patient is disturbed, the patient's family is often disturbing. (R.D. Laing, *The Politics of Experience.*)

The move from individual to family treatment, to John Elderkin Bell's (1970) 'The family is the problem', marked a very important stage, even a turning point, in the history of the psychodynamic treatment of disorders.

'It is,' wrote Skynner, 'as if we have suddenly discovered how to apply a lever to the point of balance of a great boulder, previously moved only with difficulty and against enormous forces that repeatedly undid our efforts and restored the previous equilibrium' (Skynner 1976, p.xi).

And yet work with families was nothing new. Family therapy, as it now came to be defined, was an altogether new mode of treatment, but treatment centred upon families had been with us for a long time. Even in the early days of child guidance, when it was still customary to look on a disturbance as an illness in the child, the family could not be ignored. Unlike an adult, a child cannot initiate any changes in his circumstances himself, but is dependent upon the actions and decisions of the adults around him.

For some decades before this, case workers had been describing the family rather than the individual as their unit of concern, and their work largely in terms of the maintenance and restoration of family functioning. The voluntary organisations which state their aims in their titles, the family welfare associations and the family service units, have been around for most of this century. So have child guidance clinics.

In all these fields of work, however, despite the recognition given by helping professionals from all disciplines to the key importance of family relationships, the focus had to remain for a long time upon the individual client or patient, or upon separate individuals in conjunction. Interviews with other family members were undertaken mainly as a diagnostic aid, or in support of the individual treatment that was being given to the primary patient. Family casework likewise was broken down into casework with key family members, who were probably seen separately. It was not until the advent of family therapy as a new specialism that concepts and techniques became available that made it possible to intervene within the family process and treat the family unit seen as a whole, the target of treatment then shifting from the relationships between family members onto the total interaction within the family.

But for some time before this happened, the ground was being prepared by a growing awareness of the limitations of individual treatment, which reached as far as mainstream psychiatry itself. The helping professionals were beginning to take note of the way in which treatment was often hampered or interrupted by interventions on the part of other family members who often had not appeared to be directly involved up till then. It was observed that there were times when improvement on the part of the patient would be followed by the breakdown or illness of some other member of the family network. There were other times when a recovery in hospital would be followed by a relapse as soon as the patient returned home. It seemed as if the boundaries of the problem could no longer be equated with the personal boundaries of the person who was seeking help.

In short, the time was now ripe for a new perspective, including a form of treatment which would take into account some of these new insights, and which would make it possible to extend the treatment process to include groups of individuals whose problems seemed to be dovetailed together in complementary ways. This was particularly apparent in child guidance and child psychiatry where the identified patient was a child.

The family network has an additional and fundamental significance since it is the network of origin and the prototype for all subsequent networks. Every family unit is a link in the chain whereby disturbances are perpetuated and become rooted in family configurations inherited from previous generations and passed on to the next. For many mental health workers concerned with primary prevention the mental health of a family as a whole has come to be considered a matter of legitimate concern, over and above the requirement to treat a particular disturbance. The problems do not remain contained within a family. Similar malfunctioning configurations of personal relationships occur repeatedly in many settings such as education and industry: the tensions between rival peers, between senior and junior, the attempts of the young to usurp power and of the old to hold on to it, the hostility between the boss and his or her deputy, problems in the relationships of men and women, very often appear to have originated in early family patterns that have persisted and been inappropriately transferred.

It needed once more the near laboratory conditions of the small group, in one room with an observer, to identify the family group processes at work. The family had to be turned from an often largely unseen network of interdependent roles and relationships into a small face to face group whose interaction could be directly observed and experienced by the therapist.

From the 1950s onward there have been rapid developments in the progress of family therapy and its applications. It may seem paradoxical, however, that this progress has been made at a time when the very existence of the family seems to be coming under increasing threat, and when families are breaking up, or breaking down, at an accelerating rate. It seems as if a mould is being broken; but the purpose of family therapy is neither to repair the mould nor to find a new one. As Kubie (Dicks 1967) has said, 'The psychoanalyst is not a marriage broker, nor a marriage saver, nor yet a marriage wrecker.' Neither is the family therapist any of these things for the family.

But although family therapy cannot be given the task of preserving the unity of families, it does require an acceptance of some notion of family unity. There has to be some consciousness of a family structure, even if, at the same time, doubts are being expressed as to the nature of that structure. Both the awareness and the doubts are needed, for where there are no doubts there can be no possibility of change. In the past, when there were rigidly structured patriarchal (or matriarchal) families, there was not room for any doubt and so no opportunity was offered for therapeutic change. This perhaps may explain why family therapy has developed along with an increase in family turmoil and vulnerability.

Group therapy and family therapy compared

Knowledge about families has to come from many directions, and the new discipline of family therapy did not draw upon group dynamics and group psychotherapy alone, important as these were. It has also taken theoretical concepts and inspiration from many other sources, often seeking out theory after first establishing practice. These sources include systems and communication theory, encounter methods, family casework, sociology and anthropology, as well as all the knowledge of family life recorded and communicated in myth, literature and art. But it is from the group process that the central concepts of the family process have been to a large extent derived.

Family therapy will now be set alongside the group therapy which has already been discussed, the family process alongside the group process, and the relationship between the two explored. They may be similar in many repects, but there are also important distinctions to be drawn between them, for the family forms a special and unique group. The similarities and the differences are revealing, and throw light upon both treatment modes.

In both these forms of treatment a small group of patients comes to sit in a circle with the therapist who has a commitment to facilitate change at the level of the group as a whole, and to work with and through the processes that operate in all interpersonal networks.

But, as settings for therapy, there are also important differences between groups made up of strangers and groups made up of close relatives; and so there are important differences in the therapeutic opportunities that the groups provide and in the type of demands that are made on the therapists.

A treatment group of strangers is a group made up of people who come with unrelated problems and unrelated solutions. Even if the group members are selected on the basis of similar problems as, for example, would be a group composed of alcoholics, the problems and solutions are still brought by individuals, and the group will contain a range of different attitudes and responses. This diversity is important. Even in such a group, there are likely to be times when it will become a collusive alliance of people united in their efforts to maintain a shared solution and resist change; but the fact that the group includes members with different histories and different and conflicting viewpoints will take some of the force from the collusive alliances and prevent them from hardening into more permanent groupings.

In a group of strangers, the group conductor can expect that the natural processes taking place in the group will, in the longer run, help to challenge existing solutions and discourage the establishment of entrenched positions. It is through the operation of these processes that much of the therapeutic result is achieved. While monitoring what is going on, the conductor is usually able to keep interventions to the minimum required to release the natural potential of the group itself.

In a family group, however, the position is in many ways reversed This is no group of strangers. On the contrary, it is a collection of people who are bound together permanently by the most intimate of ties; by a complex web of obligations and expectations and by a common history of inheritance. These family members have solutions as well as problems in common, and these will be solutions established by collaboration, perhaps inherited from a previous generation. And there will also be potent family traditions, and family myths and secrets, in which they have all come to have a share.

Moreover, the members of a therapeutic group come on an equal footing, but not so the family members, who are part of a hierarchical structure of young and old, weak and strong, inexperienced and experienced, inarticulate and articulate. The family group may contain young children whose communications are still largely non-verbal, and who may require special provisions if their contributions are to be recognised and accepted as part of the whole. The children will be within the circle, but they may be on the floor with play or drawing materials, or they may be moving freely among the other members and adding to, or interrupting, the conversation.

The members of a family group enter the treatment room within their roles as spouses, parents, children and siblings. Since these are the roles that they recognise as relevant to the treatment process, they may come with the intention or the expectation of leaving other aspects of themselves outside. And what they are bringing into the treatment situation is not something transferred from family networks that have been left behind at home; it is the living family network itself *in propria persona*.

It follows from this that, in the family group, we do not have an assortment of different problems and different solutions brought in from various outside contexts. Instead we have family members who are sharing in the same family problem and joining in the establishment of a common solution in which they all have some serious investment. It is a solution which is now under pressure, having become too painful or too inadequate for changing needs, but the family is tied to it because of the difficulty of finding an alternative. Some family members may be protesting against it, or may appear to be excluded from it, but they cannot escape for their very exclusion forms part of this family solution.

One of the paradoxes of family therapy is that while, on the one hand, the family is appealing for help and seeking change, on the other hand the family is struggling to maintain its familiar solution and is fighting to stave off the 'calamity' which a different pattern of behaviour might bring. Present pain may have brought the family into treatment, but that very pain is likely to be part of the means by which the family is avoiding another situation which would be even more painful. In systems language, the family is occupied in trying to maintain a steady state by means of its relationship rules and patterns of mutually reinforcing transactions.

It follows from this that any challenge to the family's established pattern of behaving, any proffering of alternatives, and any exposure to new possibilities, is not likely to come through the processes that are already operating within this particular group itself. Some new element is required that will challenge established solutions. The person in a position to introduce this new element, and bring the possibility of therapeutic change into the family group, is the family therapist.

Whereas the problems and solutions brought by group therapy patients have different sources, the family members have problems and solutions in common, arising in the same family network. Prominent in the sequence of events which has brought the family to this encounter is likely to be a complaint about the behaviour of one of the children. But the traditional medical model on which a family's expectations are likely to have been been formed in the past is now being challenged and replaced. The notional family that we have been carrying in mind, coming for help with its 'problem child', is now being given an opportunity to move away from traditional practice and fit into a new pattern of therapy. This pattern is the one that the family therapists are carrying in their minds as they reach out for the techniques that can give it concrete form and bring the whole-family concept to life in the treatment room. A family bringing a child for help is now more likely to be offered the idea that the problem is not confined to the one child with the symptoms, is not even seen as centred on that child, but, rather, is the problem of them all equally and in conjunction.

The family as a whole

When a family opts (or perhaps is induced to accept) family treatment, and the family members agree to come together for therapy, they have to rely upon the therapist to hold the total pattern of family relationships in mind, to look beyond the individual and to direct any intervention to the welfare of the whole. The therapist will perceive each family member in relation to this perceived pattern which encompasses them all, and will not single out individuals and attribute responsibility or blame.

This focus is comparable to the focus of group therapists, and, as with the small face to face groups already considered, this encounter in the one room has to provide conditions which make it possible for the interaction among a number of people to be viewed as a whole in a concentrated and encapsulated form. It is here that the family problems and the factors which created them have to be identified. It is not a question of how A behaves, or of how A behaves towards B, or of how A and B behave when C is present. ABC makes up a whole, and any single piece of behaviour derives its meaning from this total context. For the therapist, it is a question of the total behaviour of a network which includes them all, which the therapist has now joined for a particular purpose.

In the treatment room, the family is to be observed behaving in its habitual ways, with all its harmonies and dissonances, compromises and rigidities, understandings and misunderstandings, and all the patternings of its roles and relationships. The full range may not be openly demonstrated at every session, but all the potentiality is there and cannot be left at home. The family therapists have to make use of what is going on in front of them, all that is needed is contained here if only they can see it and make use of it. And the therapists, too, form part of the total pattern, contributing along with the family to what is taking place.

Furthermore, the main emphasis is placed upon what is happening in front of them all, witnessed by them all, rather than upon events that are experienced by one member and then reported subsequently to the others or to the therapist. So what is said by any one member in the session becomes a commitment which cannot be denied or conveniently forgotten. The members of the group are committed to their own insights, in the words in which they have revealed them, and cannot easily withdraw from the new position achieved.

The family group matrix

In family therapy it is not merely the individual family members who are linked together to form part of a single entity: individual events can also be treated in the same way. Every event which takes place in the family treatment room can be related to every other event and to the family process as a whole, and so every event can throw light upon the problems which have brought this family into treatment.

Here we can return to the concept of the group matrix formulated by Foulkes. Applying this formulation to the family, we have the concept of a family group matrix which is built up of all the past happenings in the family and the meanings that the family has ascribed to these happenings, including the family myths and traditions and the memories and secrets inherited from past generations. This matrix is the family inheritance seen as a whole, and every event in the present is linked to this matrix and contributes to it.

Every detail is important. In the treatment room, the question of who sits in which seat, of who speaks first, and of what, and to whom, the challenges and the withdrawals, the responses and the silences, all have their significance in this context and all form part of the one total pattern. Perhaps mother enters the room first and directs the others where they are to sit: perhaps father and one child sit close together; perhaps another child edges his chair away from the circle. None of these happenings is seen as a random event, each has its place and its relationship to the family matrix, to the family problem, and to the pattern of relationships as a whole. It falls to the therapist to recognise and (where appropriate) to reveal these relationships.

Here, in the family treatment room, is the real-life family network itself. The confrontation is with the actual problem *in situ*, the raw, unprocessed situation within which the distress is to be found. But here the therapist is the one outsider, who does not know what was said yesterday, or last year, in this family group. The other members of the group have a long, complex and intricate experience of life together, a whole history of which the therapist will never know more than a fragment. The therapeutic group of the family (whatever structure may be contrived for it by the therapist who is carrying family concepts in mind) remains part of the continuum of a particular family's life. Whatever happens in this group is still only a part of that family's life. It is an addition to it which has come in order to make change possible, and any change introduced here will go on developing when the therapist is no longer present.

The activity of the family therapist

There are now several well recognised schools of family therapy, each with its own adherents.

Family therapists bring to their work their understanding of family structures, systems, and processes (within the particular framework in which they have done their training) and their conceptions of change and of the ways in which change can be introduced. They bring their experience; and they also bring their own personalities and of course their own family histories which they have to put to disciplined use. Personal styles and preferences have their importance.

Some schools of family therapy have been founded by powerful, confident and charismatic personalities who believe in intervening actively in the treatment sessions in order to challenge and sometimes to disrupt the existing patterns of behaviour, attempting to force the family to behave differently. In contrast, there are family therapists of other persuasions who keep their own value systems and their own personalities in the background, allowing themselves to experience, and react to, the family pathology, so that they can share their understanding of what is happening.

These two different ways of working tend to be based upon the family systems approach on the one hand and on the psychodynamic approach on the other, but these bases are far from exclusive, and some family therapists, including Skynner, have attempted to integrate aspects of both.

In the systems approach, the primary focus is upon the problem in the present and upon the current pattern of interaction by which the symptoms are being maintained; and the aim is to introduce, or even to force, change into the here and now situation of the treatment room.

Therapists with a psychodynamic approach, on the other hand, place the problems within historical context in addition to the immediate social context. They consider that there is room in family therapy for concepts of the transference of attitudes and relationships formed in the early childhood of individuals. At a more specifically family level, such concepts relate to the internalised models of past family members, and to the family history, myths and legends inherited from the past generations. These therapists are ready to work more slowly, uncovering and working through past influences which are affecting current relationships. They aim to develop insight, and to identify and remove the obstacles which are preventing the family from finding an alternative solution to its current problem for itself.

Beeles and Ferber, (1969) in an attempt to classify the activities of the leading family therapists, divided them into the 'conductor analysts', those who actively force change, and the 'reactor analysts', those who try to remove the obstacles that are preventing the patient families from finding new solutions or improving on their existing ones. They also added a third group, the 'systems purists', made up of those family therapists who think most systemically and who look for the pattern of established rules which govern the behaviour of the family as a system. They then try to expose, challenge and alter these rules as they are demonstrated in the treatment situation, and they include in this the relationship with the therapist. They are, so to speak, trying to disrupt the game in progress by moving the goal posts.

In the literature there may appear to be clearer distinctions between these different ways of working than are to be found in practice, where the differences are often more of emphasis than of exclusive orientation. There are many practitioners of family therapy who do not identify themselves exclusively with any one school, but feel free to draw from a range of different formulations and techniques.

Family therapists of all different orientations, comparing their work with other forms of therapy, frequently emphasise the need to take a more active role than do therapists working with individuals or with stranger groups.. The very strength of the family group, which makes this necessary, also makes it possible for the therapists to move more freely and intervene more directly, drawing upon their own personalities and experience within their professional discipline. The family as a unit is less vulnerable to the effect of a therapist's interventions; and transference, though considered important by many family therapists, is not such an important therapeutic tool as it is in individual psychoanalysis. In the family group transference is present in a more diluted and dispersed form, and an additional or alternative focus can be found in the interaction taking place in the present situation.

Roles

By the very nature of their function, all family therapists have one thing in common. Unlike group therapists, in their treatment groups they start off in a very unequal position *vis-à-vis* their patients. In this situation, they are the outsiders, the newcomers, with a very powerful alliance set in opposition to them.

Whatever their orientation and their personal style may be, family therapists inevitably become more quickly (and more completely) drawn into the conflicts of their family groups than therapists in other situations would be, and they are less able to maintain some detachment from the problems confronting them. Should family therapists try to remain outside the conflict, they risk appearing to the family as intrusive aliens, inviting it to close ranks as it would against any other threat coming upon it from outside. Nor can the family therapist appear to be exploiting existing divisions within the family, and searching out the chinks in the family armour, without incurring the danger of aligning a family sub-group in opposition and thus increasing the splitting and polarisation. This possibility always has to be taken into account, but there are family therapists who are willing deliberately to incur this risk and then to deal with any subsequent splitting.

In order to take on the role of catalyst, or facilitator of change, family therapists cannot altogether escape the double role of participant and observer.

Whatever their framework and orientation, they have to enter into the family process and become part of it. But while they have to expose themselves to the family means of communication, and experience the operation of the family processes, they must also remain apart from what is going on in order to challenge it. So if a therapist is to become, at least temporarily, a member of the family group, it must be as the one member who is not caught up in the family fear of a calamity, and who is able to reduce such fears while challenging the family defences.

Many of the practices of family therapy have been developed on the basis of this ambiguous position of the family therapist. There are a number of different modes of working and available strategies which family therapists can employ so as to obtain some space and a measure of detachment from the problem.

The conflict may be dramatised, participant members being given different roles to play (their own or those of other members of the family as they perceive them). There is *sculpting*, in which each member of the family is invited to create a living tableau representing the family relationships as he or she experiences them. Families may be given games to play, or specific tasks to carry out, inside or outside the treatment session. Family trees may be compiled. These techniques have several advantages. In addition to providing some structure for the therapists, they can be used to provide access to more material, to allow the expression of a wider range of feelings, and to encourage the active involvement of all the family members from oldest to youngest in the treatment process.

Co-therapy is often employed, with colleagues working together to support each other and monitor the involvement; and there are the one-way screens which permit colleagues to have a part in each other's work as observers, supervisors, or even as participants making contributions from time to time although remaining outside the visual range of the patient family.

Since no family therapists can altogether escape being drawn in as participants in the family network, they have to be aware of the ways in which they are being aligned in one manner or another with the family activities. There are usually a number of different possibilities here, and different positions or successions of positions available in a gallery of traditional or archetypal family representations.

It could be, for example, that the therapist will be experienced by the family as if a member of the grandparents' generation, representing and highlighting the inheritance from the past and from the parents' families of origin. Alternatively, contact might be made by the therapist entering the family as if another parent, challenging existing assumptions about parenting and authority, and even modelling a different parental role (which the family may then need to reject). Another possibility for the therapist would be to enter the family processes as if in the position of one of the children, accepting exposure to the experience of the family pathology as it impinges upon a child, acting as a mirror or as a sounding board, and articulating the experiences of the younger and weaker members who are less able to do this for themselves. Sometimes a therapist may move through all these positions and more.

This is the transference situation, and it plays its part in the therapy. The different roles may be consciously assumed by the therapist, but they are also a product of the minds of the family members. Which aspect predominates will be influenced by the extent to which the therapist actively sets out to introduce new experiences, or alternatively concentrates more upon responding to what the family is bringing.

There is an ambiguity about generational roles. As a matter of physical maturation, the distinction in the behaviour of these different roles is perfectly clear. But, psychologically and emotionally, an adult carries living traces of former levels at all times, and there are occasions when earlier levels may reassert themselves and dominate behaviour.

The transfer of generational attributes can take place in two directions. As the infantile parts of the parents are never completely outgrown and always stay included within the family relationships, so the desired and undesired qualities of the grandparents, and of the parents themselves, may be absorbed by the children and given a new expression.

The overlapping of roles takes place at different levels and in different ways. In the natural course of the development of families, different members are permitted from time to time to relive earlier stages or to anticipate later ones. When a member is not well there is an entitlement to be nursed like the precious infant; or, to take another example, a junior school child may be given a brief taste of later independence when going on a school trip. These role shifts can be permitted because of an understanding that a restoration of the previous state will follow.

Thus, in appearing to take up one particular position in a family, the therapist can be making contact with them all, at all the different generational levels, and with the family process as a whole.

Boundaries

The boundaries between different individuals and different generations make up an important part of the structure of family life. One of the functions of a family is to help in the formation of boundaries between individuals, starting by enabling the infant to differentiate the self from the other, and going on to provide sufficient security for the growing child to ease the transition from one developmental stage to another.

A family has its natural history of growth and development, and is always placed at some particular point in a lifecycle which ranges through the establishment of the newly committed couple, the symbiotic relationship of mother and infant, the child's achievement of a sense of personal identity, and the breaking away of the adolescent. At every stage of family life there is some balance of togetherness and separateness which is shifting all the time. Those who have been held securely at the appropriate stage, when their dependency needs were uppermost, are able to let go later on with confidence and trust. But, at any stage, an inappropriate separateness leaves the family unable to perform its tasks and the individuals unnurtured. By the same token, an inappropriate togetherness freezes the family at an immature level with the infantile problems unsolved and the inevitable pathology preserved, divided out, and passed around amongst them.

It is usually thought necessary to the well-being of a family that boundaries between the roles of the different members should be recognised. Roles and boundaries provide limits and controls; and they also confer entitlements and obligations so that the individual members better understand what they are expected to do themselves and what they can expect from the others.

Difficulties arise when these boundaries are poorly defined, but they can also arise when boundaries are rigidly maintained. In some families the expression of individual opinions is discouraged and there is a family line which has to be adhered to: in other families each member may be assigned a set attitude from which departure is not permitted. There are other families in which roles become reversed. For example, father is 'just another boy', excused or denied a father's role, leaving a gap which has to be filled by someone else; or a young girl is expected to take on adult responsibilities and be 'a little mother' to her younger siblings, losing her rights and the freedom to engage in the individual activities appropriate to her age group.

Some family therapists directly challenge inappropriate roles. Others, who do not see their therapeutic task as one of commanding change, might give recognition to the need to behave in a particular way at a particular time while also giving permission to change that behaviour. All members of the family can have an urgent need to be taken seriously in their (temporary) roles before they can relinquish them. Therapists may be able to demonstrate, through the questions they ask and the responses they give, that change is more possible and less dangerous than the family believes, and then they may try to establish conditions in which some safer experimentation is possible. Some change takes place in the sample of behaviour which is brought into existence in the therapeutic session, and which is there to be explored and for every member of the family to witness, take part in, and remember. Any progress that takes place in the family session cannot subsequently be withdrawn altogether.

Communications

Problems with communications and problems with boundaries go together, so that attention paid to the one usually includes attention paid to the other. In fact, all the dimensions of family life are interrelated, and intervention at any level can introduce changes which percolate throughout every aspect of the family system.

Since the application of general systems theory to families, particular attention has come to be paid to the interpersonal communications taking place within a family; and there are many family therapists who make this level their main focus. These therapists may define their primary task as that of clearing up the muddles and mystifications, clarifying the conflicting and incompatible messages, and removing the blocks and obstacles placed in the way of clear communication, which are a feature of the life of disturbed families. Sometimes a few of the family members seem to be trying to resist the passage of certain communications; sometimes all the members of a family are colluding to this end. There may be things that are never referred to, and other things that have become secrets to be shared by some family members and withheld from the rest. Communications may have become blocked so that they can no longer be made openly and they then remain undisclosed until such time as they erupt in the form of physical or mental symptoms, such as illness or disturbed behaviour, perhaps located in one particular family member. And when the deferred communication is finally made it is likely to be given in an incomplete, distorted or ambiguous form.

It was Bateson (1971) who first labelled a communication containing two contradictory messages a 'double bind'.

Many examples can be found. A child may be praised in one sentence and all the approval snatched away in the next. A child may be urged to go to school, while at the same time the urging contains a subtle message about the dangers of the playground. Boys are expected to stand up for themselves but must not be rough. 'I'd like some help with this – but of course its a bit late now to be any real use.' 'I do want you to go out and enjoy yourself – I really don't mind being left on my own again.' Words may say one thing, while at the same time gestures are conveying something else. A gesture itself may contain two meanings, for example an embrace may be stiff and unyielding.

The escape from this situation lies in pointing out the ambiguity and asking the speaker for elucidation. But in some families there is too much fear of hurting and being hurt, or of something unacceptable emerging, for anyone to be able to challenge double-sided messages. Children in particular are frequently too vulnerable and too dependent upon their parents to be free to question the communications.

If there is no way of pleasing, and any response at all is held to be wrong, if you are 'damned if you do and damned if you don't', the tendency is to make no response. At the extreme, where there is no escape from the situation, the victim who is doubly bound may withdraw into a personal inner life with phantasies which have their own satisfactions. This formulation has sometimes been used to explain the origins of some cases of schizophrenia, but the process is familiar enough in all families though at varying degrees of intensity.

Communications in the family are of interest to all family therapists. Some who pay particular attention to this level of work will do so by exposing themselves to the consequences of the faulty communications in order to be able to demonstrate what the family members are doing to each other; they receive the ambiguous messages and draw attention to the confusion which makes it impossible to know how to respond. They may identify and highlight all the hidden messages – the two-edged communications and the latent hostility – doing what the family members have become unable to do for themselves. They may ask firmly for clarification whenever confused communications, verbal or non-verbal, are made. In this, as in all other therapeutic encounters, the therapist who feels confused always needs to say so clearly.

Satir (1964) quotes the following interchange to illustrate her own way of responding to discordant messages.

Daughter to mother: May I go to school?

Mother to daughter: When I was a little girl, I never had an education.

Therapist to mother: Now your daughter asked you if she could go to school and I'm wondering if she got an answer from you. Should she go to school or shouldn't she? (Satir 1964, p.176)

Those therapists who play a more direct and active role may take control of the family communications system themselves in order to reshape it. They may, for example, refuse to allow one member of the family to speak on behalf of another, silencing the parents perhaps so that the children's views have to be heard, or controlling the noisy behaviour of the children that is being used to silence the adults. They may make it impossible for the family to communicate in their habitual way, breaking up the existing pattern and making the family go back to the beginning and start all over again. Their interest is likely to be focused upon the present rather than upon the past, on the current manifestation of the problem rather than on its origin and function within the family developmental process.

Problems from the past

Those therapists (including many of the ones Beeles and Ferber (1969) have classified as 'reactor analysts') who look at the family process reductively within historical framework, are interested in the way in which problems develop and are passed on and perpetuated within families. They look beyond the immediate observations for the hidden origins of the problems and are ready to consider long sequences of time. Some of the developments in systemic family therapy have come as a reaction to what has been seen as the slowness of this type of work and its reliance upon inference and interpretations. It is also criticised for tending to use a linear model of causality, in which events are assumed to have prior causes, in place of the circular model of continuous interaction.

Therapists who work psychodynamically may look, for example, for the particular area of family functioning in which the fears seem to be located, and may feel that the most relevant point of intervention is where unmet needs are carried over from the parents' families of origin, so that the unsolved problems of former generations are being passed on to involve the children of today. This is an approach which may well make use of object relations theory and the formulations of Melanie Klein at a family level. Sometimes family therapists go back over the history of past generations of the family in a structured way; a family tree, or genogram, may be drawn up in order to uncover and demonstrate the means through which the family pattern is continued and problems from the past are being brought over into the present.

Byng-Hall (1973) has described work with family myths and legends, those episodes of family history which are told and retold to successive generations. He finds that these stories are often moral tales which convey the rules and obligations, the shared beliefs, convictions and assumptions, of family life; and which are subtly adjusted at each telling in order to retain their relevancy within current family preoccupations. They play a part in controlling or discouraging change within the family system, and so can act as powerful defences, all the more powerful and difficult to challenge because they play an important part in the family's sense of identity. To the therapist, family myths and legends can be a valuable source of information, and they are also a powerful tool for the introduction of change, since challenging and re-editing the family myths and legends can lead to a reformulation of the family rules.

The long past and the immediate present

A distinction can be made between two broad groups of family therapists in terms of their use of time. On the one hand there are those we have just been mentioning who work with long sequences of time, with segments of family history, and who look for the control processes, or 'governing concepts' – the family rules and the family myths and legends which support them – which keep patterns even of dysfunctional behaviour in existence, to be transmitted from generation to generation. And on the other hand there are those other family therapists who concentrate upon the current situation, the 'here and now', and deal with the small segments of family behaviour that are presented to them, finding the family pathology demonstrated within the short sequences enacted in the brief duration of a therapy session, and making their interpretations at this level without finding a need to look any further afield.

Two different models of change are involved. In discussing the ways in which these two models are related to each other, Cooklin (1981) uses the analogy of the holograph, that is, the photographic plate containing a three-dimensional image which changes according to the position from which it is viewed. If the plate is shattered into fragments, each fragment continues to contain an image of the whole object but the image is now a much smaller one and only represents one single viewpoint.

Cooklin describes the two different contexts in which change can be introduced as being related to each other in a way that is analogous to the relationship between the whole holograph and its fragments. The different approaches have had to be distinguished for purposes of clarity, but the distinctions can be misleading if the relationship between them is not also acknowledged.

The same family problems and family solutions can be viewed in both these different time contexts, and they can be identified and treated as they are passed on within long sequences of family history or, alternatively, as they are enacted within short sequences of family interaction. Family therapists may focus their work upon one or other of these two levels, but there are also therapists who aim to carry both levels in mind, and there are some who seem able to work at both levels and to move flexibly from the one to the other.

Work to change the means by which family transactions are regulated over time is undertaken on the assumption that changes at this level will lead to changes in the short sequence interactions between family members in the future; and that such changes can only be introduced within the current family context. Though the past is gone and cannot be altered now, new meaning can still be given to it in the present. Equally, active interventions within short sequences of time are made in the belief that each small sequence contains the pattern of the whole, and that the parts are linked together, in time as in space, in such a way that change introduced in one component will affect every other component and bring change throughout the whole.

The family of therapists

Whatever may be the chosen focus and mode of intervention employed, the central feature of all family therapy is the introduction of change throughout the family network through the intervention of the family therapist as change agent.

Out of this need for a conscious and controlled personal involvement within the family process has come the widespread use of co-therapy, with two, or sometimes more than two, therapists participating together and monitoring each other's involvement. For many therapists, this provides a safeguard against the dangers of being sucked personally, and not always appropriately, into the family pathology: it could also provide some protection against the danger that one therapist's interventions might come to dominate the family interaction. It also reduces the disproportion between the united strength of the patient family in resisting change and the weakness of a single therapist.

In this conjoint work, the family group is confronted with another group in the form of two or more members of a therapeutic team, that is a 'therapeutic family' ready to demonstrate another shape of family interaction, and to model alternative solutions to interpersonal problems. The therapeutic team needs to to be aware of the existence of interpersonal conflicts and show that it is not afraid of them. No apology need be made for differences of opinion among the team members. They are not claiming freedom from the type of conflicts which are contained in the patient family, and are ready to display differences and difficulties spontaneously and demonstrate that there are alternative ways in which such differences might be handled.

Thus the diversity in the therapeutic group restores to family therapy some of the advantages of group therapy which the seemingly united nature of families has taken away.

Whatever their training, family therapists have to construct for themselves their own ways of working, drawing upon many sources inside and outside themselves. In few other areas in the helping professions can it be harder to define the role of the key worker with any precision.

Outside family therapy: brief interventions

Professional workers who have to respond to the problems caused by family conflicts may find themselves contributing to a complex, multi-professional treatment plan: alternatively, they may find themselves on their own and being required to make an immediate response. Sometimes even a very brief intervention can be valuable.

For example, a general practitioner was treating a young married woman with terminal cancer. On one visit the patient's mother, who was the principal carer, said to the doctor in the patient's presence, 'I wish you could speak to my daughter's husband. He came home drunk last night and was sick on the kitchen rug.'

The doctor exclaimed spontaneously, 'Oh, the poor man', and saw the dying wife's eyes light up with gratitude.

The patient knew that the doctor was acknowledging her husband's grief, and the fact that 'his grief was very great'. Figuratively speaking, the family superego had been invoked by the mother, but the doctor refused to respond at that level. Instead he made his brief comment containing an interpretation which recognised the underlying family conflict and offered an alternative perception. It extended his concern to include the husband, and it brought the husband's behaviour within tolerance and back into the context of the family as a whole. It needed someone from outside the family, but carrying in mind a concept of the family as a whole, to do this.

Although such a response can be unlearnt and intuitive, it is also part of a method of working which can be acquired: and it can only be taught on the basis of concepts which make it possible to approach family interaction and family process as a whole.

CHAPTER II

Comparisons and Contrasts

Foulkes maintained that all the different systems of group work can be brought together within group-analysis, as group-analytic principles apply to all group situations and link them together. In a review of a previous book that the present author wrote with Dr Jack Kahn, Foulkes wrote

> In group analytic theory it is a fundamental tenet that its principles must each time be tailored to the particular purpose, task and conditions of any group. All these conditions, including the mandate of the leader, are called the group situation, and it is held that this situation determines all part processes as well as the nature of the interventions of the leader. The situation in turn is set by us according to the purpose and realities of any group . . . The phenomena are all there, always. It is the use we make of them which determines what becomes figure and what ground. (Foulkes 1970 p.191)

This tailoring to the particular purpose, task and conditions of the group depends not only upon a clear formulation of what the group is there to do: it also depends upon an understanding of the samenesses and the differences within the group systems, including the different foci and the different mandates or contracts between leader and members, implicit or explicit, that determine what has been sanctioned. These provide the context of that total situation, and determine what techniques are appropriate.

Obstacles to clarity

The sharing of many concepts and techniques, and all the areas of overlap, mean that the boundaries between the group work systems can often appear blurred rather than clear cut.

There are different schools of psychotherapy, differing in their theoretical bases and in their techniques. The members of some psychotherapeutic groups may have been selected on the basis of some problem, for example drug addiction, which they all have in common. Group counsellors define different aims in different groups, and vary in the use they make of interpretative techniques and of their own relationship with the group; some may widen their focus to include more aspects of their clients' past and present experience. Group discussion can be used to serve very different needs; and it can be adjusted to meet the disparate requirements of groups which may be varied in terms of age, education and degree of personal commitment. Some discussion groups may focus upon a topic containing personal and intimate preoccupations of its members which cannot remain unexpressed.

Group psychotherapy is not only the first among the group systems we have considered but is also the one which has made the most progress towards the establishment of a firm conceptual basis. It is from group psychotherapy that much of the knowledge of group dynamics necessary to all group workers is derived. Social workers who work with groups are frequently, and by their own choice, trained and supervised, if not by group psychotherapists then by other social workers who have themselves been trained and supervised by group psychotherapists. So it is not suprising that such social workers have sometimes appeared unable or unwilling to consider their work as belonging to a separate system, that counselling, individual and group, is sometimes treated as if it were a diluted and attenuated form of psychotherapy, and that in consequence any advance in skills is seen in terms of an ever closer approximation to the work described by group psychotherapists. While usually disclaiming use of the actual term group psychotherapy, they often appear to be doing their best to adopt the methods and much of the terminology.

Social workers may disclaim the term but others do not. The difference between the different systems is further obscured when the term psychotherapy is treated as medical property and 'group psychotherapy' is the only term it is thought appropriate to use when the leader of the group has a medical qualification, whatever the purpose and focus of the group and whatever may be actually taking place at the group meetings. It is unfortunate if group leaders who are medically qualified feel precluded from using an appropriate terminology to describe what they are doing because they do not feel free to make use of terms which they associate with the work of other disciplines.

Group discussion is conducted by members of many different disciplines. There is not always sufficient recognition of the fact that group discussion needs to be treated as a separate technique, and that competence as a group discussion leader is not automatically conferred by training or experience in group counselling or group psychotherapy. At one extreme, group discussion can be dominated and controlled by a leader with a mission to instruct. At the other extreme, group discussion can merge into a form of group psychotherapy simply because psychotherapy is the only technique that the leader of that group has at his or her disposal.

Other opinions have been expressed. The distinction between therapy and professional education, including the education of doctors and therapists, may seem elusive to some, or may not always have been considered of importance. For example, a paper published by the World Health Organisation (Matte-Blanco 1961) on teaching psychiatry to medical students discusses the use of group psychotherapy as a teaching tool that can be used to achieve a number of different aims. These aims include teaching the student about himself, about his conflicts and the ways in which they interfere with his personal life, about the ways to mitigate these conflicts, about the workings of mental mechanisms in himself and in others, about handling people under stress, and about the leadership of groups. It is the opinion of the author of the paper that 'didactic analysis' does not differ essentially from 'therapeutic analysis', and that the limits between therapy and learning are more conventional than real. However, he goes on to say that they did have difficulty at first in employing a form of therapy as a method of teaching, and that tact was required to introduce it into the medical curriculum. 'We therefore called it *group activity* ' (italics added).

A group work project is sometimes undertaken without any prior formulation of aims and terms of reference, or any appreciation that such a formulation is needed. This may be the result of a belief that therapeutic forces reside in the group itself, and that the very act of bringing people together is therapeutic. This seems to be a half truth. A group contains both therapeutic and anti-therapeutic potential, and the group forces may help or harm. Group work always carries its risks, and this is particularly the case when it is unfocused and undirected and the risks involved are not appreciated.

Groups in organisations

Similar processes are at work in all face-to-face groups, so whether the purpose of a group is defined as therapy, counselling, or education, or whether it is a work group set up for some quite other purpose, the effectiveness of the group will depend upon the sense of safety that is generated, the development of appropriate group norms, and the ways in which cohesion can be fostered and disruptive forces contained.. In all these groups the events taking place will be linked together within a group matrix, roles will come to be shared out, group focal conflicts will emerge and will be resolved in ways that are more or less enabling, more or less restrictive, and the group will retreat from time to time into basic assumption activity in the face of primitive anxieties.

Work groups in industry and other organisations fit within the present framework in that their effectiveness depends in no small part on their members' sense of personal security and ability to find constructive and enabling solutions to the inevitable problems of working together as a team.

In any work environment that is experienced as being insecure, employees will have to devote energy to protecting their personal position and avoiding risk and criticism, and this is likely to be at the expense of creativity and engagement. Personal insecurities will detract from individual and joint performance and interdepartmental rivalries may follow, sometimes bringing attempts to solve internal problems by exporting them into other areas of the organisation. An organisational structure may develop which has the unacknowledged purpose of containing anxieties, and once established such a structure may become hard to change.

While the same basic dynamic processes will be at work, understanding derived from small therapy groups that are contained within strict boundaries of space and time cannot be directly carried over into this different situation. Work groups operate within a relatively unbounded time span and within an organisational or systems context, and so will be caught up in additional intergroup dynamics with additional problem-solving opportunities. Work groups are often able to find temporary solutions to problems by projecting unwanted aspects, and attributing responsibility up and down an established hierarchy or sideways onto another department. Experience of large and median groups, which operate within a wider context and take in sub-grouping and inter-group relationships, could perhaps increase the areas of understanding.

Menzies (1970), in her well-known study of the nursing service in a general hospital, undertaken because of concern about high staff turnover and wastage of trainees, demonstrated how anxiety, experienced in the first instance by individual nurses and related to the responsibilities and hardships of their work, can bring the defence systems of individuals together to form a shared social defence system. This can then become incorporated in the structure, culture and mode of functioning of the hospital and be given a permanent shape. In the institution she studied she found many examples of the operation of such a social defence system. For example, attempts had been made to reduce anxiety about the responsibilities of individual nurses in this hospital through a system of ritual and fragmented task performance which removed personal discretion; and through the establishment of a rigid vertical hierarchy which offered a means of splitting and projecting onto superiors and subordinates. The more adult, responsible and controlling functions were all vested in the senior nursing staff, leaving the junior nurses to be typecast in contrast as spontaneous and human but irresponsible and careless and in need of constant supervision. So each nurse, put into a confining role of one sort or another, had to split off aspects of her personality and project them into nurses at another level of the hierarchy. The anxiety may have been partially contained but it was not addressed and additional anxieties were generated. The work schedules that resulted were wasteful and exhausting, job satisfaction was reduced, and relationships among staff and with patients were affected.

Stock Whitaker (1992) has posed the question whether concepts derived from group psychotherapy can be applied to groups in organisations, and has answered 'yes and no'. She has emphasised that when it comes to work groups understanding does not necessarily open the door for intervention. Differences with respect to purpose, and the prevailing culture, may make it impossible or inappropriate to transpose understandings derived from therapy groups directly to the workplace without intruding into areas that the norms and culture of a work environment do not sanction. The norms of a work environment may require that personal feelings be concealed and personal privacy be respected. We return to Foulkes' fundamental tenet that any work undertaken must each time be carefully tailored to the particular purpose, task and conditions of the group within its total situation.

However, an understanding of group dynamics can inform and improve a team leader's work, can increase the possibility of being able to recognise the wood as well as the trees, can suggest some possible strategies, and can improve the chances of his or her personal survival through difficult times, even though some of the interventions that would seem highly desirable, even obligatory, to a group therapist may have to be withheld.

Some interventions

In all the groups considered, one can envisage situations in which the groups may attempt to solve an immediate problem by adopting or permitting methods of behaviour which are inimicable to the very purpose of the group. The solution may be a temporary one which will be abandoned spontaneously with the next step in the group's development. It may, in contrast, be prolonged to the point where the leader finds it necessary to intervene.

The techniques that a group leader might use in these situations can be discussed most readily in connection with group discussion. Indeed, one would not presume to be so specific about the role of the leader in either group psychotherapy or group counselling. But the relationships within a discussion group are nearer to the realities of everyday life, and so permit the use of more immediate and more direct intervention strategies. Group counsellors and group psychotherapists should be able to learn something from considering the methods of group discussion even if their own techniques have to be selected according to other criteria and serve other purposes.

The leader of a discussion group has an educational role and a responsibility to see that learning can take place in the group. For this purpose there are times when the leader is likely to intervene more frequently and more directly than a group psychotherapist or group counsellor would be likely to do. 'Reliance on the untrammelled operation of group forces,' and 'confidence in the group's capacity to solve its own problems' may represent valid aims in some circumstances, but in others could be explanations offered by inexperienced leaders to account for inadequate leadership. Group discussion may, in fact, never become established in those groups where the leader elects to play a very passive role, perhaps modelled on that of certain group psychotherapists but transferred to a situation where conditions for the practice of group psychotherapy are absent.

In group discussion the intervention of the leader is likely to occur at an earlier stage than in the other groups considered. One of the dangers that the leader has to see and forestall is the establishment of a permanent 'culture' or habitual mode of behaviour, which will prevent the group from carrying out its particular function. This may happen if freedom of discussion becomes seriously limited, if certain conventions of speech and behaviour come to be imposed, and if certain topics, or the contributions of certain members, are not allowed. It may happen when a single member, or a sub-group, comes to dominate the proceedings and other members permit this or find they cannot deal with it.

There is, for example, the situation in which the group allows itself to become dominated by a monopolist. The monopolist, and there may be more than one if this is not a contradiction in terms, may introduce a theme himself or may use one supplied by someone else as a vehicle for the transmission of his views. He may attempt to keep the whole of the discussion period focused upon the theme which he has introduced or selected and effectively impede the introduction of other themes and other aspects. He may direct his remarks to another member or to the leader and use the response he receives, whatever it may be, for a reaffirmation of his view point in a slightly different form, or as an opening which permits him to produce new examples. The topic he selects may be an interesting and important one, and the discussion group leader may feel tempted to respond to it if it seems relevant to the group and provides an opportunity for debate. Other members may tolerate or even enjoy this for a time, but eventually they will feel that they are being by-passed and excluded from the discussion.

This behaviour on the part of different individuals and of the group as a whole will have its explanations, and the leader needs to try and find these and consider every event as a communication with a number of different levels. But the leader may also need to have to hand a practical technique for dealing with it. This could simply be to allow such a member to have a second question or interjection as a supplementary to the original one, and then, at his third contribution, to say 'Let us leave this for the time being, we will return to it,' (and this promise must be kept) and then to say 'Can we have another example?' addressing the members of the group comprehensively. If this is done, it becomes the duty of the group leader at some stage to find some connecting links between the subsequent discussion and the first contribution.

Another situation that poses its own problems is the presence of a 'paranoid' member within the group, and indeed nearly every discussion group contrives to include in its midst someone who is ready to play this role, although the term 'paranoid' is not intended here in any clinical sense. Such a person is likely to find fault with every formulation, looking for alternative explanations, in one way or another, in the damaging effect of external forces upon individual behaviour. The difficulties under discussion may be attributed to society, to class influences, to economic conditions, or, in a more general way, to established authority. A favourite theme these days is racism, which can be brought forward as an explanation to prevent a situation from being explored in any other terms.

Such attitudes and opinions may lead to divisions in the group, drawing hostility from some members and support from others. This 'paranoid' member may even succeed in eliciting from the group as a whole compassionate attempts to make up for the deprivation so obviously suffered, and from the leader an attempt to provide a 'cure'. Alternatively, the leader may find herself becoming involved in a battle, and in an attempt to exclude or secure the withdrawal of the trouble maker, with supporters and opponents among the other members. One can hazard a guess, however, that if this member were to withdraw because of action taken by the leader alone another would be likely to succeed to the same place. Such behaviour must have additional meaning for the other members who permit it or who oppose it, and it may represent some aspect of their situation that they wish to have expressed in this way.

Apart from expressing this general aspect, such a member could be looked upon as valuable to the proceedings. The value lies in this member's ability to penetrate the falsity of many established views which might otherwise be accepted uncritically by other members and even by the leader, and the way in which he may be able to challenge the leader's statements and to prevent an easy and shallow acceptance of points which the leader puts forward. Such a person must therefore be listened to; and, as leader, one must be prepared to be surprised at the validity of some of this member's contributions and at the comparative inappropriateness of some of one's own.

If, as may happen, some of this member's contributions seem a little odd, it can be the task of the leader to add something to them and give them a structure that will relate to the general theme. Some of these contributions may be disturbing, and the leader will have to repair the situation by remarks which also add something to it. Essentially, these remarks begin with the word 'Yes', and not with 'Yes, but . . .' but with 'Yes and . . .' Thus they are used to demonstrate the possibility of a response to the unanticipated, and a readiness to find creativity in something presented in an unfamiliar way.

The procedure somewhat resembles Winnicott's (Winnicott 1971) use of the 'Squiggle' as a device for communication between two people. In this device, both parties take a piece of paper and produce a scribble (squiggle is a more expressive term), and then the papers are exchanged. It is up to the recipient of each paper to make something fresh out of the original drawing of the other, and skill and satisfaction are found in giving shape and meaning with the minimum addition. There is more than communication in this; it is the accepting of something which is apparently chaotic, and, in accepting it, the turning of it into a structure which has value as well as meaning. This is what a parent does when turning a child's first babbling sounds into words and a child's first tentative movements into purposive activity. It is also one of the functions of the teacher which goes beyond imparting given knowledge. In an incidental way it may be 'therapeutic', but it is still related to education more than to any other primary process. The message to be learned is the need to accept the first product as the basis for the final construction.

There is still the problem of the other members' position in this situation. They may openly express frustration, but it is likely that there will be some recognition of the fact that this awkward and argumentative member also speaks for them. The leader's tolerance (which need not be unbounded) is in the long run reassuring to the other members of the group. And perhaps they are glad that one member is prepared to stick his neck out and be the one to risk having his head cut off.

But it is important to bear in mind at all times that in dynamic group work the major means through which psychotherapy, counselling or discussion takes place should be the action of the group itself, and that in education too the group must not lose opportunities to solve its own problems, establish its own methods and make its own connections because of over-activity on the part of the leader.

In every group, the interventions of the leaders will be influenced not only by the particular disciplines to which they may belong but also by personal leadership styles, interests and experience and personal make-up. This influence cannot be considered an improper one for group leadership is not a mechanical skill; rather, it is a process in which the spontaneous use of the leader's personality plays an important part. There is much that can be learnt, a disciplined framework and a theoretical base are essential, but within this framework and upon this base each group leader develops a personal style of leadership and gives the group something no one else could give.

Conjoint family group work

One reason given for defining the boundaries of group psychotherapy as firmly as possible is the need to release the group processes and the concepts derived from group psychotherapy for disciplined use by workers in other areas, under appropriate labels which make it clear that it is not an attenuated form of group psychotherapy that is being attempted. Likewise many professional workers who do not call themselves family therapists but who work directly with families, or with individuals with families in mind, may be able to enrich their professional work through a knowledge of family group processes.

Work that is carried out with groups of family members derives its concepts from many sources and it can be said to contain something from each of the other three systems of group work.

Those who work with whole families often need to employ the comprehensive range of skills of the group therapists, including the ability to recognise and respond to unconscious processes at both interpersonal and transpersonal levels.

They also require the freedom of manoeuvre, and the ability to focus and limit their work within a comprehensive framework, which is more characteristic of the work of a group counsellor.

In addition, they may need the skills to handle sensitive themes at an abstract level, and this brings in group discussion. This has been described as an educational process with a personal application to all the participants, even though this is not always made explicit, and even though the communications may focus upon abstract and general topics. The power of the group work here depends upon the way it reaches these areas of unconscious as well as conscious personal concern of its members. Without in any way riding an idealogical hobby horse general questions may be asked of and by the family therapist and some generalities may be thrown into the discussion to be picked up and developed by different members of the group. Many problems of parenting are approached at this level, as are the problems of growing up and handling interpersonal relationships in family, school and peer group.

In addition, amongst our family groups are those who have moved from one culture to another, creating something greater than a generation gap between parents and children. It is difficult to explore the interpersonal problems which these families bring without some reference to the generalities of cultural adaptation. This is not in itself part of the therapeutic process but it cannot be completely excluded from it, even if its deployment is unobtrusive and incidental for most of the time.

Strategies compared

The ways in which the role of the leader in the different systems of groups work needs to be related to the purpose of the group is illustrated in the following example. It deals with a situation which must be familiar to all group workers.

Let us suppose that a new group assembles and that at the first few meetings a predominant feeling in the group is anxiety at being in a new and uncharted situation. Although they react in different ways, all the members share in this group tension and in the efforts that are made to deal with it. Typically, they turn to the group leader and put pressure on him (or her) to take a more active part and to give structure to the proceedings.

To group psychotherapists, this tension provides the very material with which they work. They will do nothing (or little) to lessen it in order to allow the group members to feel more comfortable. On the contrary, they will allow it to develop until it becomes expressed and resolved, or until it appears appropriate to make an interpretation or other intervention not primarily in order to lower the tension but rather to permit further development. Challenging experiences are necessary to psychotherapeutic progress, and members of such a group must be prepared to face some discomfort.

If a similiar tension were to develop in a counselling group, it would be dealt with in a different way. Here there is no sanction, in the bargain between leader and members, for the same level of discomfort; and outside a psychotherapeutic framework it would be likely to have a disruptive effect, perhaps even leading to the break-up of the group. In a counselling group there is not the same need to foster free communication and the unhampered growth of transference relationships, and so the leader has a wider choice of approaches and is free to play a more active part.

Group counsellors have to decide what to do in the light of the particular aim that has been defined for their group, and in the light of the needs of its members. There are situations in which it might be appropriate to accede to the wishes of the group for the time being, and to play the more active part that the members are asking for.

For example, in a counselling group of ex-mental hospital patients, a common problem for all the members might be difficulty in leaving the ordered regime of a paternalistic institution. Stress in the group will involve stress on individual members; and such members may, temporarily or permanently, have both a limited capacity to tolerate stress and a need to form a dependent relationship with the group leader during the period of transition. The behaviour of the leader would need to be adjusted to meet the needs of such a group. Alternatively or in addition to making direct use of the relationship to help the group, the leader might decide to make an interpretation or draw a comparison. This could be done through a comment on what is taking place in the group, linking it to the problem which provides the group's focus, in this instance the problems of adjustment to life outside the hospital. The relationships that are finding expression within the present group could be compared by the leader with the new relationships that individual members have yet to make outside the hospital.

In group discussion the leader would have to handle the tension in relation to some aspect of the group's topic and task, using it if possible to clarify and stimulate but avoiding such a degree of stress as would expose the inadequacies of the most vulnerable. Such a situation would be very relevant to the particular theme of groups concerned with discussing problems related to dependency. This could be dependency in relationships betweeen parents and children, between marriage partners, between teachers and students, or between professional workers and their patients or clients. In workshops for staff of residential homes, for example, any (controlled) tension allowed to build up in the here and now situation of the group could be used as part of an exploration of the feelings experienced in entering a new situation, and thus could be linked, via any here and now discomfort at the unfamiliar, to the situation of elderly people giving up their own homes. It might, in fact, be an advantage to such groups to be able to experience, and then discuss, a situation in which dependency is both sought and denied.

Although in group discussion less stress on individuals is sanctioned, the capacity of the group and of individual members to tolerate new and experimental situations may be greater. But this cannot be assumed and the leader needs to assess this and to reassess it as time goes on. While the behaviour of the group as a whole may be used by the leader to illustrate the theme, no direct attention will be drawn by the leader to individual personal problems that may be revealed in the course of the exercise.

Yet, while stressing the differences in the different forms of group work being discussed, it has to be acknowledged that all these processes are utilised by people seeking help of some kind or another. The word *help* like the word *change* contains the blessing of vagueness which does not always call for a definition. Yet an attempt at some precision has to be made. This is particularly important when dealing with therapy because here the words imply a specific engagement with a person chosen for a particular range of skill and experience. But in all situations the words *change* and *help* have therapeutic overtones. If a group member's well-being increases while taking part in a group not designated as a therapeutic group, so much the better for that member and for the group process.

Responsibilities

So each of the three leaders in the three different group systems may be confronted with a very similar situation in the group. Each will be required to respond to this situation in some way. In their responses, all three leaders use an understanding of the dynamic processes which take place in all groups, and all three look beyond the individual members to the group as a whole; but each one handles a comparable situation in a different way because each relates the response to the aims of the group and each gives regard to what has been sanctioned.

Members may join a group with ideas about its purposes and processes that are distorted, inaccurate, and incomplete; the responsibility is not theirs. The responsibility belongs to the leader, and it is his (or her) ideas which must be clear.

The leader's perception of the group is all important, and determines much of what will follow. The dangers of a blurring of boundaries and consequent confusion as to what is, or should be, taking place in a group are very real.

In all these groups, the actual proceedings of the group, and the group processes taking place, form a principal vehicle through which the purposes of the group are achieved. In each group the leader is required to recognise, understand, and in some way influence, these proceedings and processes, without unnecessarily distorting or hindering their natural development. It is, however, impossible to say that any one technique belongs exclusively to one particular system and has no place in another. We cannot say, for example, that interpretation is a technique of group psychotherapy, and that direct intervention to divert the course of the proceedings of the group from a particular path can only be considered in group discussion. This very lack of explicit technical demarcation highlights once again the importance of a clear conceptual basis in every instance rooted in an understanding of aims and limits.

A group leader, in every kind of group, has responsibility for seeing that the group exists as a group and does not remain for long at the stage of being a mere conglomeration of separate individuals centred on the leader or of being a collection of sub-groups. The foremost duty is to help the group to function. Every leader has to lead, and even in a psychotherapeutic group with unrestricted verbal interchanges, the conductor still has to impose some limitations upon what takes place. The leader always occupies a very particular and important role. Even though members and leader are arranged in a circle, the point on the circumference where the leader sits becomes a special position.

Remembering this special role, there are certain types of behaviour that every group leader needs to avoid so that the spontaneous development of the group is not distorted. The leader must make communications to the group in such a way that these communications are not addressed with any particularity; rather, they are thrown into the middle of the group so that any member may be allowed to pick them up. When questioned the leader must answer, but should answer *incompletely* in order to leave room for further comments on the same topic. A complete answer from the leader silences the group.

In all these groups, periods of silence are likely to occur. They should be permitted but not insisted on. The leader will not be in a hurry to break a silence, nor permit it to continue so long that it arouses a level of anxiety that is inappropriate to the circumstances of that particular group. The leader will need to try to understand the meaning of silence. There are hostile silences, thoughtful silences, and those silences that are a consummation. A hostile silence may need an interpretation to permit the group to proceed. A thoughtful silence may need an interruption, since the members may feel, as the length of the silence increases, that the next contribution that breaks the silence must be at a correspondingly meaningful level. The silence which is a consummation may need to continue until the group feels itself ready for a fresh experience.

Questions

Communications from the group leader are likely to take the form of questions rather than statements. Questions open doors in situations where statements would only close them Questions will be used to point out certain links and make certain connections, although in different groups the links and connections will be different ones.

The approach to the group as a whole means that the questions are likely to be phrased in such a way that any personal attribution is minimised. For example, the question is not 'How do you feel?', but 'How does one feel in this sort of situation?'; it is not 'How did you deal with it?' but 'How have different people dealt with it?', or 'Does it make sense to do this or to do that?', 'Is there another problem that is similar?', or 'Is there a different problem?' These may perhaps be the questions that would be most likely to be asked by a group counsellor, but they illustrate the generality that belongs to all groups.

The group discussion leader will ask *'What else?'* Focusing upon the group topic, his question will be 'In what other context... related to what other themes ... for what other purposes?' The group counsellor will ask *'How else?'* or *'Who else?'* 'How else do you think such a situation may be handled and with what result ...how might this seem to other people?' The question *'Who else ...?'* can be used to bring other participants into the discussion and to illustrate the universality of a problem. The question *'When else...?'* can be used to elicit the connections of any event with similar examples in the history of individual members. The characteristic question of the group psychotherapist, with the least direct focus but the greatest particularity, is *'How come?'* This question can lead directly to the unconscious processes.

CHAPTER 12

The Individual in the Group Context

A case

This case, which comes from a social worker employed by a local authority, cannot be described in any way as a success; rather, it is one of the cases that leaves one dissatisfied so that one continues to ask questions and search for alternatives.

Miss Winifred C., recently discharged from a mental hospital, was in her mid-forties, a short stocky woman with frizzy grey hair wearing wrinkled stockings and a dirty cardigan which incongruously gave her the air of an unkempt school girl. When first seen by the social worker, she was sitting on the edge of her chair in the waiting room, ready and eager to jump up when summoned, her expression anxious and expectant.

In this and subsequent interviews, her life history unfolded. A diabetic from childhood, she had never had a job and was still living alone in the little terraced house which had been her home for the whole of her life. Her father had been a tailor, hard working and respectable with quiet, retiring domestic habits; and she would proudly display to visitors his great tailor's shears, still kept with tender care. They had been a close united family; her parents were 'the most wonderful parents in the world' and they gave her (their only child) 'everything.' Whenever she wanted anything, she said, she only had to cry and they would provide it. They were particularly indulgent after she developed the diabetes (a family illness) at the age of eleven.

She recalled how her parents were always home to welcome her when she returned from school. Then incongruously, she set this against another vivid memory. She remembered coming up the little garden path to the front door, which opened directly into their living room, wondering as she came whether they would be in or not, and starting to snivel as she peered through the letter box in case they had gone out and left the door key hanging on a string.

She left school at fifteen, her poor progress compounded by many absences, and no employment was ever considered for her; she was too delicate, she needed looking after, and there was enough money for her keep. Besides, she was needed at home. She gave her mother some help in the house, kept to a high standard with the brass gleaming and the kitchen range blackleaded. There were shopping expeditions, an annual holiday to Southend, and infrequent visits to friends and neighbours. The visits were few because 'we didn't need friends, we had each other'.

And so her girlhood and young womanhood passed away, with apparently little change in her manner of living, until she reached the age of forty. Then, in the same year, her father died of 'stomach trouble' long taken for granted, and her mother, also diabetic, 'just wasted away' and died a few months later. Miss Winefred C. always wept when she came to speak of her parents' deaths. At times she would say, in a burst of anger, 'How could they leave me . . . I never thought they would do this to me . . . that they would both go away and leave me like this.'

She went on living in the little house, drawing regular small amounts from her parents' savings. It did occur to her occasionally that the sum was diminishing and that when it was gone there would be nothing left, and at times she felt both angry and afraid. The house, which her father had kept in good repair himself, began to deteriorate. The roof started to leak, the plaster fell from her bedroom ceiling. She shut the door on that bedroom, (it had been her parents') and moved herself back into the smaller bedroom that had been hers before.

A relative visited once or twice and then stopped coming. She didn't know why. There were neighbours who were quite well disposed at first, and she would borrow milk and a spoonful of tea when she didn't want to go to the shops, and would call to them over the fence. But then they stopped being friendly, and no longer opened the door when she knocked.

As frustration and loneliness grew, she began to cry and then to bang on the walls and howl. The neighbours reappeared, and then a doctor and a social worker came. She agreed to go into hospital for a time 'for her nerves'. She liked the hospital. But now she was home again with a bottle of tablets, a distant appointment at the outpatients' clinic, and a new social worker.

The social worker assigned to Miss Winifred C. ('You can call me Winnie if you like' was the first thing said) found herself quickly caught up in a situation in which it seemed that only regular visits and sustained personal interest could defer a recurrence of the disturbed behaviour. Attempts to bring changes in her circumstances met with very qualified success, and only uncovered her paramount need to be coaxed and cajoled, to accept suggestions and then to be able to change her mind so that the process of explanation and discussion would begin all over again.

In all the group situations in which the social worker was able to observe Winnie, in social club, welfare centre, holiday home and hospital ward, she appeared happy whenever she could find for herself a position as a specially favoured dependent. She strove to create for herself an interpersonal network in which this need could be met, manipulating the other members to provide the responses she wanted. Her aim was to be treated as the one good child, the focus of parental approval: when this aim conflicted with the needs of other members, or of the group as a whole, she changed from being the good child to being the defiant and destructive one. Always she was very alert to the effect that her behaviour was having upon others.

At the holiday home to which the local authority sent her for a week, she was the youngest woman in the group and the only unmarried one, and afterwards she asked when she would be able to go there again. In the general hospital ward, to which she was admitted for stabilisation of her diabetes, she was the only ambulant patient, able to take round cups of tea to those in bed at the request of a motherly and responsive ward sister. In other group situations, where such a role was not available to her, or where she met with competition, she became provocative and demanding. In a busy day centre, where some of the clients were more visibly disabled than she was, her behaviour was like that of a wilful and jealous child bent upon attracting attention and annoying the grown-ups.

Her second admission to the mental hospital, again preceded by an episode of disturbed behaviour at home, occurred when the social worker was away on holiday. This time Winnie was moved from the admission ward, which she had liked before, to a back ward of chronic patients. Here she received the social worker tearfully and reproachfully, begging to be 'rescued'. But when her discharge was arranged, she appeared to change her mind and had to be coaxed and persuaded to leave the hospital.

After some experience of Winnie's demands, of vacillating mood changes from ingratiating and compliant to wilful and obstinate, the social worker began to see her as a child who was addressing her communications not to one parent figure but to two. The inconsistencies and shifts in position, the capriciousness in her relationship with the social worker, became easier to understand as behaviour directed towards two people whose relationship with each other had come to be dominated by her. She was like a child who says something to cause dissension between her parents and then sits back gleefully to watch their reaction. This was the situation she was still trying to create, but now she was in a relationship with one person, not two. The social worker, attempting to establish a consistent and reliable relationship in which the two of them could work together on some of the problems, found that all her resources were needed to preserve the casework relationship against Winnie's manipulations. Later on, she came to perceive these manipulations as attempts to split her in two and 'triangulate' their relationship.

When she came to make a final report on the case, the social worker wrote as follows:

> The work I have been attempting to do wth this patient reminds me more than anything else of child guidance. By this I mean that the problem is essentially that of the relationship of a child and her parents. The patient is a girl born to a united and self-sufficient couple who did not have enough space in their relationship to include a child. She is extremely dependent upon her parents but has little confidence in their will or capacity to give her what she wants. She only feels safe when she is in a dominant position and able to control and manipulate them, and divide them from one another in order to make room for herself. She dare not leave them, lest she should find no place for herself when she returns. Neither side can free themselves from this circular situation in which the parents' resentment at their bondage increases the daughter's mistrust, and hence her need to continue to manipulate them through her dependency. In such a case, treating the child on her own is not likely to be successful. The parents and the child need to be brought together and the family unit treated as a whole. But in this case the parents have been dead for some years. The disturbed family network persists and is being transferred into other relationships, but the child guidance formulation is being made forty years too late.

Discussion

If we can go back in our minds to the period when Winnie was a young child, and attempt to reconstruct what was happening at that time, we can envisage a family situation that could have led to a referral for child guidance or family therapy. The reasons for referral might have included school refusal, or sleep disturbance, or psychosomatic symptoms accompanying chronic ill health, depending upon the way in which the family shaped the problem and the way in which the helping agencies responded to the shaping. And at that time, it would have been in the late 1940s, some form of individual treatment would probably have been offered for the child and perhaps for the mother too.

Individual treatment might have had limited success at best. It requires a degree of separateness, a recognition of the individual boundaries marking the subsystems in the family system as a whole, that did not exist here. This lack of differentiation weakened the parts and the whole. Within a vicious circle, the weak family system was unable to provide a firm framework within which a child could feel safe and could go through the process of internalising, projecting and re-internalising, in the interests of growth and development. In the absence of this type of progress, a child may remain tied forever to the original family network.

Needing extra support and confirmation, this family had to rely for their sense of identity on the old-fashioned virtues which prevented them from sharing and enjoying the changing lifestyles of their neighbours. This increased their tendency to turn inwards and to cut themselves off from the community. The undoubted qualities which gave them a feeling of worth only increased their tendency to separate themselves from a deteriorating outer world, and left Winnie, the survivor, with insufficient resources to sustain her. And in the outside world were located it seems, and by family consensus, the shapeless fears which turned the home into a much needed retreat from the dangers that might be encountered elsewhere.

Had it been possible at that time to see this family together, the therapist might well have chosen to focus upon the family communications, including the ambivalent messages and double binds which were a feature of the relationship between Winnie and her parents. This faulty communication pattern was a necessary consequence of the absence of appropriate boundaries to their separate personalities. Clarity of speech might have forced open acknowledgement of the hostile component and of the anger contained in the ambivalence.

Although Winnie was never observed within the family group, she was seen in other group situations. She was seen entering existing groups, bringing with her, and transferring into these new situations, needs and expectations derived from her experiences in the group situations of the past. These new groups tried to make room for her, making some adjustment to their proceedings in order to accomodate her, and partially meeting and partially failing to meet her needs. When she did not get what she wanted she responded vigorously, falling once more into the role of demanding and manipulating child, addressing the internalised parental figures. It seems that she never gave up hope of obtaining what she wanted.

The social worker felt impotent, as indeed Winnie's parents may have felt impotent. It seemed to her that the frustrating and circular nature of their relationship was the source of much gratification to Winnie. What else might have been done?

Had group therapy been available, with a proxy groups of strangers able to represent both the internalised network of the past and its counterpart in the present, it might have been possible to provide a second opportunity to pass through the experiences that her family of origin provided and failed to provide. Had she wished for and been able to make use of such an opportunity, she would have been likely to find her habitual responses challenged and alternative responses offered which could superimpose new experiences upon the experiences of the past. She might have been able to separate out the component parts, test the reality of her expectations and her fears, and learn to relate to others in a different way.

Alternatively, a counselling group, with its restricted aim and focus, in which the idea of support would be more prominent and the sharing more specific, might have been more acceptable and appropriate.

Some group opportunities in fact were provided for her, or came her way incidentally. Though not designated therapy, they might have been some help by providing surrogate family situations, modifying rather than reinforcing the internalised representations of the past. Some very limited changes did in fact take place, none of which proved to be lasting. It seems that the opportunities were insufficient and came too late.

CHAPTER 13

Professional Choices

- When an individual comes for help, how does the professional worker respond?
- What are the choices that are available?

The need to shape

It is still the case that most clients come singly, most problems are initially presented by individuals, and most distress first comes to notice as individual distress (even though it may well contain complaints about another family member, or about a service or institution.) So the starting point is still usually an individual, and the individual has to remain an ever-present preoccupation.

What are the tasks of the professional helper in surgery, consulting room, clinic or social service department? One of the first professional tasks is to find a shape for the distress.

A client or patient who approaches a professional person or agency for help will already have given the problem some preliminary shape, however indeterminate. Very often the first professional task is to recognise the proffered shape, to search behind it for the original unshaped distress, and then to reshape the problem so that it can fit within the professional framework available.

This process of shaping and reshaping distress can be considered through the activity of the distressed person, through the activity of the helping professional, and through the activity that the two of them are carrying out together. It takes place in the context of all the assumptions that are made about the nature of mental activity and about the relationship between man and society. It is made within the social and cultural framework of the day which may permit some shapes and provide no room for others, Yesterday's permitted shapes may seem as old fashioned as yesterday's hats.

It can also be related to the range of help which is currently available and much of the reshaping of the distress is likely to take place so that the helping person can respond effectively within the resources available. It could be that the distress will in time come to be shaped and reshaped and shaped again as part of that complex series of transactions between the parties concerned that has become known as the helping process

This process of shaping and reshaping distress is fundamental to a consideration of the work of the helping professions. It is also fundamental to the main theme of this work, that is, *the understanding and use of the range of contexts in which human activity can be located.*

The client shapes

'It's my leg, doctor,' says the patient in the GP's surgery, and an injured leg may leave little choice.

But there are other situations where an inevitable shape does not present itself, and where there is no clear pathway leading from the distress to the shape, and from the shape to a helping person. Sometimes the distress which is presented in one form could have been presented in many others.

An overburdened mother, with many children and few resources either material or psychological, may look for relief in a number of different ways. She may go to the doctor, to the health visitor, the head teacher, the housing department or the priest. She may blame her troubles upon her husband, the hostile neighbours, the unhelpful teachers, her poor housing conditions, her legs, her back, her nerves, her children's health. Somewhere in this confusion, she may find a shape which offers a course of action, the route to a helping person, a possible remedy and a future hope.

So the helping professionals, in office or surgery, are presented with distress which has already received some shaping for their acceptance. A number of different factors will have influenced the shape which the distress has acquired by this stage. The range of helpers known to one particular individual may be limited. One well-worn path to a particular agency's door may suggest itself, and may determine whether the distress takes the form of a problem of physical or mental illness, housing, child-rearing or education. Our overburdened mother may have had help in the past from a responsive headteacher, or from a health visitor, or from the chemist in the corner shop, and so her current difficulties may cast themselves into a pattern that will enable her to go to the same resource again

The professional worker reshapes

Once the person's distress reaches the office, consulting room, surgery or chambers, another set of factors is brought to bear upon the problem; there are two different parties to the process now, and together they have to set to work on reshaping the problem so as to find an area relevant to them both on which they can work together. Some agreement or contract has to be made.

The helping person does not stand alone. He, or she, is the representative of a particular profession, and probably also of a particular service or agency which operates within defined terms of reference.

It is the helpers' job to bring to the problem their professional training and any resources which are available, augmented by personal skills, perceptions and inclinations, and augmented, too, by concepts added through additional training or through borrowing from other disciplines. Professional helpers have to pick up the problems that are presented, distinguishing the distress from the subsequent shaping, identifying the people and areas involved. They have to look for things which can be treated and areas which are suitable for intervention, and they may have to consider transposing problems into different areas, adding to what is presented or subtracting from it. Some reshaping is, indeed, inherent in all professional functioning.

Inward and outward looking professions

There are many helping professions at work today whose job is to respond to distress that will have been given some sort of shape in order to be presented to them. Some professions offer a particular and specific method of treatment and only take on patients or clients who are suitable for that treatment. There are other professions which take on particular problems or particular client groups and have to find appropriate treatments for them all within their existing repertoire.

Marital therapists, for example, are likely to have a primary commitment to both a particular treatment approach and to a small and selected group of people in distress who are able and willing to benefit by that method. Their responsibility is limited in range (though not in depth) and does not extend to distress at large.

Generic social workers have a more general orientation. They may indeed have their specialist and preferred areas and their statutory responsibilities, but their primary commitment is not to one particular method but to a range of problems or forms of distress.

We can look at these two groups as the *inward-looking* and the *outward-looking* disciplines. The inward-lookers, for example the neuro-surgeons or the traditional psychoanalysts, have been accustomed to keeping themselves separate and exclusive, seeking to deepen and refine their skills rather than to extend their range. They maintain their boundaries and mix mainly with their own colleagues, reading the same journals and learning from one another.

The outward-lookers, on the other hand, have been concerned to extend the range of their treatment methods, and to provide more choice, more variability and more flexibility, in the skills they have to offer. They are more likely to look beyond their professions and to try to learn from others.

Both inward and outward-looking professionals have the task, at the first encounter, of responding to the distress as it has been shaped by the client. They have to hold in mind the different options that come from the client and those that they themselves can provide, and they have to try to find a fit and make a bargain about the treatment.

In this encounter the inward-lookers often offer a clear shape of proven effectiveness in which they are likely to have total and justified confidence. But the firmer the shape, the more limited is its application likely to be. There is always room for the outward-looking professionals with their search for new shapes to apply to the problems before them. And the more options that the helping professionals have in their repertoire, the more options are likely to be discovered within the contributions of the clients, and the greater will be the flexibility that can be brought to the reshaping process.

The power of individual professional workers to reshape distress may be considerable or it may be very limited. Their professional training and their terms of service within the context of their clinic or agency gives them their primary authorisation. In some clinics, such as those providing psychoanalytic treatment, the staff have the task of deciding whether a particular person will, or will not, profit from the treatment they are able to provide, and any redefinition of the distress will be done to include it or exclude it from their terms of reference. Social services, or more eclectic psychiatric services, may have less power to exclude, and be under more pressure to provide some sort help and have a wide repertoire available. The approaches vary from finding suitable cases for treatment to finding suitable treatments for cases.

Apart from the requirements and limitations of their agencies and services, and the frameworks of their specialist trainings, professional workers bring to this task of reshaping their own personal talents and inclinations and the sum of their personal and professional experience. They also bring all the extensions and developments of their original training, and the concepts and models which they have created for themselves within their own professions or have borrowed from other disciplines and made their own. They will have a range of different shapes at their disposal, and an understanding of some of the different shapes which are at the disposal of colleagues in other disciplines. They will have the capacity to collaborate with these colleagues, and this will help them to place the problems in a wider context than that of their own particular specialisation.

The search for a fit

So the search for a fit among the shapes on offer goes on, and there are times when an agreement cannot be reached. Sometimes the person in distress has come to the wrong door, or has brought an inappropriately shaped problem. Sometimes the gap between the conceptions of the person seeking help and the conceptions of the helper are too great to be bridged. Sometimes the helper tries to reshape the problem in a way that is unacceptable to the other party.

Example

An extreme example can be found in the case of young man of nineteen suffering distress about the size of his nose. He wished to have plastic surgery, and accepted referral to a psychiatrist hoping for a recommendation which would enable him to have the operation performed free of charge under the National Health Service. The problem had been placed by others, but not by the patient, in a psychiatric framework; though the psychiatric framework, in this case, was proposed as a means to an end.

The psychiatrist did not accept the assignment in these terms. He interpreted the patient's complaint about the shape of his nose as a sympton of a psycho-sexual problem, and made an offer of psychotherapy in lieu of surgery, an offer that was indignantly refused. The interpretation may have been valid, but in the circumstances it did not lead to effective action because the patient and the psychiatrist had each started with preconceptions from which neither was prepared to budge. The young man had settled his distress into the shape of his nose, and the psychiatrist was determined, with some theoretical justification, to find the location of the problem in another area of the body. There was rigidity on both sides, and a refusal to reshape together in order to look for a meeting ground. Too few alternative shapes were made available or found to be acceptable.

In other cases, where psychiatrist and patient have a more viable area of negotiation, they may together be able to shape the miseries into some sort of agreed pattern so that the two of them can work together, perhaps even finding a pattern which can be matched with the descriptions of an illness in psychiatric textbooks. For traditional psychiatric diagnosis can be considered as a process of shaping and selective matching in which the imperfect approximations of the patients have to be measured against the model or 'ideal' illness of the textbook.

In the example given above, the psychiatrist wanted to reshape the problem while keeping it within individual psychopathology. Other professional workers respond in their different ways. Some may try to narrow the area that is presented, calling their patient or client back to the point, wishing to concentrate more upon one specific aspect they recognise as relevant to their own particular framework and to the model that they are carrying in mind. It may be the bad cough, the child's failure to learn or the need for supplementary benefit. 'I tried to tell them all about it,' the client may say afterwards, 'but they didn't seem interested. They only wanted to talk about Billy not being in school.' The mother of a child about to be taken into care complained, 'They only seemed interested in the baby.' Granted that the baby was indeed the primary concern, she still felt that some thoughts should have been spared for her, as yet unexplored, personal distress.

In other cases attempts to widen the area of discussion may be equally unwelcome to the clients. Unsupported mothers, seeing their problems as economic rather than psychological or even social, can be indignant when a social worker enquires into their personal relationships and offers casework help in addition, or even instead of, the practical support which they are seeking. Social workers, no less than psychiatrists, have their framework in which financial difficulties seldom stand alone and are often taken as symptoms of a wider maladjustment which needs exploration – a 'cry for help' that the crier may not wish to acknowledge.

Though one person comes, or is brought, the problem is unlikely to be confined to the one person. Indirectly or directly others are involved. The presence of a network, which may remain undisclosed, always has to be taken into account.

Some alternative shapes: a hypothetical encounter

To illustrate the process of shaping and reshaping in the transactions between client and helper, we can return to the general practitioner's surgery where the doctor and the man complaining about his leg are working together to define the area of their joint concern.

1. 'It's my leg, doctor.'

With this statement, the problem is defined by the patient as the problem of part of a person. If he stops at this point, and if the doctor accepts this definition and also stops here, the doctor would presumably limit his area of concern to the leg. The patient then might only expect to take off the one sock.

A number of situations occur in which it seems appropriate and sufficient to remain at this level. The dentist pulls out the bad tooth and the medical practitioner excises the wart or straps up the sprained ankle. This is similiar to the situation in which one leaves one's watch with the watch mender or one's pans with the tinker, treating all other aspects of one's life as irrelevant to the problem presented. The person seeking help defines the problem and decides which areas to hand over for expert attention.

This level of working is not much favoured among the helping professions. Since there is always likely to be more to a problem than the fragment that is presented, it can be argued that additional areas should at least be sought out and examined.

Conversely, it can also be argued that this level is very often sufficient and that wherever possible the helping person should remain at this level without seeking any authorisation to take the enquiries further. Different levels of work are appropriate in different circumstances: the optimum level being that which achieves a 'good enough' result with the minimum of disturbance. The problem for the helper is to distinguish such cases from the others where it is proper and necessary to make enquiries that extend beyond the presenting facts.

Irving Goffman (1961) described work at this level as belonging to the 'tinkering trades', comparing it with the work of the tinker repairing a broken pan. In tinkering trade transactions the tinker deals with a disordered possession brought by the client, with an implicit bargain that he should maintain a disciplined unconcern towards the client's other affairs and even towards the reasons which brought the request for the service in the first place.

Applied to the helping professions, work of the tinkering kind requires closed and discernible physical symptoms, allowing a distinction to be drawn between the client and the client's malfunctioning object.

It was Goffman's contention that the profession of medicine had attempted to pattern itself upon the tinkering model, resulting in some strange and inappropriate practices. Patients may find themselves being treated as if they were possessions handed in for repair. And, becoming possessions, they may find that the role of client or customer has been taken away from them and transferred to others. A relative may be pressed into service as the customer who brings a malfunctioning object for attention, to be given information about the patient, to consult with the experts, and to be involved in decisions about the treatment.

If our doctor accepts the leg as the object to be tinkered with, it may be because he has an image of himself as an expert repairer of defective objects. Or it may be that he is aware of other possibilities, but judges that this level is all that is available to him, or all that is needed in this instance. Or he may feel that the other levels are not of medical concern and should be attended to by members of other disciplines.

However, either doctor or patient may be dissatisfied with intervention at this level alone. It may not be easy to stop at the knee. The patient may wish to continue and the doctor may (or may not) permit him to do so. The doctor may wish to explore further and the patient may (or may not) respond to his continued interest. Should they agree to continue, they could pass together to position 2.

2. 'It's my leg, doctor. *But I don't feel well in myself.*'

Now the leg is no longer a defective object to be tinkered with on its own, but has been related by the patient to the rest of his person.

This is the level at which the watch mender might feel able to extend his interest beyond the watch to the owner, feeling that the information given by the watch alone is incomplete, and ask 'Have you ever dropped it?' And the garage mechanic might turn from the car to the driver and ask 'Do you drive with your foot resting on the clutch pedal?' A doctor or social worker might turn from the symptom or situation presented to ask 'And how do you feel about it yourself?'

The professional worker is assuming authority to reshape the problem in a wider context and enter into other aspects.

3. 'It's my leg, doctor. But I don't feel well in myself. *My wife isn't being much help to me either.*'

Now the problem is no longer bounded by the person of one individual, but has been widened to include a relationship with someone else.

There are two main possibilities at this level. The patient has disclosed his wife's involvement in the problem, but he still keeps the problem as his possession; his wife is being no help to *him*. The doctor, while accepting this extension, can still remain focused upon the one patient, with the wife a factor in the patient's environment which may have to be modified in the patient's interests. To this end, he might advise the patient how to behave towards his wife, or he might seek to talk to the wife in an attempt to explore her attitudes and feelings.

But there is another possibility. The doctor could redefine the boundaries of the problem so that it is becomes a joint possession of the husband and wife with the focus now upon the relationship between them. We move from the level of concern confined to the inner and outer life of a single person to the interpersonal level where it is the interaction between two people which is important. This is a level in which many family doctors now take an interest, although it may be even more familiar to marital counsellors.

The doctor might say: 'Next time you come to see me, would you ask your wife to come along too. I would like to talk to the two of you together about this.'

4. 'It's my leg, doctor. But I don't feel well in myself. My wife isn't being much help to me either, *but it's not just that … The children seem to have got out of control since I had this bad leg.*'

This new situation can bring a move from an interpersonal to a transpersonal level, from the dyad to the group. When we are focusing selectively upon the relationship between two people, we are likely to have in mind a closed, two-way interactional system in which an action performed by A has an effect upon B, and B's reaction comes back to have an effect upon A in its turn. But with the introduction of the children we move into a wider arena, and have to have in mind a model of a much more complex pattern of relationships; we are now confronted by the family process itself. A watch mender would be unlikely to try to enter this area, although one might conceive of him asking 'Do your children ever play with the watch?' if he thought the problem being presented could not be understood without an extension into this area. At one level a problem can be considered to belong to a single individual: at another level the same problem needs to be related to the family as a whole.

Example

An anecdote can be used to illustrate this. The patient was a man with bowel symptoms who had had extensive and repeated examinations, all negative, and all, it appeared, carried out in the spirit of the tinkering trade. Only after all these procedures had failed to help was he sent to a psychiatrist in order that the disorder might be related to the whole person. But the psychiatrist wanted to go a step further. After listening to the patient's description of his symptoms and the way they troubled him, the psychiatrist put the following question. 'I know that these symptoms are painful, and that you are in constant discomfort. But sometimes symptoms like these do serve a useful purpose in the life of a person all the same. Can you think of any way in which these symptoms have done any good?' The answer came back without hesitation. 'No good at all. Quite the contrary. And they have been very upsetting to my mother, my sister, and my wife.' It needed very little more acquaintance with the family history to realise that the upsetting of his female relatives was a consummation devoutly to be wished. This patient continued to retain his symptoms.

An awareness of family interaction, and a readiness to enter into this area, can be used in different ways. Some workers might continue to focus upon their primary patient while questioning what meaning the presenting problem might have for other family members and how the patient perceived this. Others, faced with a problem which had become identified as family property, might try to separate out the component parts. This might involve dealing with the different individuals in turn in their special roles as parent, wife, husband, child and sibling, against a background in which all the other relationships have their place. The problem is defined as one of family life, but the work remains focused on separate individuals.

A third method would be the family therapy approach that takes the family as a whole and treats it as if it were a single entity subject to its own group processes which include but transcend the activities of any individual member.

But this may not be enough. A family is a group with a history and a context. In addition to concepts of the family as an entity, the worker will need to have conceptions of a family life cycle and of family growth and development in which different patterns can be recognised.

Our doctor still has a primary patient with a leg condition. His role is not that of a family therapist *per se.* But, nevertheless, he can make his interventions with an awareness of the family dynamics as a whole and of the part which he himself may now be playing within them. He has himself been brought into the family network.

5. 'It's my leg, doctor. But I don't feel well in myself. My wife is not much help to me either, but it's not just that. The children seem to have got out of control since

I've had this bad leg. *A very rough type of person is moving into our street now, and I'm worried that its having a bad effect on our boys.'*

The boundaries of the problem are extended yet again. We pass beyond the family to its social context and find relevance in the relationships between the family and the society of which it forms a part. In order to understand this relationship, there are certain new questions which need to be discussed. What are the boundaries of the family? How are these boundaries maintained? How does the interaction between the family and the surrounding society take place? How does the family see itself in comparison with other families? What are the crucial differences which help to give this family its sense of identity? Some workers may wish to study the social context in order to understand the family better. Some workers may attempt to intervene at the interface betweeen the family on the one hand and the community, street or neighbourhood on the other. Some may even, within the terms of their job descriptions, feel called upon to consider a whole community as their client and try to help this community to work towards a solution of its problems.

Most workers in most situations would not feel that they had the authority to turn neighbouring families into clients or patients (even as parts of a greater whole) but there are group and family psychotherapists and community social workers who have felt able to do this. There have been well documented cases in which psychotherapists have formed whole neighbourhood networks into treatment units, intervening in the first instance in the interests of one disordered family and then locating the pathology in a social network or 'tribe' and bringing upwards of forty persons together in one therapeutic enterprise. Speck and Rueveni (1970) in the United States can be taken as early examples of this method of working. They have described network therapy (or sometimes tribe therapy), defining a social network as that group of persons who maintain an ongoing significance in each other's lives by fulfilling specific human needs. Starting with a particular patient diagnosed as schizophrenic, they take the whole family as their unit of concern and then go further. They try to assemble all members of the kinship system, all friends of the family, the neighbours, and where possible, friends and neighbours' kin. Typically, they claim to be able to assemble at least forty persons in the house of the focal family for a series of lengthy meetings with a therapeutic team. Introductions to the friends, relatives and neighbours are provided by the focal family, who thus do the preliminary selection. And of course, out of this list, those who then accept the invitation and turn up for the therapy must constitute a particular and self-selected sub-group.

Behind this approach is the hypothesis that pathology, and in particular, schizophrenia, involves higher social levels than the nuclear family alone and is equally present in the kinship system and in the neighbourhood and social group. Speck and Rueveni described the pathology as a failure in communication, with 'mad modes' of communication being maintained in the entire social network round the labelled 'schizophrenic' family, this social network being the mediator between the madness in the culture, where this particular disturbance originated, and the madness in the particular family which had become identified and labelled. Their goal was to increase the communication within the social network, and in particular between individual members of the schizophrenic family and their kin, friends and neighbours.

For a precedent they looked back to prehistory, when tribal assemblies were gathered together in crisis situations, and to the tribal meetings for healing purposes that take place in different cultures. By convening the social network of the 'schizophrenic family' they were trying to bring into the open a concealed network, in the hope of being able to make the group as intimately involved as possible in each others' lives and so supply a strong sense of tribal support, reassurance and solidarity.

6. 'It's my leg, doctor, But I don't feel well in myself. My wife isn't being much help to me either, but it's not just that. The children seem to have got out of control since I've had this bad leg. A very rough type of person is moving into our street now, and I'm worried that it's having a bad effect on our boys. *I've been up to the Town Hall about it, but they don't seem very interested in our case.*'

This last level is that of the more formal social and political structure in which the family carries on its existence, including the helping agencies and those agencies which the family sees as withholding help.

The staff of these agencies may be treated as colleagues or auxiliary workers, to be approached, co-opted or manipulated in the interest of the patient. They may be seen as an integral part of the problem, to be included in any treatment plan. The boundaries of the problem may have to be redrawn to include housing department personnel, if a family has a claim to be rehoused or if it has difficulty in paying the rent. A school may have to be included if the problem involves the failure of a child to learn, his fear of his teachers or his disruptive behaviour in the class room. Our doctor might wish to influence what is happening in housing department or school, he might know who to approach at the Town Hall, or might feel he should help his patient to present his appeal more effectively. Or he might well feel that none of this is of direct medical concern and put aside this aspect of the patient's problems.

Or, alternatively, the doctor might be working as a member of a team with social workers and health visitors and thus be able to intervene therapeutically within a wider field, and include more dimensions of a problem, than would be possible were a single discipline working on its own.

There are other aspects to problems which have been left out in the interests of a tidy formulation that has moved by stages from the part person via the family to society at large. One important area is that of employment. Suppose that the patient were to say to the doctor:

7. 'It's my leg, doctor, *and it's making it difficult for me to carry out my job.*'

Here the disorder, located in the leg, is linked to the whole man in the role of worker and breadwinner, and so is linked to the work situation which includes him. Starting from this point, there are again a number of ways in which the problem could be approached, and a number of different contexts in which it could be placed.

There is the leg; there is the man as worker with the focus upon his capacity to do his job; there is the work situation which may need to be modified if he is to continue in the same job; and there are the alternative jobs which might be available to him now with his altered capacity. Then we have the man as provider for his family and here we are back in our mainstream again, taking into account the family relationships. It might be necessary to explore, for example, his fears that his family will suffer hardship, or that he will lose status in the family or will have to put up with criticism or hostility. There may be an unconscious wish to punish his family, or to repeat or avoid some pattern carried over from a previous generation. Or there may be a conscious or unconscious feeling of gratification at the prospect of giving up an irksome responsibility and taking up again a more dependent role. We could go on adding to the possibilities, and the range of our perceptions will depend upon the range of the shapes that we are able to carry in our minds.

The minimum sufficient network

Different ways of working all have their advocates; and training, personal skills and inclinations, may encourage people to think in terms of wider or of narrower contexts. Amid such complexity criteria are hard to find.

When faced with the problem of defining and selecting areas of intervention, a useful concept is that of Skynner's (1987) *minimum sufficient network*. For this purpose Skynner defines a network as 'that set of psychological structures which needs to be connected to one another if the total system is to be autonomous and capable of intelligent responses and adaption' (Skynner 1987 p.5–6). These structures may all be found within one person or they may be shared round among different people or groups of people. This network needs to include all the elements that are relevant, but at the same time it should be no bigger than it has to be so that the task is not made unnecessarily complex.

If we think in terms of functions, we need to consider the following questions.

- Who is disturbed?
- Who is disturbing?

- Who has the motivation to change the situation?
- Who has the capacity to change it?

Individual treatment is offered in the belief, or hope, that the patient is the one who is suffering, the one who is wanting things to change and the one who can be helped to bring about the change that is needed. An adult patient who has not suffered severe social or family deprivation in the past may have sufficient integration to justify this belief, and so the minimum sufficient network needed for this purpose is sometimes assumed to be contained within the one individual.

But this is not always the case. The four functions may be carried by four different people, who may or may not be members of the same family. The network may extend beyond the family. One of the four functions may belong to an institution such as a school, if the complaint is of the disruptive behaviour of a child, and in this case the school, perhaps in the person of the class teacher, would need to be included in the network.

A capacity to change the situation may be hard to discover or mobilise in the identified network, and there may be pressure for some other body, such as therapist or child guidance clinic, to take on this function. Skynner draws attention to the mistake that is made when a clinic accepts, explicitly or implicitly, the responsibility for changing the people referred to suit the demands of the people referring them. This automatically makes the clinic into the part of the network that carries the motivation and may prevent another part of the network from taking on this role.

Once the four functions have been identified and brought together within the one treatment network, the task of the professional worker is not to take over responsibility for any one of them but to try to bring these split-off parts of the problem together by clarifying communications between them and making the links that are needed if the network is to start to work as whole.

The identification of the minimum sufficient network forms part of a treatment plan that is drawn up within a particular context. It may have a particular practical relevance to work in a child guidance setting. In other settings the resources available, including the training, experience and personal skills of the workers involved, may be more circumscribed. So may be the expectations of patients or clients and their readiness to become involved. Sometimes the relevant parts of a network cannot be brought together and intervention may have to be focused on just a part of an identified network, even perhaps on just a single person. But the concept remains a useful and valid tool. In these cases it is the function of the worker to carry the whole network in mind, including the parts and functions that are present and the parts and functions that have stayed away, and one of the treatment aims can still be to clarify communications and to bring the different parts closer together.

Knowledge that is exclusive and knowledge that is shared

The transmission of concepts between disciplines is a complex process, and difficulties can arise when insufficient attention is paid to it.

Before one is able to communicate profitably with a member of another discipline, whether as teacher and student, borrower and lender, team members or co-workers on a shared task, one needs first to be sure of one's own professional identity and traditional boundaries. Professional identity is built up in complex ways, through extended professional training, continuing education and practice, as well as the perception and absorption (or rejection) of some of the personal qualities of teachers and supervisors.

It is a process which becomes ever more important as the knowledge base expands and as the perception of problems becomes more and more complex. Professional workers are expected to acquire a deepening knowledge of their own profession, and, in addition, a knowledge of the range of work that colleagues are carrying out beyond the range of their own experience.

They are likely to have had a continuous exposure to teachers and workers in other professions, sometimes because of multidisciplinary work and sometimes because of deliberately arranged training courses bringing different disciplines together to discuss specific themes. Shared areas of theory and practice need to be recognised in addition to the areas where each profession can lay claim to exclusive authority.

Some knowledge is specific to a particular profession. But, in addition, each professional worker also draws upon a wide area of knowledge that is shared with others, and it is these overlapping areas that make professional collaboration possible. Without this overlap, members of an interdisciplinary team can only work separately and in parallel, and the coordination then has to come from an overlord who gives orders concerning the final objective.

We can look on the knowledge used by any profession as being, figuratively, contained within three concentric circles.

- First, there is the inner circle containing knowlege that is exclusive to that profession.

- Second, there is the middle circle containing knowledge that is shared with other professions.

- Third, there is the outer circle containing knowledge that is very relevant to professional practice, but which is outside that professions's specific training and professional experience.

The expansion of knowledge, and developments in areas belonging to other professions, can remove a particular theme or skill from the exclusive possession of one profession and move it outward into the shared area. Alternatively, there can be a movement in an inward direction, as sometimes happens when a change in thinking brings a piece of formerly shared theory within the territory arrogated to one particular profession. For the purpose of illustration it is convenient to apply this model to medicine because here the exclusive area is more clearly differentiated than in other caring professions.

Within the doctor's inner circle are the specific medical knowledge and skills, the authorisation which the doctor has to deal with acute illness and the responsibility which the doctor has for the conduct of treatment. Here the doctor carries full responsibility and any work done by any other profession is done 'under doctor's orders'.

Within the second circle are the problems of family interaction, many aspects of the development of children, occupational problems and knowledge of social conditions, and all the knowledge that is shared with social workers, psychologists, administrators, educationalists and others. The doctor makes these areas part of his enquiries, but cannot make prescriptions based upon them alone, although they influence his decisions and he has influence in his turn. It is influence, but it is not exclusive professional authority. If he does elect to speak with authority in this area, he cannot speak with the finality he could employ if he were within the first circle, for here there are other professions which have a different but at least equally valid voice.

In the outer circle are all the questions of public policy and of everyday living which affect the lives of the doctor's patients, which the doctor has to know about and should have opinions about, but of which he can only speak with such authority as comes from personal qualities and everyday knowledge. 'What do you as a doctor think about modern youth?' he may be asked. The doctor may have a lot of opinions about modern youth but they are not strictly medical opinions and care should be taken not to allow them to be invested with medical authority.

The doctor has been taken as a convenient example, but these considerations are equally valid for many other professions.

The boundaries shift

Example: school refusal

An example of the shifting boundaries of professional areas that comes to mind is the response to the failure of some children to attend school

For a time this behaviour was dealt with within the educational system, having at first been considered to be a social and legal matter and not the province of the psychiatric services. However some cases remained intractable; and when patients began to consult family doctors, searching for additional explanations of the behaviour, a number of cases found their way to psychiatrists. The involvement of psychiatrists led to the coining of the term 'school phobia', after which it became possible to recognise a syndrome and place it within the province of child guidance clinics. Criteria were then laid down in order to distinguish 'school phobia', now recognised as an emotional disorder, from 'truancy' which remained a social problem. However, the boundaries were not altogether clear. For some time it remained a matter of dispute between the clinical and educational services as to to whether school phobia had any existence or was just a fancy name to excuse particular children from the consequences of their refusal to go to school.

Gradually, the concept of emotional disorder related to school attendance came to achieve general recognition. This was followed by the further recognition that there were social aspects to the school phobic cases, and emotional factors in many of the so-called truancies. The result of this was that the condition was renamed. The term 'school refusal' began to be preferred to 'school phobia' in order to recognise a continuity of problem behaviour (in interpersonal terms) which could be related to food refusal in infancy and occupational problems in adulthood.

During all this time these problems were considered to be personal to the child, or appertaining to the area of family relationships, and for the most part the school was disregarded. The school was merely the place where the behaviour came to light.

The next stage came when the workers in the educational field, including the teachers, began to recognise a psycho-social dimension in their work. The practice of advising or counselling began to form part of the general or specialist teacher's activities. This brought back an educational interest in the whole range of the problems of school attendance, and made it possible to think of ideas of prevention and treatment outside the range of the psychiatric services.

Thus there has been a shift back and forth, from education to psychiatry, and then from psychiatry back to education; with the inclusion along the way of psychology, social work and general medicine as the different professions have been drawn together in multidisciplinary team work. Wherever such a shift is made it brings members of different professions together to work alongside one another, at the same time allowing the professions to continue their own independent approach within their own disciplines.

Boundaries are shifting in many other areas. For example, as the understanding of dynamic psychology has increased, new treatments have become available within psychiatry for forms of personal distress hitherto not considered treatable. These disorders are then taken into the inner circle of the psychiatrist, until such time as the spread of skills to other professions (who meanwhile have been making independent progress of their own) brings these disorders out once more into the circle where knowledge is professional but shared.

Expectations of teachers and students

There are few professions today that do not face demands for an extension of their work into areas which are concerned with feelings, motivations and relationships. Doctors and clergy, teachers and nurses, are now expected to take part in 'counselling', and this means that that it is often psychologists, social workers, and psychiatrists who are cast in the role of teachers of other professions. Willingly or unwillingly, many of them accept this role; and they also take part in the teaching of each other.

Where members of different professions meet in a situation in which one is designated teacher and the other one student, what is the one expecting of the other?

Is the student expected to take on the attitudes and ethos of the one who is designated teacher? Is the student expected to become the teacher's disciple, subordinate, or rival? Or to become associated with the teacher's profession, even if barred from joining it?

These are confused and covert expectations that need to be examined in order to consider another alternative – that the purpose of the encounter is the development of something new. This might become the property of the student's profession, or, to take the process one step further, it could become a shared possession. For, where members of two different professions meet, each could and should have something to learn from the other and so the roles of student and teacher may be shared and even at times reversed. Teaching is then turned into a creative experience, and both professions grow.

So here again teaching is not didactic teaching but is contained within the parameters of group discussion, requiring from teacher and student a joint exploration in which each gives and each receives.

CHAPTER 14

In Conclusion

As the creeper that girdles the tree trunk, the Law runneth forward and back –
For the strength of the Pack is the Wolf, and the strength of the Wolf is the Pack.
(Kipling, *The Jungle Book*)

This book has been concerned with the group context at large and with the contexts of particular groups. It has been concerned with finding ways to understand the group process and then with ways of applying that understanding for specific purposes both inside and outside the confines of therapy. It has been concerned with the problems involved in transferring concepts and techniques from one setting into another.

Starting with the special situation of the psychotherapeutic group, and using models of group dynamics derived from group psychotherapy but valid in other group situations, we have moved onwards and outwards through counselling and problem solving to experiential, training and educational groups, to work teams and institutions, from small groups to median groups to large and massive groups, and then to work with families and with individuals.

Therapy has its strict parameters, and the importance of understanding and observing these parameters before drawing upon the concepts and techniques of group therapy for other purposes has been stressed. But nevertheless all group situations can provide opportunities for personal growth which can be encouraged or discouraged, and what is gained in one group situation can then be carried over into others. Groups contain an inherent potential for developing constructive understanding and for facilitating positive change and development, and a group leader or conductor can work with a group to serve a variety of different ends. But if this potential is to be realised certain conditions have to be observed and these include the provision of a safe and containing space and the recognition and observation of appropriate boundaries. These conditions are the initial responsibility of the group leader.

One theme has been particularly important in considering the group context and has run through all the work with groups and families that has been considered. This theme is the simultaneous approach to the parts and the whole.

To group analysis in particular this is a foundation concept, central in the theory and demonstrated in practice, with a universal application which has facilitated the transfer of concepts to other forms of focused group work not only in the helping professions and in education but also in organisations and industry. Individual and group are two aspects of the one process and understanding at the two levels at the same time is needed. The ability to carry in mind the individual and the group is translated in clinical practice into an ability to move flexibly from individual member to the group as a whole and from group back to individual, carrying both levels simultaneously in mind in the knowledge that the same process is being addressed through interventions at either level. This flexible movement was characteristic of Foulkes' own work and teaching. Like Kipling's Law of the Jungle it runneth forward and back. This gives meaning to Foulkes' statement (Foulkes 1990) that the distinction between group and individual psychodynamics is meaningless except by abstraction. Anything that affects an individual member affects the whole group: anything that affects the group affects every individual member.

Foulkes illustrated this by means of an analogy. A car journey through unfamiliar country requires a small-scale map to show the whole route in which a town may be indicated only by a dot. But on entering the town we need a different map on a larger scale, a town plan in fact in which all the individual streets are indicated. The town plan and the way that the streets are arranged organises and rearranges the passing traffic and sends it on again changed in direction and in speed. Foulkes used the town here to represent the individual, and like the individual the town serves as a nodal point within a greater communications network. And so transpersonal processes reach the individual, moving through her and being influenced by her in turn before they are passed on through the network, now changed in form and direction as the form and direction of traffic is changed by passing through a town. To understand the traffic flow, and to complete the journey, a town plan on its own does not supply enough information. The larger map is also necessary. And vice versa.

Consideration of traffic provided Foulkes with a further analogy. People who study traffic are interested in the particular frequency of accidents at certain places. Accidents can be linked to a particular location, but they are also linked to the drivers who have played their own parts in causing the accident, bringing their own problems, mental and physical, and their own accident proneness. So understanding at two levels is necessary. Knowledge of the state of the roads and knowledge of the state of the individual drivers involved are both needed.

So patient and therapy group, student and class, worker and team can be looked on as if two sides of the same coin. Work with families and with groups needs some foundation in a knowledge of individual growth and development and of individual psychodynamics (supposing for the moment that there is such a thing as individual psychodynamics). And conversely when we work with individuals we need a knowledge of the dynamics of the groups and of the families of which the individuals form a part. Any problems which show themselves through disturbances in relationships can be linked back to disturbances in networks in the past, now brought forward to reappear with some new protagonists in networks in the present. So when we turn to work with individuals it follows that the patients or clients who come for help are not really alone but are dragging behind them as an invisible presence all the networks of which they are, or have been, a part.

The introduction of questions of context has brought changes into many professions. When the concepts of group and family dynamics first began to be formulated it was as if they had come in response to a need, at a time of dissatisfaction in which new approaches were being sought. Existing concepts and existing treatment methods based upon individual psychology were then no longer found adequate as a response to the problems that clients and patients were bringing. If there had not been a change in the problems themselves, perhaps there had been a change in the way that they were being presented, or perhaps the change was in the perceptions of the helping professionals.

Wherever the change came from, the new concepts, and new forms of treatment which resulted opened up the possibility of working with whole groups and whole families in mind, whether clients or patients come singly, or in pairs, or in larger aggregates, and whether they themselves present their problems as individual ones or as part of a larger disturbance.

Professional workers in different fields have had to become aware of a wider range of possibilities, and have had to become sensitive to a larger number of aspects, as knowledge and techniques originating in other disciplines have become available to them. Members of a number of different professions who have acquired a knowledge of group and family psychodynamics can now carry a range of models in their mind. These models help them to recognise the existence of processes at different levels and make it possible for them to respond to the material presented at these levels. They do not have to cover all these aspects on their own and they do not have to leave their own discipline. They can take their own particular tasks and relate them to a wider perspective, refining their own responses and at the same time opening up the possibility of collaborating with a larger number of colleagues of different trainings and different orientations.

These changes can all be related to the adoption of more open systems concepts in the place of the more static closed systems of the past. Formerly, as

Skynner (1976) has described, a training was considered to have been completed when 'enough' knowledge had been acquired, after which the worker would remain within her own professional boundaries and try to protect them from encroachments and disturbing change. However there is now an acceptance of more open systems and of more permeable boundaries that permit the passage of information in and out and enable professional workers to pool resources and to learn from each other. But for all that the boundaries, even if more permeable, still need to be acknowledged and preserved.

Finally, for all group workers, some words of advice from Alexander Pope (1951 [1711]) with thanks to Kevin Power for pointing out these lines.

> Be silent always, when you doubt your sense;
> And speak, though sure, with seeming diffidence.
> Some positive, persisting fops we know,
> Who, if once wrong, will needs be always so;
> But you, with pleasure own your errors past,
> And make each day a critique on the last.
> 'Tis not enough your counsel still be true;
> Blunt truths more mischief than nice falsehoods do;
> Men must be taught as if you taught them not,
> And things unknown proposed as things forgot.
> Be niggards of advice on no pretence;
> For the worst avarice is that of sense.
> With mean complaisance ne'er betray your trust
> Nor be so civil as to prove unjust.
> Fear not the anger of the wise to raise;
> Those best can bear reproof who merit praise.

Bibliography

Abercrombie, M.J.L. (1981) *Group Analysis 14,* supp. 2.

Abercrombie, M.J.L. and Terry, P.M. (1978) *Talking to Learn.* London: SRHE Monograph.

Agazarian, Y. and Peters, R. (1981) *The Visible and Invisible Group.* London: Tavistock/Routledge.

Austen, Jane, (1932) *Letters.* Oxford: Oxford University Press.

Balint, M. (1957) *The Doctor, the Patient, and his Illness.* London: Pitman.

Bateson, G. (1971) 'A systems approach.' *International Journal of Psychiatry 9,* 242–244.

Beeles, C.C. and Ferber A. (1969) 'Family therapy: a view.' *Family Process 8,* 280.

Bell, J.E. (1970) 'A theoretical position for family group therapy.' In N. Ackerman (ed) *Family Process.* New York: Basic Books.

Bentovim, A., Gorell Barnes, G. and Cooklin, A. (eds) (1982) *Family Therapy.* Vols. 1 and 2 London: Academic Press.

Berne, E. (1967) *Games People Play.* New York: Grove Press Inc.

Bion, W.R. (1952) 'Group dynamics: a review.' *International Journal of Psychoanalysis 33.*

Bion, W.R. (1961) *Experiences in Groups.* London: Tavistock.

Boswell, J. (1884) *Life of Samuel Johnson.* [ed A. Napier.] London: George Bell & Sons.

Byng Hall, J. (1973) 'Family myths used as a defence in conjoint family therapy.' *British Journal of Medical Psychology 46,* 239.

Caplan, G. (1961) *An Approach to Community Mental Health.* London: Tavistock.

Conan Doyle, A., quoted in Hardwick, M. and M. (1964) *The Man who was Sherlock Holmes.* London: John Murray.

Cooklin, A. (1981) 'Change in here and now systems vs. systems over time.' Vol. 1. In A. Bentovim, G. Gorrell Barnes and A. Cooklin (eds) *Family Therapy.* London: The Academic Press.

Cox, M. and Theilgaard, A. (1994) *Shakespeare as Prompter.* London: Jessica Kingsley Publishers.

De Board, R. (1978) *The Psychoanalysis of Organisations.* London: Tavistock Publications.

De Maré, P. Piper, R. and Thompson, S. (1990) *Koinonia.* London: Karnac Books.

Dickens, C. (1854) *Hard Times.* London: Collins Library of Classics.

Dicks, H. (1967) *Marital Tensions.* London: Routledge & Kegan Paul.

Eden, A. (1994) 'The internal consultant'. In R. Casemore *et al. What Makes Consultancy Work?* London: South Bank University Press.

Erikson, E. (1950) *Childhood and Society.* New York: Norton.

Ezriel, H. (1950a) 'A psychoanalytic approach to group treatment.' *British Journal of Medical Psychology 23*, 1–20.

Ezriel, H. (1950b) 'A psychoanalytic approach to the treatment of patients in groups.' *Journal of Mental Science 96*, 774–779.

Fairburn, W.R.D. (1952) *Psychoanalytic Studies of the Personality.* London: Tavistock.

Ferrard, M. and Hunnybun, N. (1962) *The Caseworker's Use of Relationships.* London: Tavistock.

Ferron, E. (1991) 'The black and white group.' *Group Analysis 24*, 2.

Foulkes, S.H. (1964) *Therapeutic Group Analysis.* London: Allen & Unwin.

Foulkes, S.H. (1970) 'Review.' *Group Analysis 111*, 3.

Foulkes, S.H. (1975) *Group-Analytic Psychotherapy. Methods and Principles.* London: Gordon & Breach.

Foulkes, S.H. (1990) *Selected Papers.* ed. E. Foulkes. London: Karnac Books

Freud, S.H. (1926) *Inhibitions, Symptoms and Anxiety.* St. Ed. Vol. 20. London: Hogarth Press.

Freud, S.H. (1963) *The Interpretation of Dreams.* St. Edn. Vol. 5 London: Hogarth Press.

Goffman, I. (1961) *Asylums.* New York: Doubleday.

Halmos, P. (1965) *The Faith of the Counsellors.* London: Constable.

Harding, D.W. (1970) *Social Psychology and Individual Values.* London: Hutchinson.

Harrow, A. (1997) 'Group analysis in education by accident.' *Group-Analytic Contexts 10.*

Henry, J. (1972) *The Pathway to Madness.* London: Cape.

Herman, J.L. (1992) *Trauma and Recovery.* New York: Basic Books.

Hutten, J.M. (1996) 'The use of experiential groups in the training of counsellors and psychotherapists.' *Psychodynamic Counselling 2*, 2.

James, H. (1884) 'The art of fiction'. In *The Critical Muse*. London: Everyman's Library.

Kahn, J. and Thompson, S. (1970) *The Group Process as a Helping Technique*. London: Perganon.

Kahn, J. and Thompson, S. (1982) *The Group Process and Family Therapy*. London: Perganon.

Klein, J. (1987) *Our Need for Others*. London: Tavistock.

Klein, M. (1963) *The Adult World and Other Essays*. London: Heinemann.

Kreeger, L. (ed) (1965) *The Large Group*. London: Constable.

Kubie L.S. quoted in Dicks, H. (1967) *Marital Tensions*. London: Routledge & Kegan Paul.

Levi, P. (1990) *The Mirror Maker*. London: Methuen.

Lewin, K. (1952) *Field Theory in Social Science*. London: Tavistock.

Main, T. (1964) 'Some psychodynamics of large groups'. In L. Kreeger (ed) *The Large Group* London: Constable.

Matte-Blanco, I. (1961) 'The place of psychiatry and mental health in medicine and in the medical curriculum.' *Teaching of Psychiatry and Mental Health*. Geneva: WHO Public Health Paper No. 9.

Menzies, I.E.P. (1970) 'The functioning of social systems as a defence against anxiety.' *Centre for Applied Social Research*. London: Tavistock Institute.

Nitsun, M. (1991) 'The anti-group'. *Group Analysis 24,* 1.

Osborne, J. (1972) 'Introduction' to Ibsen's *Hedda Gabler*. London: Faber & Faber.

Parsloe, P. (1969) 'Some thoughts on social group work.' *British Journal of Psychiatric Social Work 10*, 1.

Pines, M. (ed.) (1983) *The Evolution of Group Analysis*. London: Routledge & Kegan Paul.

Pope, A. (1951) 'Essay on criticism.' *Collected Poems Epistles and Satires*. London: Everyman's Library

Russell, B. (1960) *Sceptical Essays*. London: Allen & Unwin.

Satir, V. (1964) *Conjoint Family Therapy*. Palo Alto: Science and Behaviour Books Inc.

Skynner, A.C.R. (1976) *One Flesh: Separate Persons*. London: Constable.

Skynner, R. (1987) *Explorations with Families*. London: Routledge.

Skynner, R. (1989) *Institutes and How to Survive Them*. London: Methuen.

Slavson, S.R. (1950) *Analytic Group Psychotherapy with Children Adolescents and Adults*. New York: Columbia University Press.

Speck, R.V. and Rueveni, U. (1970) 'Network therapy.' In N. Ackerman (ed) *Family Process*. New York: Basic Books.

Stock Whitaker, D. (1992) 'Transposing learnings from group psychotherapy to work groups.' *Group Analysis 25, 2.*

Stock Whitaker, D. and Liebermann, M. (1965) *Psychotherapy through the Group Process*. London: Tavistock.

Turquet, P. (1964) 'Threats to identity in the large group.' In Kreeger (ed) *The Large Group*. London: Constable.

Winnicott, D. (1971) *Therapeutic Consultation in Child Psychiatry*. London: Hogarth Press and Institute of Psychoanalysis.

Yalom, I. (1970) *The Theory and Practice of Group Psychotherapy*. New York: Basic Books.

Zinkin, L. (1984) 'Three models are better than one.' *Group Analysis 17, 1.* Reprinted in H. Zinkin, R. Gordon and J. Haynes (eds) (1998) *Dialogue in the Analytic Setting*. London: Jessica Kingsley Publishers.

Subject Index

Author Index